PENGUIN BOOKS
HUSBAND OF A FANATIC

Amitava Kumar was born in Ara, Bihar, and grew up in Patna, famous for its poverty, corruption and delicious mangoes. Kumar's writings on the experience of migration, as well as his poetry and criticism, have been widely published in India and abroad. He is a professor of English at Pennsylvania State University. Kumar has also written the script for a prize-winning documentary film. His earlier books, *Passport Photos* and *Bombay–London–New York*, have also been published by Penguin Books India.

Books by the same author:

Passport Photos
Bombay–London–New York

Husband of a Fanatic

AMITAVA KUMAR

PENGUIN BOOKS

PENGUIN BOOKS

Published by the Penguin Group

Penguin Books India Pvt Ltd, 11 Community Centre, Panchsheel Park, New Delhi 110 017, India

Penguin Group (USA) Inc., 375 Hudson Street, New York, NY 10014, USA

Penguin Group (Canada), 10 Alcorn Avenue, Toronto, Ontario, Canada M4V 3B2 (a division of Pearson Penguin Canada Inc.)

Penguin Books Ltd, 80 Strand, London WC2R 0RL, England

Penguin Ireland, 25 St Stephen's Green, Dublin 2, Ireland (a division of Penguin Books Ltd)

Penguin Group (Australia), 250 Camberwell Road, Camberwell, Victoria 3124, Australia (a division of Pearson Australia Group Pty Ltd)

Penguin Group (NZ), cnr Airborne and Rosedale Roads, Albany, Auckland 1310, New Zealand (a division of Pearson New Zealand Ltd)

Penguin Group (South Africa) (Pty) Ltd, 24 Sturdee Avenue, Rosebank, Johannesburg 2196, South Africa

Penguin Books Ltd, Registered Offices: 80 Strand, London WC2R 0RL, England

First published in India by Penguin Books India 2004
Copyright © Amitava Kumar 2004

All rights reserved

10 9 8 7 6 5 4 3 2 1

For sale in the Indian Subcontinent only

Typeset in Sabon by InoSoft Systems, Noida
Printed at Pauls Press, New Delhi

This book is sold subject to the condition that it shall not, by way of trade or otherwise, be lent, resold, hired out, or otherwise circulated without the publisher's prior written consent in any form of binding or cover other than that in which it is published and without a similar condition including this condition being imposed on the subsequent purchaser and without limiting the rights under copyright reserved above, no part of this publication may be reproduced, stored in or introduced into a retrieval system, or transmitted in any form or by any means (electronic, mechanical, photocopying, recording or otherwise), without the prior written permission of both the copyright owner and the above-mentioned publisher of this book.

For Mona, and our daughter, Ila

I asked him for instances of this progress—any evidence to show the least sign of reconciliation between Mohammedans and Hindoos, and he replied that a Hindoo was now able to receive betel from the hands of a Mohammedan.

— J.R. Ackerley, *Hindoo Holiday*

He writes that he wants to talk
that he's thinking of converting
and I know, it isn't to me.

— Mona Ahmad Ali, 'The Wolf's Cry'

Contents

Lunch with a Bigot

Mr Barotia was talking to someone when he opened the door. Speaking into the phone that he held in his left hand, he gave me his right fist, which I couldn't quite decide whether to touch or to hold. Mr Barotia said to the person on the phone, '*Haan, haan*, we will sit down and talk about it.'

The apartment, with the sunlight falling on the bulky white furniture, some of it covered with transparent plastic, appeared clean and bright, especially after the darkness of the corridor outside with its musty carpeting. I was happy that I had got so far. I had spoken to Mr Barotia for the first time only during the previous week. On the phone he had called me a *haraami*, which means bastard in Hindi, and, after clarifying that he didn't mean this abuse only for me as a person but for everyone else who was like me, he had also called me a *kutta*, a dog.

Although I had no idea of Jagdish Barotia's identity till recently, I had wanted to meet him for well over two years. I wanted to meet face to face a man who thought I was his enemy, to see if I could understand why he hated me so much, and why he hated other people who were different from him. My name had appeared on a hit-list put on a web site in the year 2000. The web site belongs to a group called Hindu Unity—none of whose members, including Mr Barotia, were named on the site—and it presented links to other right-wing Hindu groups. My name was on a list of individuals who were regarded as enemies of a Hindu India. There was special anger for people like me, who were Hindus but, in the minds of the list's organizers, traitors to Hindutva, the ideology of a resurgent, anti-left, ultranationalistic Hindu cause.

The summer after the site was established, the *New York Times* carried a report on the alliance that Hindu Unity had formed with Rabbi Meir Kahane's group. This is how the article began: 'A web site run by militant Hindus in Queens and Long Island was recently shut down by its service provider because of complaints that it advocated hatred and violence towards Muslims. But a few days later, the site was back on the Internet. The unlikely rescuers were some radical Jews in Brooklyn who are under investigation for possible ties with anti-Arab terrorist organizations in Israel.' The Zionist organization as well as the Hindutva group had come together in New York City against what they considered their common enemy, Islam.

The news story had mentioned that Hindu Unity was a secretive group. It had been difficult for the reporter to meet the men who ran the web site. I had sent several e-mail messages to the address provided on the site—the address where one was supposed to write and report the names of the enemies of the Hindus—but no one had responded to my requests for an interview. Then, while I was having lunch at an Indian restaurant with a leader of the Overseas Friends of the Bharatiya Janata Party, Mr Barotia's name came up. The BJP is a right-wing Hindu party within India; the Overseas Friends is an umbrella organization of Hindu groups outside India, zealously presenting to anyone who cares to listen the details of what they regard as the menace of the minorities (that is, non-Hindus) in India. When I told the man that I'd like to meet Mr Barotia, he gave me his phone number and just as casually, mentioned that Mr Barotia had been instrumental in establishing the web site for Hindu Unity. (When I asked Mr Barotia directly about this, he said, via an e-mail message: 'I am a supporter of Hindu Unity and all the organizations which support the Hindu cause ... . I think there is a difference between being a member and a supporter. I do not pay any subscription for membership in Hindu Unity.')

Half an hour later, I was on the phone with Mr Barotia. When I gave him my name, he recognized it, and his voice lost its warmth. He told me that he had read an article of mine describing a visit to Pakistan, and he asked me to confirm what he knew about me, that I had married a Muslim. When I replied that I had, he said, 'You have caused me a lot of pain.' I didn't know what to say. It was then, after I told him I wanted to meet him, that he called me a bastard and a dog. He also said that people like me were not secular, we were actually confused. We would learn our lesson, he said, when the Muslim population increased in India, and the Muslims came after us and chopped our legs off.

I guess I could say that I felt his pain when he said that he didn't understand what had happened to the Hindu children, how it had come to be that they were surrounded by so much darkness. I said to him that I was not a child any more, but I sounded like one when I said that.

Mr Barotia invited me to his home, saying that he was sure that after he had talked to me and given me 'all the facts', I would change my mind about Muslims. He was the secretary of an outfit which he called the Indian-American Intellectuals Forum; he was also the organizing secretary of the Hindu Swayamsevak Sangh, the overseas wing of the RSS (Rashtriya Swayamsevak Sangh, or National Voluntary Organization), a militant group to which the murderer of Mahatma Gandhi had once belonged. The Internet was a gift to Mr Barotia's propaganda. It made him a better long-distance nationalist. He said to me, 'If the Hindus will be saved, it will be because of the Internet. I send out an e-mail and am able to talk at once to 5,000 Hindus.' And so it was that less than a week later, I went to Elmhurst, Queens, to meet Mr Barotia.

In the summer of 1999, when India and Pakistan were engaged in a conflict near Kargil, in Kashmir, I had got married. In the days leading up to my wedding, I often told myself that my marriage was unusually symbolic: I was doing my bit to help bring peace to more than a billion people living in the subcontinent because I am an Indian Hindu and the woman I was about to marry, Mona, is a Pakistani Muslim.

The wedding took place in June, and it was hot when I drove up to Toronto, where Mona's parents had recently moved from Karachi. Driving home alone (Mona had stayed behind with her family for a few days because they were returning to Pakistan), past Niagara Falls, where I had heard that honeymooners often go, I felt good about myself for marrying 'the enemy'. The thought gave me a small thrill. I was suddenly awash in altruism; its tepid tide cleansed me of a narrow, binding form of self-love. I also found that I wanted others to partake of this feeling of well-being which I was experiencing—and I began to compose in my mind a brief newspaper editorial about how my marriage had opened a new track for people-to-people diplomacy.

Every day in Toronto the news bulletins brought to us the war in Kashmir. But we had other preoccupations. Along with Mona's brothers and father, I would wake up at five in the morning to watch India and Pakistan fighting it out on the cricket fields in England, where the World Cup tournament was being played. A day before our wedding, India beat Pakistan in the match in Manchester. During that match, one lone spectator had held a sign, 'Cricket for Peace'. Watching the match on television, I wondered whether I too could walk around with a placard hung from my neck, saying 'Marriage for Peace'.

The article I eventually wrote for an Indian newspaper was what first brought me to Mr Barotia's attention. We became enemies.

At least, that is how he thinks of his relationship with me. We hardly know each other. The issue is not personal; it is political. After reading my articles about my marriage, and later, my visit to Pakistan, Mr Barotia denounced me as an enemy of India. I went to meet him in his apartment in Queens because I wanted a dialogue with him. I also wanted to see his face. I found the idea of a faceless enemy unbearable. That wasn't a psychological problem so much as a writer's problem. I wanted detail and voice. Mr Barotia had said to me on the phone that the Hindu rioters in

Gujarat, who burnt, raped, or slaughtered more than a thousand Muslims earlier that year had taught the Indian minorities a lesson they would never forget. I wanted to meet Mr Barotia so that I could ask him about the process through which he had come to think of the Muslim as the enemy. I did ask him, but his response revealed little to me that was new.

Nevertheless, our meeting was a discovery because it made me think not simply of our differences but also our similarities. What is it that divides the writer from the rioter? The answer is not very clear or simple. There could be more in common between the two than either might imagine—a vast hinterland of cultural memory and shared prejudice, for example. Was it an excess of sympathy on my part—or, on the contrary, too little of it—that made it difficult, if not also impossible, for me to draw a plainly legible line between a man in a mob and myself?

*

There was a woman in the house, she was Mr Barotia's niece, and she called out to him when she saw me enter the living room. He was being asked to put on a shirt. Mr Barotia was short and had a round face with grey eyebrows. He put on a pair of gold-rimmed glasses after I told him that I doubted his statement that we had met before. Mr Barotia touched his glasses and frowned. He said, 'But your face looks familiar.' I suddenly thought of the Hindu Unity web site, where my photograph had appeared, picked up from the newspaper pieces. Perhaps that was the reason why Mr Barotia thought that he had seen me before. He had seen my face on the site's so-called black list, along with my name and address. But I couldn't bring myself to tell him that. Instead, I drank the tea that I was offered. And then, Mr Barotia began to tell me about what he called 'the poison of Islam'.

The litany of complaints was familiar and quickly wearying. Mr Barotia began with the names of all the male Indian filmstars who were Muslim and married to Hindu women. 'Sharmila Tagore is now Ayesha Begum and that Aamir Khan is also married to a Hindu girl.' These women had been forced to convert, he said, and now Muslims were having sex with them, thereby defiling them. When Mr Barotia told me this, he moved his right forearm back and forth against his paunch in a pumping action. He was using a vulgar Hindi word for what he was describing, a word common on the streets in India, and he said it so loudly, and so repeatedly, that I was startled and immediately thought of his niece in the kitchen. I was a stranger and she had not come in front of me; it was Mr Barotia who had had to get up and go to her to fetch the tray with tea and biscuits for us. Her manner had suggested that there was a great deal of traditional reserve in the household. What did she think of Mr Barotia carrying on so obscenely about circumcised cocks and fucking?

The BJP leader in the Indian restaurant, when he had given me Mr Barotia's phone number, had told me that Mr Barotia's family had been massacred during the riots in 1947, during the Partition of India and Pakistan. I found out now that wasn't true. Mr Barotia said that his family had left Sindh, in Pakistan, and crossed the border quite safely more than a year after the Partition. This revelation left me without a convenient explanation for his bigotry.

When I asked Mr Barotia to tell me about how he had come to acquire his well-defined worldview, he sputtered with rage. 'I was a liberal like you; liberal, stupid and ignorant. In Islam, there is no space for your secularism. There is no humanity in it. They extol the virtue of violence, they want to kill infidels ... . Islam is not a religion, it is a political ideology to capture land and rape women.'

I had begun taking notes. Mr Barotia would now and then point at my notebook and say, 'Write!' and then he would say things like, 'Hindus were being killed in Pakistan and Gandhi was giving speeches. *Saala tum ghoomta hai haraami* ... . When Gandhi was killed, that day I felt relaxed.' A little later, a friend of Mr Barotia's joined us, a fat, bearded man with a red tilak on his forehead. This man pedantically recited Sanskrit shlokas when he made his polemical points, and I sometimes turned back to Mr Barotia's plainer speech, and his abuses, with a sense of relief.

Soon, it became clear that Mr Barotia was going to buy me lunch. We walked to an Indian diner about ten minutes away, in Jackson Heights. Mr Barotia behaved like a friendly host, urging me to try the different dishes, putting bits of warm *nan* on my plate. He also ate with gusto, refilling his plate several times, and as I looked at him, his shirt front flecked with the food he had dropped there, I saw him as a contented, slightly tired old man who was perhaps getting ready to take an afternoon nap. Earlier, Mr Barotia had told me that because the Hindus had killed so many Muslims earlier that year in Gujarat, a change had come about. 'We have created fear,' he boasted. '*Yeh garmi jo hai, main India mein phaila doonga.* This heat that is there, I will spread it in India. And those who write against us, their fingers will be cut.' But, for now, he was quietly stuffing pakoras into his mouth: a retired immigrant worker eating in a cheap immigrant restaurant.

Mr Barotia had told me earlier that day that he had come to the United States in 1972. For twenty-five years he had worked as a legal secretary in Manhattan—the BJP man in the restaurant the previous week had told me that Mr Barotia had been 'a typist', and I had seen from the gesture of his hand that he was being dismissive. Mr Barotia said that he had got along well with his colleagues at work and they treated him as 'a partner in the firm', and one of them had even called him after the attacks of September 11 to say, 'Jagdish, we thought you were obsessed with Muslims. But you were right.'

After our lunch, one other matter of business remained. Mr Barotia was going to give me newspaper-cuttings and booklets. We walked back to his apartment through the crowded streets of Jackson Heights. The exercise brought Mr Barotia back to life. His home is in a locality where Indians and Pakistanis immigrants live together; Elmhurst is said to be the most diverse zip-code area in the whole of United States. When I asked Mr Barotia about his experience of living in this part of the city, he looked at the Muslims milling around us, the men with beards and caps, women with headscarves, and he spat out abuse. They harass our women, he said, and there is a lot of tension here. Then, suddenly, he began to talk of my wife whom he has never met. We were passing in front of the Indian grocery and jewellery stores, and Mr Barotia turned to me and said, 'It is okay. You fuck her. And you tell everyone that she is Muslim, and that you keep fucking her! And through her, you keep fucking Islam!'

'What did you do when he said that?' This is what
Mona, my wife, asked me when she heard the story. I had
called her from a public phone near Mr Barotia's apartment.
Above me was a large sign with black letters painted on
a white board, LEARN ENGLISH APRENDA INGLES.
There was a pause before I replied to the question. I told
Mona that I had done nothing. Wordlessly, I had kept
walking beside Mr Barotia. It would have been more
accurate to say that I had made a mental note of what he
had said. I said to myself that I needed to write down his
words in my notebook as soon as I was back on the train.
And that is what I did. Sitting in the train, with three men
on the seat opposite me, each one of them wearing identical
yellow jerseys and holding aluminium crutches against their
knees, I took down notes about what Mr Barotia had said
during our walk back from the lunch. The strange thing
is, although perhaps it is not strange at all, that later Mr
Barotia's words crossed my mind, just when my wife and
I had finished having breakfast in our kitchen and there,
next to the sink with the empty bowl of cereals, I had
begun to kiss her.

*

During lunch, Mr Barotia had told me that I was ungrateful
if I forgot how Hindu warriors had saved our motherland.
He must have got to me because when he asked me why I
believed in coexistence with Muslims, I said a phrase in
Hindi that essentially meant 'we are Nehru's bastards'. It
was an admission of guilt, of illegitimacy, as if Nehru, the
socialist first prime minister of India, had done something
wrong in being a liberal, and those of us who believed in

his vision of an inclusive India were his ill-begotten offspring. Nehru is often accused by his detractors of having been a profligate person, and my remark had granted him a certain promiscuity. But the more serious charge hidden in my comment was that the former prime minister had produced a polity that was the result of miscegenation with the West.

I was being disingenuous—and so was Mr Barotia. Our lives and our histories, with or without Nehru, were tied up with links with the wider world. I am an Indian writer who writes in English. Mr Barotia's parent party, the RSS, had been inspired by the Nazis and revered a German man, Hitler. Today, Mr Barotia is a fan of the Internet. We both live and work in the United States. We are both struggling, each in our way, to be *like* Nehru, whose eclecticism was exceptional. But Nehru was also exemplary because, unlike many of his Hindu compatriots, he had an unwavering belief that Hindu-Muslim conflict had nothing to do with tradition but was a modern phenomenon, which could be corrected by means of enlightened policy.

In the train, flipping over some of the papers that Mr Barotia had given me, I began to read what the Hindutva brigade had to say about Nehru. An article provided 'circumstantial evidence' that Nehru was a Muslim. One item of proof offered was the following: 'He had "Muslim" morals while "chasing and pursuing" a married woman (Edwina Mountbatten) and professing love to her. If he were a Hindu he would have respected married women and looked at the unmarried girls as "devis".' Another piece, this one about Gandhi who had preached love among different religions, began by asserting that there are two kinds of bastards: those who are 'born of illicit sex' and those who are 'despicable in word and conduct'. 'The remarkable thing about Mohandas Karamchand Gandhi,' the writer said, 'is that he was a bastard on both counts.'

Mr Barotia had given me a set of typewritten sheets collected under the title 'Wake Up! America! Wake Up!' These pages, each one carrying exhortations printed in emphatic bold letters and followed by a series of mercilessly underlined sentences, were his response to the tragedy of September 11. ('The macabre massacre of around 15,000 people [mostly Disbelievers] in less than 120 minutes. The inciter, the instigator QURAN is the CRIMINAL CULPRIT, which incites millions of Muslims around the World to the ghastly, ghostly crimes of this enormous destructive nature on the Disbelievers; and UNASHAMEDLY at the same time, tells these are all HOLY! So, Oh Disbeliever World! UNDERSTAND THIS COLD, CHILLING TRUTH.')

As I read the above words, it was as if I could hear Mr Barotia's hectoring voice. His interest in alliteration had not been evident to me before, but it didn't distract me from his real interest in producing a phony history and linking it to language. 'As the history of Mohammed goes, he was banished by his family and the society of his times,' Mr Barotia wrote. He followed a little later with a bogus disquisition on the etymology of the name for Muslims. The Prophet, in order to avenge the lack of respect shown him, founded 'gangs of powerful youth (Muscle Men), offering them girls of their choice, food and wine'. And, the word "Muscle Man" came to be mispronounced as "Musalman". Over a period of time, this mispronunciation became an accepted pronunciation!' The ten-page text ended with a question not about September 11 but an earlier unresolved crime that is still an obsession for many conspiracy-theorists in America and to which Mr Barotia was only giving a new twist: 'Who was behind the planning, plotting and planting the Death of the Dearest JFK?' The answer: 'It was ISLAM, ISLAM and ISLAM, the ever valiant villain.'

*

There are various things that could be said about Mr Barotia. One would be that he is a fringe element that gives a dangerous edge to an increasingly powerful and mainstream ideology in the subcontinent. Mr Barotia is also a member of the group that claims success in raising funds in the West—including investments made by expatriate Indians, allegedly to the tune of four billion dollars—to support the Indian government after economic sanctions had been imposed on India following the nuclear tests in 1998.

But, what interests me, as a writer, are the words that Mr Barotia uses. Their violence and ferocity—their absoluteness compromised and made vulnerable in different ways, not least by the repeated eruption of a sexual anxiety—carry the threat most visible in the rhetoric of rioters in India today. That rhetoric leaves no place for the middle-class gentility of Nehruvian liberalism. Indeed, its incivility is a response to the failures of the idealism represented by the likes of Nehru and Gandhi. Mr Barotia's voice is the voice of the lumpen that knows it is lumpen no longer. It almost has the legitimacy of being the voice of the people, which it is not, and its aggressiveness is born through its own sense that it is pitched in battle against those who held power for too long.

I am not sure whether I would ever, or for long, envy Mr Barotia's passion, but I find myself sympathetic to his perception that the English-speaking elite of India has not granted the likes of him a proper place under the Indian flag. Once that thought enters my head, I am uneasily conscious of the ways in which I found myself mocking Mr Barotia's bigotry by noticing his ungrammatical English. Like Mr Barotia, I was born in the provinces and grew up in small towns. For me, the move to the city meant that I learnt English and embraced secular, universal rationality and liberalism. Mr Barotia remained truer to his roots and retained his religion as well as a narrower form of nationalism that went with it. His revenge on the city was that he also became a fanatic. I do not envy him his changes, but I can't think of those changes without a small degree of tenderness.

There is also another reason why Mr Barotia's words hold my attention. His stories about heroism and betrayal share something with the fantasy-world of my own childhood, whose half-understood atmosphere of rumour and prejudice was a part not of a private universe but a largely public one. What Mr Barotia and I share in some deep way is the language of memory—that well from which we have drawn, like water, our collective stories. After my meeting with Mr Barotia, I thought of a particular incident from my childhood and wondered whether he, too, had similar memories, linking him and me, all of us, to all the bigots of the world.

My memory concerned a dead lizard. I must have been five or six at that time. The lizards, the *girgit*, were everywhere. In the small garden outside our home in Patna, they would creep out of the hedge and sun themselves on the metal gate. (Many years later, in a mall near Washington, I saw the lizards being sold as pets, and was reminded of my childhood fear of them.) These lizards were yellow or brown, their thin bodies scaly, and many of them had bloated red sacs under their chins. Although I was scared of the lizards, I also wanted to kill them. I often daydreamed about killing one by throwing a stone at it when it wasn't looking. I would try to imagine what its pale exposed belly would look like when it fell through the air, from the gate to the ground.

A boy who was a year ahead of me in school actually killed one of them, bringing it to me in a plastic bag. It was he who told me that the lizards were Muslim. He pointed out the sacs under their chins and said that they used to be beards. Here is the story he told.

During the riots that accompanied the Partition of India in 1947, the Muslims were running scared of the Hindus. If the Hindus found the Muslims, they would murder them. If the Hindus did not kill the Muslims first, the Muslims would instead butcher the Hindus with their swords. Or they would take the Hindus to the new country, Pakistan, where the Hindus would be converted and become trapped forever. One day, the Hindus saw a bearded Muslim running away. They caught him and were about to chop off his head. The man was a coward. In order to save his life, he pointed with his beard towards the well where the other Muslims were hiding. Because of this act of treachery, that man was turned into a lizard with a sac under his chin. That is why when we Hindus looked at these lizards, they bob their heads as if they are pointing towards a well.

Weddings in a Camp

Shama was sitting in the back of the car. She was going to take me to the Shah-e-Alam relief camp, which was the biggest camp for those who had lost or simply fled their homes in the riots in Gujarat. I had known Shama years ago when I was in college in Delhi. She was now a prominent political activist there. The driver turned to look back once, and then again—because Shama was breaking thick wads of notes behind us. For a long while the only sound in the car was the dull crack of the stash of hundred-rupee notes being freed from the metal staples holding them together. Shama had probably got the money from a political party in Delhi. Earlier, from the floor of her car, she had picked up a booklet and handed it to me. It was entitled *Genocide in the Land of Gandhi*. She also gave me several flyers about the protests that had been planned in Ahmedabad and in Delhi. One of the flyers carried a small poem by the Urdu poet Bashir Badr: '*Log toot jaate hain / Ek ghar banaane mein / Tum taras nahin khaate / Bastiyaan jalaane mein*' (People are broken in the struggle / To build a house / You feel no pity / In burning down whole settlements).

On the way to the camp, we stopped at a house where a few women widowed in the riots were living along with their children. A social worker was waiting for us there and she quietly took the money that Shama had brought. Then, the woman began saying that there was a lot of anger among the children. They had witnessed the deaths and the rapes. She said that the children had not even been washed for many days. It had taken almost fifteen days to get any clothes for them. Shama was listening to this, and she turned to me and said in English, 'This is the beginning of another Bosnia.' The widows in that house were from the housing colony where Ehsan Jafri, the Congress Party legislator, had been killed. One of the women asked her daughter to speak up, and the nine-year-old girl said that after Jafri had been cut into pieces and burnt, the crowd had done the same to her father. She said that he was hacked into three pieces and then doused with kerosene and set alight. She used the word 'Abbu' for her father. When she finished her story, the girl looked at her mother as if she had just given her teacher the right answer in a classroom.

We were all sitting on the floor of the large hallway. Shama let the women speak to me while she herself stood to the side with the social worker, discussing the possibility of getting the children enrolled in the 'New Age School' in their new neighbourhood. While we talked, a tall white goat entered our little circle, and the children began to laugh. Two of the taller girls pulled at the animal but it was stubborn. It became a part of our small group in the hallway.

All the rooms in the house had bare floors and empty walls. There was no furniture anywhere. I could see a woman in a yellow sari sleeping on the floor in one of the rooms. At the other end of the hallway, in the kitchen, three women were chopping vegetables. Shama finished talking with the social worker and turned her attention to the smaller children. She asked them about songs they knew and a little girl, who couldn't have been older than five or six, began to sing and thrust her little hips to a bawdy song. She sang, '*Meri phool waali sari kharaab ho gayi*' (My flower-print sari has now been soiled). Everyone clapped, and before we left, Shama handed me her camera so that I could take pictures of her with the kids holding hands and singing the Hindustani version of 'We Shall Overcome.' *Hum Honge Kaamyaab.*

From the house in which we had met the widows, Shama asked the driver to take us to the Indian Institute of Management where she was interested in talking to one of the professors. A meeting was being planned in the city for Hindus who were critical of what had been done to their Muslim neighbours. The institute was a sprawling brick building, designed in a modernist fashion by Louis Kahn. Shama spoke to the professor about the meeting for a few minutes and then it turned out that she had come with another purpose. Taking out a CD from her purse, she said that she wanted a copy made. The CD contained a pirated video made by the men who were killing and raping Muslims. The professor immediately got up from his chair and locked the door. We fixed our eyes on the computer screen. But there was a glitch. The file would not open and our host had to summon a technician. This man sorted out the problem in five minutes and then, after he had left, we began to watch the footage. This was not a snuff movie that we were seeing. Instead, it was a sanitized documentary with the camera passing steadily over rows of corpses laid out in what could have been a morgue or a hospital. I looked at Shama's face and sensed her disappointment; she was hoping to have first-hand evidence of the killers committing murder and rape.

At first glance, the dead did not look like the dead. The burnt bodies with puffy, light-coloured lips, and holes where there had been eyes, resembled the rich customers at expensive, exotic spas, covered with ugly mud which has been fortified with minerals. It was only when the camera moved closer or travelled down that you were shocked by the brightness of the exposed intestines or testicles blown up to the size of a child's football. A split sternum appeared on the computer screen. It was yellow in colour. No one in the room said anything. These are the small ways in which genocide becomes mysterious: why does the flesh inside the chest of a man—or perhaps a woman, it was impossible to tell—take on a rich yellow hue when the rest of the body is burnt black?

The air-conditioned room felt cold. And I was glad when Shama insisted that we needed to get to the Shah-e-Alam camp soon. In the car, once again we heard the repeated, now familiar sound of thousands of rupees being snapped out of the sealed wads in which the bank had delivered them. This time Shama was preparing a larger amount for distribution. Once we got to the camp, I could begin to see why.

At first, we passed a row of metal-walled toilets—'Donated by Unicef'—placed in the shadow of huge, black plastic containers for water. The toilets were on the right, twenty-two of them for anywhere from eight to ten thousand people, and the stench of crowded humanity was everywhere. The narrow, twisting street had led us under an old gateway and suddenly opened on to the

larger space of the Shah-e-Alam mosque where the camp
was housed. A canvas ceiling had been erected on the
mosque's grounds to provide cover from the summer sun.
Under it lay thousands of people, sitting on the ground or
leaning against small bundles of bedding and clothes.
Shama walked over to an enclosure on the left where a
makeshift clinic had been set up. There were about a dozen
patients standing in a line beside a desk where two doctors
sat. About fifteen feet away, there were white metal cots,
without their mattresses, and it is there that we sat down.

A few people had been expecting Shama. While they
spoke to her, Shama began to tick off some of the names
on the handwritten list in front of her. She would call out
the name of a woman and sit speaking to her in a low
voice. Each of the women received a bundle of money. I
got up and sat several feet away on a cement platform,
and decided that I would wait there till Shama was finished
with her work. A few women from the camp were sitting
around me, and I asked them to describe their daily routine
in the camp. One of them, whose name was Ruksana,
said, '*Ek din ek baras ke barabar lagta hai*' (A day seems
to last as long as a year). But there was another woman,
quiet, dark-skinned, and with very short hair, who touched
my arm and said she wanted to show me her wounds. She
had been flung on a fire after being raped. Her son, Sohaib,
was only twenty days old at that time. The woman's name
was Razia Bano. All her hair had got burnt in the fire and
that explained why her head appeared recently shaved.
Turning away from the rest of the crowd, Razia showed
me the huge gashes on her back. And then, before I could
say no, she had lifted her sari and showed me the wound
on her left thigh where the doctors had taken the skin for

grafting. It was impossible not to feel that the violence inflicted on Razia included this situation where, in search of help, she had been left without that sense of privacy in front of male strangers which till now would have been habitual to her.

I mentioned this to Shama when we were back in the car. The meeting with the women had tired her; she sat at the back in silence, smoking a cigarette. When I spoke about Razia and my embarrassment as well as pain at her suffering, Shama said in the dark, 'What she didn't tell you was that someone in the mob was carrying a cricket stump and that bastard thrust the wicket in her vagina.' I turned to look at Shama but she was gazing out of the window. She said, 'It is very difficult for them to talk about what has happened. You come to know because Reshma will tell you that this is what was done to Farzana, and Farzana will tell you that this is what happened with Reshma.' It was at the Shah-e-Alam camp that six women members of a fact-finding team had asked small girls if they understood the meaning of the word '*balatkaar*', the Hindi word for rape. A nine-year-old wanted to give a reply to the visiting women. She said, '*Mein bataoon Didi? Balatkar ka matlab jab aurat ko nanga karte hain aur phir use jala dete hain*' (Shall I tell you, Didi? Rape is when a woman is stripped naked and then burnt).

*

Long before I went to Gujarat in the summer of 2002, I had read *Underground*, the Japanese writer Haruki Murakami's book on the gas attack in the Tokyo subway. Murakami had been living in Cambridge, Massachusetts, but was on a visit home when the tragedy took place. Twelve people died and five thousand were injured when some devotees of the Aum Shinrikyo cult released the deadly sarin gas in the trains. When Murakami heard the news, he began to wonder about the victims. In an interview later, Murakami said that 'the first thing that came into my mind was "What kind of people were on the train?" and "What happened to them in the attack?" Because theoretically I could have been one of them'. It is a writer's response and, over nearly a year, Murakami interviewed sixty victims of the attack and presented their stories.

Underground was his first, and to date, only book of non-fiction. Murakami had been living abroad for seven or eight years. In a note that appeared at the end of the first Japanese edition of *Underground*, he wrote: 'Time for me to be heading back to Japan, I thought. Go back and do one solid work, something other than a novel, to probe deep into the heart of my estranged country. And in that way, I might reinforce a new stance for myself, a new vantage point.' It appears that Murakami, thinking of himself as stranded in far-off America at the moment of the attack, was moved to reclaim his share of the national trauma. What had remained for him a blank so far would be replaced by the reality he would investigate on his own terms as a writer. This was also my own purpose in visiting Gujarat which had witnessed unimaginable violence that some believed was only a harbinger of what would happen in the rest of the country.

In another interview, Murakami had said that the media in Japan had not provided adequate information about the people's actual experiences after the attacks: 'It seemed to me that people were more interested in "Who did it?"

and "Why did they do it?"' While these are reasonable questions to ask, in the writer's estimation there isn't enough attention paid to other issues. Murakami explained to his interviewer, 'We should inspect the thing from different directions and angles if we want to know the truth of it. That's why I started to meet the victims of the incident and collected their firsthand stories, face to face.'

I went to Gujarat to speak to the Muslim victims of the riots but it was never an uncomplicated affair. The whole process was tinged with ambivalence. As when I began to speak in the Shah-e-Alam camp to an eleven-year-old boy whose name was Raja Bundubhai Qureshi. When Raja told me his story—a terrible story of his mother and sisters killed—I saw from the way in which he recited the details that, in the name of charity and the need for news, this little boy had been turned into an automaton or an agony-machine. Insert a coin into the slot, and hear a recitation about rape.

Unlike Murakami, I was only aware of the fact that even 'theoretically' I could not have been one of them. I was not a Muslim. If I could identify with anyone, it was with the murderers. And what made this easy was that I could walk into the offices of the Vishwa Hindu Parishad and give my name and no one would suspect me of not being a supporter of the terrible pogrom against Muslims that had just been carried out in the state. It was in that office that I met Mr Keshavram Kashiram Shastri, the chief of the Gujarat VHP. The office was decorated with lurid photos of the burning railway carriage in Godhra, and the dead being carried out on stretchers, and captions in Hindi like 'Even the smoke is saying Jai Shri Ram'. On 28 February 2002, a train carrying Hindu *karsevaks* or religious workers had been set alight in Godhra. Fifty-eight persons, including women and children, had died. The act was believed to be the work of Muslims and, in the days that followed, Hindu mobs raped and burned with impunity in towns and villages all over Gujarat. There were no pictures on the walls of the VHP office of the vengeance brought down upon the Muslims. I had gone to meet Mr Shastri because he had justified the violence by saying, '*Karvun j pade, karvun j pade* (It had to be done, it had to be done). We don't like it, but we were terribly angry. Lust and anger are blind.' He had also excused the rioters, saying that they were '*kelvayela Hindu chokra*' (well-bred Hindu boys).

Mr Shastri told me that he was ninety-seven years old. He had fair skin and large, light-coloured, watery eyes. On his head he wore a pale saffron cap, and he had put a red mark in the shape of a V on his forehead. We were talking in a large, bare room with Mr Shastri sitting behind a large wooden desk which had a single Manila folder placed on it. Men would periodically come into the room and touch his feet and then leave. For the whole time I was in that room, for the better part of an hour, a man with a large moustache sat to my left, not speaking and not even once turning to look at me. When Mr Shastri found out that I lived in America, he began telling me that he was working on a paper entitled 'Language and Art in Navajo Universe'. I expressed surprise. Mr Shastri remained serene. He started speaking of the language that the Navajos used, '*Apni hee bhasha hai, yahin se le gaye hain*' (It is our own language, they have taken it from here).

Mr Shastri spoke at length about the Native Americans, and about Mongols and their relationship with Indians. He explained to me the intricacies of the active voice and the passive voice in Sanskrit. And about the discovery of gold, silver and glass. I did not understand the point of anything he said. Then he began talking about the lack of philosophy in Islam and in Christianity. The Muslims burnt all our scriptures, but the Christians didn't. Yet, there was enough that had endured the trials of history. He mentioned Panini's grammar, as an example, a work that had lasted two thousand five hundred years.

Then, the interview was over. Mr Shastri asked me a second time what my name was, and then he explained its derivation from Sanskrit. He raised his hand and blessed me with the word 'Shubhasheesh'. This is what I got for being a good Hindu in front of him. It was not the first time this had happened in Gujarat. I would decide I would be polite in my conversations, and begin by making harmless inquiries so as not to arouse suspicion. And then when the moment would seem to have passed I could have just turned around and popped a question like 'How can you go to sleep at night after the misery you have brought upon so many innocent people?'

In Mr Shastri's case, the fault was perhaps only mine. I had asked him, at the beginning of our conversation, 'Who is a Hindu?' All his ramblings about his Brahmanic discipline, or Panini's grammar, and even the Navajo Indians, were a way of telling me about an immemorial, mythic past. Mr Shastri was old and gentle, and I felt a little twinge of guilt for disliking him, though dislike him I did. I disliked him because he had told a journalist that the VHP had not planned the riots before the Godhra incident: it was on the morning after the burning of the train compartment that the party workers had sat down and prepared a list of the Muslim businesses to destroy in

Ahmedabad. His candour could only be the result of an unchallenged arrogance as a leader of right-wing Hindus. His innocuous interest in grammar shielded, and even sanctioned, the actions of the rioters in Ahmedabad. Those were the people who had distributed flyers which said: 'We have untied the penises which were tied till now. Without castor oil in the arse we have made them cry. Those who call religious war, violence, are all fuckers. We have widened the tight vaginas of the bibis.'

*

Mr Azad was sitting at a conference table with a small mound of women's underwear in front of him. There were four or five men sitting around the table. Mr Azad got up to greet me. He was a tall, middle-aged man, with a clipped moustache. He asked me to sit down, and water was brought for me by one of the men I had seen outside. The conversation I had interrupted resumed. A man in a white kurta, holding a cellphone in his hand, was asking Mr Azad that he be given a chance. 'We can help,' he said insistently. 'Give us fifteen minutes.' There were three other men, also wearing white kurtas, sitting next to the man with the cellphone. They looked expectantly at Mr Azad.

With the air of a man who already knew the answer to his question, Mr Azad asked, 'What will you do in those fifteen minutes?'

'We will do breathing exercises,' said the man with the cellphone.

Mr Azad held up a bunch of brown brassieres in his right hand. 'This is more important than breathing techniques.' In the local refugee camps, there was a great need for women's undergarments. Children needed biscuits. The cost of giving every child in the camps four cookies each on a single day was anywhere between fifty to seventy-five thousand rupees. With such basic needs still unmet, why would anyone in the camp want to do breathing exercises?

This was my first meeting with Mr Azad. I had learnt that he was running a small relief operation, picking up the pieces after the devastation of the riots. We had talked on the phone when I had called from Delhi. He had promised to find me a hotel and I had come directly to his office after landing at the Ahmedabad airport that evening.

The men in white kurtas, sitting across the table from Mr Azad, did not say anything for a while. They looked calm. Then, one of them, speaking with a North African accent, said that he was a Muslim like Mr Azad, but even he was convinced of the good of his Guruji's teachings. The man was handsome and he had the kind of relaxed, athletic bearing that only the very rich seem to have. He said to Mr Azad in a soft voice, 'We have centres in a hundred and forty-five countries. We have five thousand branches all over the world. You must allow us to help you.'

Mr Azad examined the grain of the wood on his desk. When no one spoke for a while, the man with the cellphone said, 'Please arrange for us to go into the camps ... . If the mind is not stable, whatever you provide will not be enough for those who are suffering.'

Mr Azad didn't seem to want to relent. I wondered whether he had thought about saying yes because to say no, for those sitting around him, made him a recalcitrant Muslim, the one who complained when he was hurt but who refused help when it came from the Hindus. He was paying full attention to the man with the cellphone who had began to quote his Guruji's teachings. 'Grace is blowing everywhere,' he said with a smile. When Mr Azad didn't respond, the man said, 'We are giving people a stable mind, so that they can experience grace within them.' He sounded as if he was selling a new line of suitcases.

The meeting ended and Mr Azad took me down to his car. He said that we would stop at his home for dinner and then he would drive me over to the hotel. Mr Azad's wife, Uzzma, had set out a variety of Gujarati dishes on the table for us to eat. Uzzma was in business with her husband; both had now given up their jobs to work in the relief effort. The couple had earlier planned to retire in New Zealand, but the riots had forced them to change their goals. When we were putting food on our plates, a young man came out of a room on the side. He was their son, and while he was still there, Mr Azad said; 'It is unnatural for a father to say goodbye to his son in the morning and wonder whether he is going to see him again in the evening.'

The line had been used by Mr Azad before. He now set the plate of food aside and allowed the moment of silence to grow. It was clear that the riots had been a dramatic event, and they had given Mr Azad a role. Although I was eager to provide audience I was also hungry and I liked the food that Uzzma had cooked. Despite the plate of food in front of him, Mr Azad remained unmoved, just as he had been in front of the men at the meeting. While I ate the hot puris and the meat curry, Mr Azad spoke of the way in which the government in Gujarat had refused to help the victims. A sum of Rs 1250 was all that was first offered as compensation if all your moveable property had been destroyed. How much was that—I asked myself—twenty-five dollars? By the time the riots ended, there were a 125,000 people in the camps in Ahmedabad. For the first five days, the government did not even provide toilets there. Soon after September 11, Mr Azad said, George Bush had made a public appeal that innocent Muslim citizens should not be targeted and attacked. In Gujarat, after the train-burning in Godhra, the ruling Bharatiya Janata Party leaders had exhorted people to do precisely the opposite. Gujarat had become a graveyard. There were six thousand homeless victims of the riots living in a Muslim cemetery near Mr Azad's house. The people in the cemetery survived without a shred of support from the government. They had to make do with the absolute minimum. The space between two graves was where a whole family would sleep.

*

My room in Ahmedabad's Hotel Aaram had a new door. The wood was shiny and light brown in colour; the room number had been written on the top of the door panel with chalk. Three months earlier, on 1 March 2002 a mob had broken down the old door. Abid Ali Aljibhai, the young owner of Aaram, told me that the rioters wanted things they could steal. From the room in which I was staying, they had carried away the wall-clock and the colour TV. On the previous evening, a larger group of rioters had arrived with petrol. The group had set fire to a restaurant in the basement of the same building. The mob, directed by a leader of the ruling Hindu party, had also tried to get into the hotel upstairs but hadn't succeeded because the shutters had been locked from inside. Aljibhai, who is Muslim, was hiding in the hotel with five of his hotel guests. All his guests were Hindu but the murderous crowd, Aljibhai said, would not have waited to find out such details.

Downstairs, the Red Carpet Restaurant was gutted. The metal gates were torn open and everything inside burnt an ashen grey; the only bit of colour that now remained was a strip of melted red plastic on one side of the charred marquee. There were other businesses in the same complex— there was a travel agency as well as a phone service company—but they were owned by Hindus and had been left untouched. This was a pattern that was repeated everywhere in Ahmedabad. You would see a row of white flats built together: all of them were intact except for one or two which appeared to have been smudged by an inky thumb.

The devastation was remarkable. It is what the visitor first saw: the skeletons of burnt buildings. And yet, what I have described so far is still not quite as shocking as the sight of the burnt houses in parts of Ahmedabad like Naroda-Patiya: there, along with petrol and kerosene, the rioters had used cylinders of cooking gas. Those homes were wrecked by explosions. The fire consumed everything. Only the damaged walls and sagging, burnt-out roofs remained. In one house, the blades of a ceiling fan had drooped in the fire, and resembled the wilted petals of a flower. In another, a sack of sugar had turned to dark amber syrup and flowed onto the steps outside where it had dried. An umbrella, folded and hanging from a nail on the outer wall, absurdly signalled a past life in the abandoned quarters. Those who used to live there were either dead or crowded into makeshift relief camps in the Muslim areas of the city.

If you asked anyone in Ahmedabad why this happened—why what amounted to an ethnic cleansing had taken place—they would very likely tell you one of two things. They would say that the killings and the destruction was a just response to the torching, on 27 February, in a town to the east of Ahmedabad, of a train-compartment in which fifty-eight Hindu karsevaks had been killed. Or they would say that in India as a whole, and in Gujarat in particular, the Muslim is a second-class citizen and, in the current environment, any excuse can be used to kill or terrorize them. The two answers seemed to present opposed truths. But the depressing fact was that they both performed the same function: in Ahmedabad, they revealed the religious identity of the speaker.

The first answer was given by a Hindu, and the second by a Muslim. This social division was the more salient truth. It was nearly inescapable in Gujarat and when you had heard it a hundred times, you stopped asking anyone for reasons to explain what happened there. More than four months had passed since the violence erupted. Although people were still in camps, there was talk of life returning to normal. The BJP, in power in Gujarat, was sensing victory at the polls because of wide Hindu support and calling for fresh elections. The party's expectations were fulfilled some months later when, in mid-December, the BJP won power in the state legislature with a landslide majority.

Next door to the Aaram was Hans Inn which had also been destroyed. When the fire started, there were fourteen people trapped inside. The mob, which was at least 5000 strong, did not allow anyone to come out. According to a human rights group report, a government minister had directed the attack on the hotel.

I would not have heard about what had happened at Hans Inn—the evidence of the fire was there, but I had not known about the deaths—if I had not inquired about the dull hammering that I heard through the hot afternoons on the other side of my hotel wall. The man who told me about the fire that had gutted Hans Inn had himself suffered during the riots. He was a wealthy businessman, a Muslim, and had to flee his home. But he wanted things to quickly return to normal. Unlike me, who wanted to know what had transpired in March, he did not want to dwell too much on what had happened. He had lived through four riots in Ahmedabad. He said, as if offering proof of the way in which the daily, healthy routine had begun to assert itself, that the schools had just reopened for the first time.

Indeed, on the other side of Aaram, there was a school called Dewan Ballubhai, and the singing of children's voices could be heard across the wall. One morning, I went to the principal, Mr Patel, and asked him if I could visit one of his classrooms. I was told to wait while Mr Patel addressed his school on the public address system. The students sat in their classes, listening to their principal's voice, while he spoke to them from his office. Mr Patel was standing with his back to me, microphone in hand, watching his own reflection in the glass cabinet where his school's trophies were stored. When the speech was over—

some of the students had begun wearing expensive, designer sneakers, and they were told that they'd be allowed to use only ordinary canvas shoes—he gestured towards me. I was going to meet the twelfth grade.

There was an item in that day's paper about Muslim passengers on railway trains. I read the news report out to the students and asked them to write down their responses. The story was fairly straightforward: Muslim passengers travelling on Gujarat trains were concealing their identities by adopting Hindu names. I had a few other questions for the students, and I dutifully put those queries before them, but it was the one about the travellers that interested me the most. When I read their responses, I found out that almost all the students had recommended that the passengers who gave false names should be chastised. Some felt that more harsh punishments·should follow. A few had taken care to mention that the riots had caused disturbances, but the passenger should be told by the authorities that what he or she was doing was wrong. One school kid, the only one writing in English, added that if the ticket collector finds out that the passenger is a Pakistani terrorist, the offender should be sent to jail. There was one student who had written that the passenger should be allowed to go on his way. By way of explanation, the student had written that there were riots going on in the state of Gujarat—except that next to the common Hindustani word for riots, he had written in English, 'war'. Only one lone student willing to identify with the traveller's fears! My eye went down to the student's name. Saiyed Mustkimm. It is a Muslim name. Everyone else among Saiyed's classmates, if I am to go by the names written on the essay sheets returned to me, was Hindu.

*

In mid-April 2002, then Prime Minister Atal Behari Vajpayee told the national executive of the BJP assembled in Goa, 'Wherever Muslims are they do not want to live with others peacefully.' These words were widely seen as an endorsement of the pogrom that had just been carried out in Gujarat, and Vajpayee's remarks were condemned as such by much of the liberal intelligentsia as well as the popular media. The prime minister said in response that he had been misquoted. If this was true, then he had been repeatedly misheard at the meeting. Mr Vajpayee had also said that wherever 'there is a Muslim population in the world, the countries live under threat of militancy and terrorism'. He had then added, 'Muslims the world over do not want to mingle with other communities ... . In Indonesia, Malaysia, wherever Muslims are living, they don't want to live in harmony. *Ghul milkar nahin rehte.* They do not live together with others in peace.'

A few days later, Siddharth Varadarajan, a newspaper editor in Delhi, published a commentary about an incident that had occurred in Gujarat on 25 March, just a few weeks before the prime minister had made his offensive remark. Varadarajan wrote that he had received from his staff in Ahmedabad a photograph which had revolted him. In the picture, a woman lay dead on the road. Her clothes had been ripped off and, in the centre of the frame, close to her bloodied body, lay a red brick. The woman was a Hindu and her name was Geetaben. It was in broad daylight, near a bus stop, that she was murdered by a Hindu mob because she had married a Muslim man. When the attackers had attempted to kill her husband, she had stood in the way and had thereby given him a chance to escape. Varadarajan wrote, 'But the killers seemed more interested in her. She was dragged out, stripped naked and killed.'

Against Geetaben, Varadarajan had placed not the mob, but the prime minister of India who had delivered his shameful statement in Goa about Muslims. In the eyes of the Delhi journalist, Geetaben had shown 'more courage, humanity and dignity and more fidelity to the Hindu religion' in her single moment of defiance than the Indian premier had done during the entire month. Varadarajan had pointed out for his readers the context in which the prime minister's words became not only ironical but deeply tragic. There was now not even one Muslim business left in Gujarat. The men manning the photocopying machines near the courts would refuse to make copies for the Muslim lawyers. Men with beards were not being served in the restaurants as well as shops in the entire state. Mothers prayed that their children wouldn't call them 'ammi' on the street and thereby identify them as Muslims. 'Instead of speaking out against this,' Varadarajan wrote, 'Mr Vajpayee actually had the gall to say Muslims do not wish to live in peace.'

Unlike the journalist in Delhi who had made a strong but fair case against the prime minister, I was more interested in Geetaben. I was unable to find her husband in Ahmedabad. There were a few stories, some of them involving insanity and even suicide, but not one of them could be confirmed. But I was still thinking of Geetaben's story when I asked a friend one afternoon whether he knew of any Hindu-Muslim couples in the city. There had to be many others. Only nine days after Geetaben's killing, a thirty-four-year-old Muslim man, Muhammad Riyaz Qureshi, had been hacked to death and then burnt in Shahpur Darwaza, Ahmedabad. According to the police, Qureshi was murdered because he was married to a Hindu. My friend knew of these items that had appeared in the news; he was himself a journalist who worked at an English language daily in Ahmedabad. He had been helpful to me before, and this time too, he did not let me walk away empty-handed. On a scrap of paper, he wrote down the names of two men and also their telephone numbers, and made me promise him that I would not reveal how I had come by the information. 'In such times,' he said, 'people are very sensitive.'

There was a small telephone booth near my friend's office. Its owner was sitting on a cot that he had pulled outside in order to escape the afternoon heat. I went in and called the first number on the piece of paper I had with me. A woman answered. I only knew her husband's name and I asked for him. She said he would be at work. There was the noise of water running while the woman spoke to me. I realized I had disturbed her at home. Then I called the number that the woman gave me. I asked the man who picked up if he was Aziz. When he said yes, I told him that I was a visitor and I was a Hindu who had married a Muslim. I was writing a book about my marriage and I was interested, I said, in talking to him and finding out, in a place like Gujarat, what it meant to be married to someone from the other religion.

There was silence at the other end. In a level, serious tone, the man asked me, 'Who told you about me?'

I do not think I even paused. I had recently arrived in the city, I told Aziz, and I had been chatting with a group of people at a party just the previous night. 'When I told them about my book, this man, who was a lawyer, I think, took me aside. He said he was a friend of yours and he gave me your name. In strict confidence, of course.'

'What was his name?' Aziz asked.

'I do not know,' I said, 'I don't think I even asked him.'

The telephone booth was a small wooden room with a single naked bulb. I could use the plastic fan nailed to one wall, but when I put it on it clattered loudly. I looked at the dusty, immobile blades of the plastic fan as I waited for Aziz to speak. I had shocked him, I knew that. I didn't know whether, if I acknowledged this fact, it would make it any easier for him to talk to me. I stayed silent. I entertained the possibility that if I ignored our awkwardness, Aziz would perhaps assume that things were normal.

'If you see this man again,' Aziz said after a while, 'please tell him that if he is really a friend of mine, he will not tell anyone else what he told you.'

He hung up.

The phone was wet from my sweat. I was suddenly aware of the smell in the tiny booth; it was the smell of the filth in that shop mixed with the rancid odour of my own body. There was no reason now to call the second number. On the piece of paper in front of me was written the name 'Sagar Rao'. Instead of calling his number, I called my friend instead and told him what Aziz had told me. My friend, whom I'll call Anil here, laughed and said, 'You did well. Don't give my name ever.' Then, he told me where I would find the second man. Anil asked me to go to the office of a Gujarati newspaper, *Sandesh*. He said that I would find Sagar Rao there. While Aziz was a

Muslim man married to a Hindu, Rao was a Hindu married
to a Muslim woman. Anil said that Rao was the advertising
manager of the newspaper. His newspaper had fanned the
flames of the riots by publishing stories about ten to fifteen
kidnapped Hindu women whose breasts had been sliced
off. The stories were false.

It was a long ride on the three-wheeler, almost forty-
five minutes through the late afternoon rush hour. The
streets were thick with traffic and fumes. At last I was at
Rao's office, a shining white, modern building with marble
floors and tinted-glass facade. I showed my press pass
from a New York agency and said that I was looking for
Sagar Rao. I was directed to an upper floor and I could
already feel my sweat drying as I made my way through
the large, air-conditioned space. Rao sat in a glass cubicle
in the middle of a large floor. He was speaking in a loud
voice to a group of men standing around him; he would
joke and they would laugh, and he would laugh too, very
loudly. I stood outside the cubicle. Rao was heavy-set and
bearded. He was wearing a white kurta which made him
look like a politician. When his cellphone rang, he
instructed the person who was calling him to buy flowers.
'You pick me up, but make sure you buy the flowers first,'
he said in Hindi.

At last, Rao noticed me and sent a peon, wearing a
white Gandhi cap on his head, to ask me what I wanted.
I gave the man my card. Rao continued with his
conversation and with his jokes, but a few minutes later
I saw him gesture at the peon again. I was being summoned.
He asked me to sit but then seemed to forget about me.
I noticed that Rao had a red tilak smeared on his forehead.
He began to tell two of the men standing to one side

about a dinner party he had attended. One of the phones on Rao's desk rang and while he was talking on it, explaining why the caller needed to talk to the editor, another phone next to it began to ring. One of the men standing beside the desk took the call and handed the phone over to Rao with a whisper. Rao carried out an intermittent conversation on both lines. Tea was brought for me and I finished drinking it. The conversation and the joking in the room went on. More people came and sat down and talked to Rao. Finally, he looked up from his papers and asked me, 'What can I do for you?'

I did not know what to say to him. For several minutes, I had been asking myself if Rao already knew why I was there, and if that would explain why he was stalling. But, this was impossible. Then, I had begun to wonder why he was so incurious. He had let a stranger come in and sit in his office. He had even provided tea. For much of the time that I had been sitting there quietly, Rao had not actually been working. Did he not want to know what I was doing in his office? And now, when he asked me precisely that, I did not see how I could say anything to him in front of all the people around him. These other people, incidentally, had all turned around and were staring at me. I switched to English and said, 'It ... is ... personal.' Rao nodded and said in Hindi, 'No problem. Go ahead.'

I thought of Aziz and what he had said to me on the phone, but I could not see how to avoid answering Rao's question. Nevertheless, I said nothing about his marriage to a Muslim. I only said that my wife was a Muslim and that I was writing about such mixed marriages in Gujarat. Rao kept nodding his head as I spoke, and everyone else continued to look at me. When I stopped, Rao said in a flat voice, 'That is fine. But what do you want me to do?'

'I was wondering if it would be possible to interview you.'

'I will be honest with you,' Rao said, 'I myself am married to a Muslim. It is not an issue between us. I am Hindu, I worship my gods. She is a Muslim, her Allah is dear to her. But in a disturbed time, things can go wrong. Just the other day, she had gone to meet some relatives. She was coming out of a Muslim locality and a man there mistook her for a Hindu and tried to attack her with a sword. Thank god, nothing happened.'

I said, 'Perhaps I could get in touch with you later and have a conversation with both of you.'

He said, 'Yes, you can do that. You can come to my house and have tea.'

Then, he gave me his home phone number and asked me to call him the next day at nine in the morning. I did and he asked me to call him at three in the afternoon. In the afternoon, a man who answered the phone every time I called said that Rao was not in the office.

It had been around this time the previous day that I had called Aziz.

I felt bad about calling him again, but I did, and almost regretted doing this when I heard his voice at the other end. When I identified myself, I became aware once more of the silence on his side.

I began to tell him why I had called. 'I felt very bad yesterday,' I said, 'I am calling to apologize for having made you uncomfortable.'

'Tell me one thing,' he said. 'My wife told me that you had called my home first and then she gave you my office number. I did not know that you had my home phone number. Who is it that you met at the party? Tell me.'

I didn't know the name, I said, and knew that Aziz thought that I was lying.

He didn't say anything more and I spoke again, offering apologies and assuring him that I wanted him and his wife to be safe. Aziz graciously thanked me. He said, 'At any other time, we could have met. But the times are very bad. It is Gujarat ... .' And then, he said goodbye.

The next morning, I got Sagar Rao on the phone but he said that he had not had a chance to ask his wife yet. 'You can come and have tea with us. We'll talk,' he said. I called him several times over the next two days and then again a week later. Rao and I did not see each other again, and I did not get to meet his wife. I could not even get the chance to ask Rao if he ever felt afraid in the way that Aziz did. And if not, why not.

*

The day I flew back to Delhi from Ahmedabad, I went to the post office in Jor Bagh to pay a phone bill for a friend. There was a painted sign on the office wall which said, 'A customer is the most important visitor on our premises'. Next to the sign was a large photograph which showed Mahatma Gandhi talking to someone on the phone.

Gandhi can be used to sell almost anything in India, but it is increasingly getting difficult to sell Gandhi himself. The previous night in Ahmedabad, I had gone to the Sabarmati Ashram to watch the sound-and-light show on Gandhi. When I tried to buy a ticket, the man at the counter suggested that I hold on to my money. 'Unless there are five persons in the audience,' he said, 'the show will be cancelled.' There was still half an hour to go. I waited. After a while, the ticket-seller came out of his little room. We began to talk. I smelt alcohol on his breath. More time passed, and I was still the only person at the gate. I asked the man if I could buy five tickets myself. 'Yes,' he said, and added, in a voice touched with resignation, 'I am here to serve you.'

The ashram was on the bank of the Sabarmati, although it should be said that the river, invisible in the dark, was only a sluggish sewer. I had come there earlier during the afternoon, and had looked down at the river and seen a few donkeys, belonging to washermen, grazing near clothes that had been spread out to dry. Waterfowl made their way over clumps of hyacinth growing in the ditches, but it was clear that the mostly dry river bed was a place where people came to defecate. Now, at night, the smell of shit and putrefaction was carried by the breeze. But the atmosphere was not unpleasant. The breeze took the edge off the heat, and the sounds of the distant city traffic were barely audible. The leaves of the neem trees rustled above me. Behind me, a stray dog that had stretched its body across two chairs, drawn no doubt by the coolness of the metal seats, regularly sighed in its sleep.

It was in 1915 that Gandhi had established the Sabarmati Ashram, and he had lived there till 1930. It was from there that he had started on his Dandi March, vowing not to return till India became free. When freedom came, at midnight on 15 August 1947, Gandhi was asleep in the wreckage of a Muslim's house. He was in Calcutta, which had gone up in flames, appealing for peace between Hindus and Muslims. Exactly a year earlier, it was also in

Calcutta that the riots over the demand for Pakistan had started. In 1947, Gandhi had gone to Bengal because, as one newspaper put it, he had been asked 'to pour a pot of water over the raging fire that was burning in Calcutta'. The papers reported that Gandhi had said that 'he would love to give his life if it contributed to the quenching of mob-fury'. On 2 September, Gandhi began a fast to death. He did not eat or drink anything for seventy-three hours, and broke his fast only after he received promises of peace from the members of both communities in Calcutta. A few months later, in late January 1948, he was shot dead by a Hindu man who believed that he was thereby snuffing out the love for Muslims from Gandhi's unpatriotic heart. Gandhi had not returned to Sabarmati since his departure in 1930.

The rooms in the ashram today display old photographs and museum artefacts—Gandhi's spinning wheel, a time-piece, his dentures, a pair of wire-rimmed glasses. Visitors walk around and read the rules from many years ago painted on the walls. One of them is titled 'Equality of religions' and it states that everyone at the ashram should 'entertain the same respect for the religious faiths of others as one accords to one's own'. But what did such rules mean in contemporary Ahmedabad?

While strolling around in the ashram earlier that day, I had fallen into a conversation with a group of Bihari workers—workers with their hands flecked with blue and white paint because they were engaged in the task of renovating Sabarmati railway station. One of them, whose name was Jagat Singh Yadav, said to me that the problem with Ahmedabad was that it had too many Muslims. He said, 'Wherever you find so many Muslims, there is bound to be trouble.' The statement sounded suspiciously similar to what Prime Minister Vajpayee had said in Goa, but it is also true that such remarks were very common in Gujarat. I gave the comment no more thought till some days later, when I was back in Delhi, and reading old newspapers on microfiche in the Nehru Memorial Library.

The newspapers during August 1947 had been full of reports of riots each day. On 24 August, for example, there was a report on the front page of the *Hindustan Times* that Prime Minister Nehru was flying to riot-affected Jallandhar in Punjab. There was an overwrought account from Lahore, in Pakistan, which said that over 1,600 houses had been destroyed in the violence. It was titled 'Eight Days of Terror in Lahore'. There was also a report from Calcutta. It mentioned that Mahatma Gandhi, while addressing the crowd gathered for a prayer meeting with him, had said that Hindus should not object to the cry *Allah-u-Akbar* which was raised by the Muslims. Gandhi had 'held that it was probably a cry greater than which the world had not produced. It was a soul-stirring religious cry which meant that God only was great. There was nobility in the meaning. Did it become objectionable because it was in Arabic? Hindus should have no hesitation in uttering the cry together with their Muslim friends'.

I must confess that when I first read the report—the scratchy print splayed across the screen of the clattering microfiche machine—I found it bewildering. The cry *Allah-u-Akbar* would have been heard by Hindus, or at least by those Hindus who had been involved in riots, when the Muslim mobs were about to attack them. (The Hindus and Sikhs had cries of their own, which were also raised when their mobs roamed the streets, but that is beside the point.) The first image that came to mind on reading Gandhi's words was of a refugee being told that he or she should join with the attackers! The religious slogans that were being used by the mobs from each community incited fear; they did not in any way stir the soul. But I also understood that Gandhi was trying to remove that fear by reading the meaning of the cry literally and reminding everyone of that basic truth. More than that, in that utterly radical appeal to Hindus that they too should participate in saying *Allah-u-Akbar*, he was underlining the respect one has to have for other religions distinct from one's own. He was laying claim to the belief that he himself, and also everyone else, was bound to God and not to religion, and hence, as he had once famously declared about himself, we were all, each one of us who were Indian, simultaneously Hindu, Muslim, Christian and Sikh.

My mind went back to Jagat Singh Yadav in Sabarmati Ashram and his statement about Muslims. The news report about Gandhi's prayer meeting now provoked a question. If Jagat believed in God, would he be prepared to say that the God that the Muslim worshipped was also his own? Would the mosque also be Jagat's temple? The same questions could be asked of a Muslim, of course, and, sitting in the Teen Murti Library, I thought of Mr Azad who, while addressing his fellow Muslims in Ahmedabad, had said that while the Hindu majority had mistreated them during the riots, were they not also themselves mistaken in giving Hindus names like kafir?

Gandhi's openness—on one of the walls at the ashram at Sabarmati were his words, 'I want the cultures of all lands to be blown about my house as freely as possible'—

had its roots in Gujarat's own plural past. The social historian Shail Mayaram has written that 'Gandhi could, arguably, only have been born in Gujarat'. The Mahatma's mother belonged to the Parnami cult which had a strong Islamic derivation; he himself adhered to the Vaishnava dharma which had what Mayaram calls 'a moral and religious philosophy with a highly incorporative vision'. Porbandar, where Gandhi was born, was a port. Such places in Gujarat had served not only as gateways to trade and commerce but also to ideas, and science, and the literary arts. Through the ages, the entire region came to acquire a political, cultural and linguistic diversity. This meant that every religious group possessed a complex identity influenced by the others. According to Mayaram, 'Gujarat is today one of the Indian States with the largest number of Muslim communities including groups that combined the idea of the worship of the ten avatars with Quranic cosmology.'

It is this rich material history of influence and interdependence that had produced the eclectic imagination of Mohandas Gandhi. So, along with the murder of Gandhi all over again, it was the idea of a syncretic culture that was being laid waste when armed brigands of the VHP and Bajrang Dal wrote on the walls of the houses that they had destroyed 'Muslims leave India'. The nearly 2000 dead, the rape of hundreds of women and the demolishing of many mosques was evidence of this.

The violence in Gujarat was still continuing when a Delhi newspaper published a brief story about a Muslim saint's *dargah* in Amreli which was being taken care of by Hindu villagers ever since the Muslims in the village had migrated after the Partition. We were supposed to feel happy about this, and perhaps I did. Is this not what I wanted from Jagat?

It would be wrong not to demand more. It is not merely respect for the other's religion that is important; what is essential is that we have respect for the other's rights as a human being. The fundamentalists in India deny the former and thereby also the latter; the secularists fight for the latter but pay very little attention to the former. Both aspects can come together in the celebration of a shared life. The world as well as the history that a Hindu claims as his own is in many ways indistinguishable from the world and the history of his Muslim neighbour's. For either of them to contemplate harming the other is to do injury to the self. All of this sounds hopelessly idealistic after the violence of Gujarat. In its aftermath, a good start would be to remember that religion plays only a small part in the riots. In fact, as Ashis Nandy has rightly remarked, religious riots have become 'one of the most secularized aspects of Indian public life'. Profane matters like profits and property often determine the course that riots take. Crass calculations of electoral politics predetermine how many members of which community are likely to die. Indeed, it would appear that very little is left to chance. During the first week of rioting in Gujarat, the police in nearby Jaipur arrested seventy bookies. These men had been fuelling rumours about the riots with the goal of encouraging bets on the chances of the violence in Gujarat state inflaming other areas. The men were using their cellphones to spread rumours of clashes between Hindus and Muslims. The odds being offered on the possibility of unrest crossing the borders of Gujarat were between 4-1 and 6-1.

*

There was a busy vegetarian restaurant close to Aaram hotel, which served a 'fixed pure vegetarian' meal for fifteen rupees. That is where I ate lunch every day. As soon as one had found a seat, the manager would bring over his notebook, ask for the customer's name, and write down a number next to it. One day a young man next to me refused to say who he was. A small group of hotel employees gathered around him, and I could hear the mockery in their tone as they explained the need for a name. What would a Muslim man or woman have said to the manager's question in the days after the riots?

There was irony in this situation too. Many such restaurants in Ahmedabad had been owned by the Cheliya Muslims, a prosperous sect of Muslims from Mehsana district in Gujarat. These establishments served mainly Hindus, and they employed Hindu cooks. Even the names that these restaurants had were Hindu ones, including names of Hindu gods and goddesses. It was only after the buildings had been torched by the mobs that many of the neighbours learned that those businesses had been owned by Muslims. Many of the Muslim owners believed that the list of their businesses had been prepared much in advance, even before the train attack in Godhra, but there was also the opposite contention made by Mr Shastri from the VHP that they had come up with the list only on the morning of 28 February.

After eating my lunch, I would take a three-wheeler to the Darya Khan Gumbat relief camp. It was there that I met Noorjehan who said that she had lost her pets on the very first day of the riots. Noorjehan was a young woman with delicate features and an air of great sadness about her. When the crowd came—they were about seven or eight hundred—Noorjehan was watering her plants. She used the English word 'flowers' to tell me that she had a small garden. Noorjehan's family owned goats. They were now gone. She had a cat which she had named Sonu; it had long hair and had been brought from Bombay. The men in the mob killed the cat as well as her other pets. Most dear to Noorjehan had been a parrot, Raja, which used to call out Noorjehan's name. I think I understood what Noorjehan meant when, between her tears, she said, 'Those animals loved me. More than human beings, I loved the animals and the birds. There is love between animals.'

Noorjehan showed the cuttings from English and Urdu newspapers which had carried her story on the day after the riots. There was a photograph of her in a national daily, her eyes swollen red, but it was clear that the photographer had been drawn by her beauty. I learned from the cuttings that the men who entered her house hit her at the back of the head with a sword and then gang-raped her. Later, a niece had to pull Noorjehan away from a fire where her assailants had pushed her.

I saw Noorjehan several times. I would get to the camp around three o'clock in the afternoon when sewing machines would be given out to a few of the victims. The women from the camp would be waiting under a tarpaulin tent for the relief workers to arrive. One day Noorjehan said that she had received some money from an agency that was helping women who had been raped. She said that she would use the money to buy back her pets if they were still alive.

The camp had been set up in an old high school building. The stairway smelt as if an animal had died there. Each room had old walls with scenes, outlined in black paint, from stories for children. Although everyone took off their slippers and shoes at the door, the floors were gritty with dirt. Everyone slept on the floors. It was in one of those rooms one day that Noorjehan introduced me to an old woman, a widow, who was the mother-in-law of Kausar Bano. It was Kausar's widely-reported story, narrated with varying details by countless victims, which had been described by the women's fact-finding team as a 'collective experience' and a 'meta-narrative of bestiality, a meta-narrative of helpless victimhood'. Kausar had been visiting her parents in Naroda Patiya. She was pregnant. Her attackers used a sword to cut open her womb and then threw her and the nine-month-old foetus into a fire.

The last time I saw Noorjehan was when she waved at me from a window: I was downstairs at a wedding for twenty young women in the camp. The grooms sat in a square, in the best clothes that they owned. It was three-thirty in the afternoon and the heat made me feel that we had all been stuffed into a well where the water had long ago gone dry. A politician appeared, clad in a white sherwani. All the brides, dressed in red, were brought to the edge of the gathering and then led to an adjoining room. The qazi, looking dignified with his white beard, went around to each groom collecting signatures on the marriage licenses. The previous day I had seen shiny new trunks being unloaded from a truck. The trunks were made of thin aluminium and now they were stacked in the corridor: in each box had been put a blanket, a bedsheet, one or two utensils, and a copy of the *Qur'an*.

These wedding gifts had been provided by the Jamaat-i-
Islami, the right-wing Islamic party. That is what Mr
Azad had complained against: the government was totally
anti-Muslim, and none of the secular groups were doing
much either. In that vacuum, organizations like the Jamaat
were showing themselves as willing to help the Muslim
victims of the riots. In the future, Mr Azad believed, the
right-wing groups would demand their pound of flesh in
support from all those they had helped in their hours of
darkness.

When the qazi was done with the signatures from the
grooms, he went to the room where the brides were sitting.
I had so far been chatting with one of the men who was
getting married, a cheerful man named Mohammed Yaseen,
but one of the bearded men from the Jamaat-i-Islami came
up and handed me a small bottle of fragrant *attar*. With
great politeness, he requested me to put a few drops of
perfume on each of the grooms. I was even taught how to
do it. Take a drop on your index finger, rub your thumb
and finger lightly, and then brush your hand against the
groom's shoulder and sleeve. I went around doing just
that, but the perfume was very strong, and made my skin
sting. By the time I was done, the qazi returned and read
out a short prayer. Then, the ceremony was over. I went
over to several of the grooms to congratulate them. But,
people had questions for me. A man who said his name
was Mohammed Iqbal wanted to know if I was related to
the Abids. Then, an older man, with a grave demeanour,
asked me whether I was a Pathan. He asked me for my
name. He had assumed I was a Muslim and, instead of
telling him that he was wrong and that I was a Hindu, I
answered that my name was Safdar Ali.

Mohammed Yaseen, the man I had been speaking to earlier, took me to meet his bride and his family. The older people made it a point to tell me that their sadness had lifted at the sight of the young getting married. But there was also more to the matter. Families with young women in their homes were fearful of further violence. Manzoor Ali, the father of one of the grooms, explained why he had given his assent. 'The girl's father had suffered during the riots. When he came to me with the proposal, I said, "Bismillah".' Those who had lost homes were now marrying so that they would have a roof over their heads. The young man Iqbal, who had earlier wanted to know about my local relatives, waited to say something to me till we were alone. He brought his face close to my cheek and said, 'Man is the only animal with a mad taste for virgins.' This hunger became apparent during the riots, he said. It was safer, then, to get young women married, even if you had to do it in a relief camp at a mass wedding.

The local papers had printed photographs of the weddings in the camps. People in the BJP government saw the marriages as a return to normal life, but a more desperate bid for normality was surely unimaginable. One evening, while talking to Noorjehan, I wanted to ask her about Gandhi. It had occurred to me that Gandhi would have wanted weddings to take place, *but between Hindus and Muslims*, and he would have wanted leaders of both communities to give away their sons and daughters in marriage. He would have found other imaginative ways to break the wall between the victim and the victimizer. But it seemed absurdly idealistic to discuss Gandhi in Gujarat. Merely two to three months had passed since the major violence and already there was talk about new elections being held to the state legislature. The BJP was feeling confident that what had happened during the riots would win for it the majority Hindu vote.

Indeed, ten months later, when the elections did take place, the party that under Chief Minister Narendra Modi had been reviled for its involvement in the riots, rode to power with a clear, sweeping majority. In the course of his campaign, Modi had declared that Pervez Musharraf, the Pakistani dictator, was his true electoral opponent. This meant that anyone who did not support him, including the Muslim voters who viewed him as the Milosevic of the Gujarat riots, were all supporters of Pakistan.

This is the self-justifying logic of the hate-mongers: We must annihilate Muslims because they are anti-nationals, and they are anti-nationals because they are Muslims. This murderous logic is not confined to Gujarat. The leader of the VHP, Praveen Bhai Togadia, declared at a press conference that after the successful experiment in the Hindutva laboratory of Gujarat, the exercise would be repeated in the rest of India. This could not be seen as an empty threat. Nor could it really be said that Togadia or Modi were lacking in public support. One week prior to the elections in mid-December, a report in *Time* magazine said that Modi asked his audience during an election rally, 'Why are so many of you here?' In answer to his own question, referring to the train-burning in Godhra, he shouted, 'Because the fire that burns in my heart is the same as the fire in yours.' The *Time* reporter had written that, for anyone missing Modi's meaning, a young woman in the front had screamed out, 'Kill the Muslim motherfuckers.'

2

Zero Point

It was raining in Patna. When she got inside the car, my sister smelt of chloroform. She had been operating on a child who had been born with a crooked spine. I had waited outside the clinic, the car's windows fogging up with moisture, and then my sister was suddenly in the seat beside me, full of apologies. I pulled on to the street that was flooded and half-empty. In the rain, it was difficult to find the place we were looking for. We ended up first at a shelter run by Mother Teresa's nuns, and then, after more directions had been shouted at us from under umbrellas, we arrived at the giant metal gates of the women's remand home.

The gates were locked. I was asked to write my name on a piece of paper and pass the chit to the female guard inside. I had written my sister's name too, and indicated that she was a doctor, because the previous day someone had said that it would be easier for me to find a way past that gate if I was accompanied by a woman. The guard disappeared inside the building. My sister began to tell me that five years ago there had been charges of prostitution at the remand home. Cars would be sent by ministers and senior officers to pick up girls. Then, more recently, there had been a report in a newspaper that women would sometimes parade naked on the roof during the evenings. Young men stood in a ring outside the tall walls and tossed love letters to the women inside. The letters were wrapped around stones. My sister is always good with such details.

The warden, Mrs Das, was waiting for us at the top of the steps where it was dry. She was dark-skinned and bespectacled, but the severity of the glasses and her hair pulled tightly back was offset by a hint of fashion. She wore lipstick and sported high heels, and I noticed this, I think, because of the dullness of her surroundings.

In a local Hindi newspaper about a year earlier, I had read that a few of the young women in the remand home had been put there because they had married men from a religion different from their own. Hindus had married Muslims, and vice versa, against the wishes of their families and ended up in this prison. I asked Mrs Das if this was true. She considered my question but did not confirm or deny what I had said. She was not hiding anything from me, it was just that she treated such questions as philosophical statements. She began to tell me that the women in her care, especially those who were under twenty, did not know the difference between right or wrong. They thought only of sex. For them, 'love was lust'. Only 5 per cent of the women who had married of their own would ever return to their parents. The parents often filed a police case against their daughters, charging that they had run away from home or had been kidnapped, and if the women were unwilling to go back home they were brought to the remand home for rehabilitation. They would stay there till their case came up in court within a year or two.

I repeated my question. Mrs Das said that there were many examples of marriages between men and women of different faiths, one Hindu, the other Muslim, and these marriages led to unfortunate complications. A pregnant Hindu woman had been admitted to the remand home because the father of her child was a Muslim. Mrs Das said that the woman lost the child and became 'mentally deranged'. I must have looked disturbed or upset, because she began to explain the bigger picture to me. Hindu girls often ran away with Muslim boys. This is because the lifestyle of the Muslims is more 'soft and cultured', although after marriage, all of that begins to fade away. Muslim girls, on the other hand, are less likely to elope and marry Hindu men. Even the court is reluctant to protect such alliances. This, she said, is because there is a fear that the matter will turn violent. Riots can take place, Mrs Das meant to say, because Muslim men will not allow Hindu men to take away their women.

Mrs Das had ordered Coca-Cola to be brought for us and a woman came in with three bottles which were wet from the rain. We were sitting in the dank room with its green walls. For a long while, Mrs Das looked out of the window distractedly, and then pressed the buzzer under her desk. When the woman who had brought us the soft drinks reappeared, Mrs Das asked her to fetch Nazrana Khatoon.

Nazrana was a young, plump-cheeked Muslim woman with red sindoor in the parting of her hair. Her eyes were round in shape and she held them wide open as if she was constantly being surprised by the world. She had married a Hindu youth in a small town in Bihar and now felt she belonged to her husband's faith. This explained the sindoor which, I must note, she had applied with the zeal of a new convert. Nazrana said that she now also had a Hindu name, Munni Devi. I asked her about her husband. His name was Ram Karan Das and he was in jail in Darbhanga. Nazrana's parents had claimed that she was not yet sixteen years old, which was false, and now her husband was behind bars on charges of abduction and rape. Nazrana had been at the remand home for six months but she was slated to appear in court soon. Mrs Das was certain that the case would be decided in Nazrana's favour.

I asked Nazrana to tell me about her relationship with her husband. She turned her wide eyes at me. She simply said that she had fallen in love. She was talking to me in Hindi but she used the English word 'love' and I had difficulty understanding it because she pronounced it 'law'. Her love had deepened when her father, Abdul Qayyum, had held a revolver at her head and told her to stay away from her lover. She had met Ram Karan at the shop where she would regularly take wheat for grinding. Nazrana's conjugal life had lasted only a few hours. She got married at eight in the evening. At one o'clock that same night she had to flee to another village because her father's house was being attacked by the Muslims in her village.

The actions of the village elders, men that she had grown up among, made Nazrana feel a sense of betrayal, but she also felt caught in a wonderful romance. This sense was something that she had got from Bollywood. Nazrana had watched the Hindi film *Gadar* in the company of her lover and been inspired by the experience. The film had been a big hit the previous year: it portrayed the love story of a Jat truck driver, Tara Singh, and a Muslim girl, Sakina, who belonged to a rich family. The larger drama of the film is the trauma of the Partition, and the hostility between the two new nations, India and Pakistan. When Sakina goes to Lahore on the other side of the border and is not allowed to return, Tara Singh follows her there, and brings her back to India after decimating half the Pakistani Army. The lovers' delayed reunion suggests the possibility of the reunification of the two nations, and it would appear that love in the time of high nationalism is not only about conquering the heart but also the heartland. But the film had found a more private echo in Nazrana's heart. She said of the film's hero and heroine, 'If they could get married—a Hindu and a Muslim—so could we.'

The previous year, when I had watched *Gadar*, I was reminded of a story narrated by Urvashi Butalia in her book about the Partition, *The Other Side of Silence*. The brief narrative in Butalia's book was pieced together from newspaper reports, a memoir, and other sources; its protagonists were a Muslim woman named Zainab and a Jat peasant from Amritsar, Buta Singh. Zainab was a young woman abducted from a refugee's caravan headed for Pakistan during the time of the Partition. She was sold to Buta Singh, who then took the step of marrying her.

'The story goes that in time, the two came to love each other,' Butalia writes. The couple had two daughters. A few years later, however, a search party looking for abducted women came from Pakistan and took Zainab away. She had no say in the matter, but she promised her husband she would return. Family intrigues tied to a greed for property had figured in Zainab's rescue, but Buta Singh could not reconcile himself to a life without his wife. In order to find money for his journey to Pakistan, he sold his land, and in a bid to get admitted into that country, he converted to Islam. He applied for a Pakistani passport, and when this bid for citizenship failed, he appealed for a short-term visa. He was successful but bad news awaited him when Buta Singh reached his wife's village. He found out that Zainab had been forcibly married to a cousin in order to keep within the family the property that she had inherited from her father.

In other words, Buta Singh had arrived too late. To make matters worse, he was asked to appear in court because he had not reported his arrival to the police—which the citizens of both India and Pakistan are required to do within twenty-four hours of their entry in the other country. When Buta Singh told his story to the magistrate in court, the official summoned Zainab. In court, 'guarded by a ring of relatives', she rejected her former husband. The next day, Buta Singh threw himself under a train. In the dead man's pocket was a suicide note requesting that he be buried in Zainab's village, a wish that her relatives did not allow to be fulfilled.

'When Buta Singh's body was brought to Lahore for an autopsy,' writes Butalia, 'it is said that large crowds gathered outside; some people wept; a film-maker announced that he would make a film on the story.' More than fifty years later, even as India and Pakistan massed their troops at the border, the film *Gadar* was produced and became one of the biggest box-office hits in the history of Hindi cinema. It should not surprise us that Buta Singh's failure in love, or even what Butalia calls Zainab's silence, should now have been turned into a tale of romantic happiness and even nationalist triumph. Yet, I found it remarkable, listening to Nazrana in the remand home describe her reaction to the film, that the story enacted across the border of India and Pakistan had found form and significance far away inside a small country-town in eastern India. It suggested to me that, given the political strife between Hindus and Muslims in the country, the border was present everywhere.

When Nazrana left the room, Mrs Das looked at me and shook her head. 'These girls,' she said, 'they pick up ideas about love from films.' She pressed the buzzer again and picked out names from the book in front of her. We met other inmates, young women who would come and stand beside the desk uncomfortably, while Mrs Das or I quizzed them, and they would quietly provide details about their fraught love without once asking questions in return. Then, a small boy rushed into the office wearing his school uniform. This was Mrs Das's son. He showed his mother his empty tiffin-box, and when she patted him on the head, he rushed out again. My sister and I were also ready to leave, but it turned out that Mrs Das had a story to tell.

She said that a childhood friend of hers, who was a gynaecologist, had called her one day to tell her of a patient who was pregnant and was seeking an abortion. The gynaecologist knew that Mrs Das was childless and wanted to adopt a baby. After she had heard Mrs Das's response, the doctor told her patient that it was too late to carry out the procedure and that she would arrange for someone to adopt the child. This prospect kept Mrs Das in a state of excitement.

At last, she got a call from the gynaecologist. The pregnant woman was in labour. After the birth, the infant was brought into the doctor's living quarters where Mrs Das was waiting. She saw that it was a boy. In the first few minutes, she found the child unattractive, but a little later, when the doctor fed milk to the baby, Mrs Das felt tenderness overcoming her. As she felt herself getting attached to the baby, even while she sat in the doctor's bedroom, Mrs Das began to fear that the infant's mother would return and ask for her child. She was afraid to go out on the street and, for that reason, she waited till six in the evening and only then did she step into the dark outside.

When she came home with the child, Mrs Das found that her husband was not very accepting of the child, even though in time, she said, he began to love him as if the child were his own. Her own affection for the boy knows no bounds. 'I still have the green sheet from the doctor's clinic in which I had brought the baby home,' Mrs Das said. I asked her if her son knew that he was adopted. 'I have not told him, and I will never tell him,' she said. Some years back, Mrs Das had surgery performed in her lower abdomen. The boy had seen the scar on her stomach and one afternoon said to her, 'This is where I came from, no? When they cut your stomach?' Mrs Das saw that I was taking down notes and perhaps because of that she said, 'Even if someone tells him that he is adopted he won't believe it.' The real romance here—for a woman who had denounced a little while ago the romance of illicit love picked up from films—was of the child's adoption. I got into the mood that Mrs Das was describing and I felt happy for her and for the boy. At the same time, I also began to think that, like the young women in the remand home, the child's mother had also perhaps found, or been forced, into a relationship that did not find social sanction.

I was writing down what Mrs Das was saying—but I kept thinking of the boy in the next room who would not believe it if he was told that he had been adopted. I wanted to ask Mrs Das a question, but didn't. Would she believe it if one day somebody were to tell her that her son's biological mother—or, perhaps as likely, the father—was actually a Muslim?

*

The border that divides the Hindu and Muslim communities in India is often interchangeable as an idea with the physical border between India and Pakistan. The mere fact that there is a territorial boundary between the nations—a line that exists as a tangible marker of an Islamic nation that was carved out of the bigger entity—is often used to cast suspicion at the Muslim inhabitants of India. Hindu children learn to believe that in the Muslim ghettoes in India, men wave green Pakistani flags and burst fire-crackers every time India is beaten by Pakistan in a cricket or hockey match. When riots break out between Hindus and Muslims, provocative slogans are routinely raised asking Muslims to pack up their bags and leave for Pakistan. The popular cry is, in fact, unimaginably crude: *Musalman ke do hee sthan—Pakistan ya Kabristan* (There are only two places for the Muslim—Pakistan or the grave). In some ways, of course, the anxiety of the ideology of nationalism, its search for purity, must make it return again and again to the other inside its own body politic, the imagined other that must be rooted out and killed. On the one hand is the division between communities inside India, and, on the other, the division between the two nations, but in the neurotic imagination of the anxious nationalist, the two are identical. Each border recalls the other, and one can always suspect that behind the invocation of one lurks the shadow of the other.

There is a further twist. The presence of the border is a concrete reality but because it must perform an abstract function—barbed wires, guards, and guns needing to symbolize, at the same time, not only nationalism but also a unified, perhaps even peaceful, community—it also retains at its heart a certain instability. This uncertainty is only multiplied in the case of India and Pakistan. To begin with, the border that exists as a geographical division is a contested one and this is evident from the fact that a Line of Control serves as an actually existing border even though the maps of each nation dispute the territory under the control of the other. In addition to that, the physical border is a proxy for the profound cracks inside civil society, namely the divisions between Hindus and Muslims. To add to it all, events and eruptions lead to a fluctuation even in this relationship between the two split meanings of the border, and this aspect, too, adds to the instability of the otherwise plain idea of the clear, dividing line.

This ambiguity of the border is of interest to me as a writer. It is the ambiguity of a liminal space that divides but also joins, and, equally important, it calls attention to the role of the imagination in giving meaning to our lives. This ambiguity is also the reason, I think, why the border cannot easily be rescued either from poetry or even a more ordinary pathos. Consider the example of a small news item from Islamabad about the arrival of migratory birds at the Charana Wetland Reserve. The bird reserve is in Jammu, in northern India, and close to the Indo-Pak border.

According to the report, the exchange of fire across the Line of Control, between Indian and Pakistani forces in the years before the ceasefire in December 2000, had led to a sharp drop in the number of birds, including Siberian cranes, that came to the reserve. The ceasefire had been announced by India during the month of Ramzan and then extended for a short period later on. The report stated that peace had granted the migratory birds a reprieve. They had started returning to the reserve. The report was no more than two hundred words long but the writer could not resist closing it with a more poetic, if also ungrammatical, conclusion: 'The migrated birds do not have any border disputes nor they have any conflict. The whole of the world is their home.'

In reality, the border is rather prosaic, flatly representing the language of command used by the state. Its principal idiom is one of authoritative signs, a semiotics of power, and the commonest signs are uniforms, guns, and imposing fences. The slightest speech of the state is coded with an ideology of assertion: an imperative ('Do Not Cross') or a slogan ('Victory to ...'). At the India-Pakistan border—which I first visited during the winter of the year 2000—there is a tall brick gateway on each side of a white line. On one side, the Hindi lettering proclaims, '*Mera Bharat Mahan*' (My India Is Great). On the other side, the sign is written in Urdu, '*Pakistan Zindabad*' (Long Live Pakistan).

I had arrived in Lahore a few days before, on a Pakistan International Airlines jet. Passport in hand, I took my place in a line before a row of desks where the customs officials were sitting. Two men in mufti fell in beside me, and one of the men asked for my papers. He had recognized my Indian passport. His right eye was filmy, and it remained fixed on something to my left while he questioned me about my itinerary: where I was going, where I would stay, how I knew my hosts. I looked up to notice that the line had disappeared. An official waved me over, ignoring the plainclothes policemen. 'Welcome to Pakistan,' he said.

It's about a forty-minute drive from Lahore, to Wagah, where the border lies. The road to Wagah wends its way through small pastoral villages, full of brick kilns, buffaloes and mustard fields. There were boys playing cricket in dusty plots by the roadside. There were gaudily decorated buses—one of them had an F-16 painted on the driver's side, with the word 'Pilot' emblazoned underneath. There were cattle, bullock-carts and turbaned men on foot. Every few minutes we passed another emaciated dog, barking insistently, guarding its stretch of broken highway. I was just thinking how similar this was to the landscape on the other side of the border when Anwar Muhammad, my driver, asked, 'Do you have wide roads like this in India, too?' I lied and said no. I was trying to be friendly to each and every Pakistani. I was going to the border, after all.

Anwar was a member of the security detail of my host, Asma Jehangir, who is a well-known human rights lawyer. She also happens to be my wife's aunt. Asma's teenage son, sitting in his room in front of a large, framed advertisement for a British beer ('Helping Ugly People Have Sex Since 1862'), advised me not to mention India at the border. Anwar, the driver, had served for fifteen years in the Pakistani Army; he was one of the police bodyguards that the government had provided my host after several death threats had been made against her. The previous year, an 'honour killing' had taken place in the office next door. That is where Asma and her younger sister, Hina Jilani, work as lawyers. A young woman named Samiya Sarwar had come to the office seeking help for her divorce from an abusive husband. She had left home and was living in a women's shelter called Dastak. Her parents pressured Samiya to meet them, and she agreed to meet her mother in Hina's office. The mother—claiming that she was having trouble walking unassisted—came with a male helper. In the office, the helper took out a gun and shot the young woman dead. The mother escaped but Anwar's partner killed the gunman. Just before I left Lahore with Anwar, Asma had been telling me Samiya's story. She pointed to the steps of the room in which I was staying and said, 'There was blood everywhere.'

Suddenly, Anwar pulled over. We would have to walk the rest of the way. Anwar explained that the only vehicle allowed to cross the border was a bus which ran between New Delhi and Lahore. The route was opened in early 1999, and Atal Behari Vajpayee had made the inaugural trip. The words '*Sada-e-Sarhad*' (Call of the Border) were painted on both sides of the bus. Vajpayee had greeted his Pakistani counterpart, Prime Minister Nawaz Sharif, here at Wagah. But only a few months later, war broke out. The fighting was once again along the Line of Control that functions as the border in the disputed territory of Kashmir. The battle was fought in the vicinity of a town called Kargil among snow-covered Himalayan peaks. Soon after the ceasefire that ended the fighting in Kargil, Sharif was deposed in a military coup. Still, the bus soldiered on, rolling through the gates at Wagah four times a week. Then, it stopped after the break-up of all relations between the two countries following the attack on the Indian

Parliament on 13 December 2001. Now, once again, the bus and train services have been resumed and, once again, from such fragile evidence, people talk of peace visiting the subcontinent soon.

When we got out of the car to walk, I noticed that Anwar was carrying a light machine gun. As I approached the border post, a young Pakistani guy walked just ahead of me, cigarette in hand. Two men were sitting on chairs by the side of the road. One of them gestured sternly at the cigarette. The *azan*, the call to prayer, had just sounded from a nearby mosque. 'It's Ramzan,' the man said in Urdu. The smoker quickly stamped the cigarette out. The man on the chair told Anwar to remove the magazine from his gun and give it to the guards farther up the road.

After passing under the arched gateway, you walk for a long stretch towards a guard who protects a white line across the tar road. This is the Zero Point. The border between India and Pakistan is approximately 1,250 miles long, but the Zero Point is the only place where you're allowed to cross. White arrows point at the line from either side, as if you could miss it.

*

There was tension in the air. And not so much because of the soldiers with guns. My problem was more personal. The visa granted me permission to visit only Lahore and Karachi. I was now standing where I was not supposed to be. But despite the anxiety, I was also thrilled. The fact that I had walked up to Zero Point from the Pakistani side seemed to me to be a minor miracle. It had not been easy to get there.

It was in the US capital that I had first applied for a visa. A couple of weeks before I did that, there was a report in the Pakistani papers about a change in visa policies. The military government of General Pervez Musharraf had decided to allow tourists from all over the world to fly to Pakistan without prior clearance from the country's consulates abroad. The only exceptions were tourists 'from India and non-resident Indians'. In other words, I would need a visa. In Washington, D.C., at the Pakistan embassy, I was told that my application would be sent to Islamabad for an inquiry. The application form I had downloaded from the embassy's web site was not the one I needed to fill out as an Indian national. There was another one for me. The form I was now given had lines like this printed in block letters: 'YOU MUST REPORT FOR POLICE REGISTRATION WITHIN 24 HRS OF ENTRY IN PAKISTAN AND PRIOR TO DEPARTURE/ARRIVAL AT EACH SUBSEQUENT PLACE OF VISIT IN PAKISTAN.' I had brought with me the ticket that showed very clearly that I would be flying to Pakistan in a fortnight. I had brought my green card, a letter of proof of permanent employment in the US, a statement from the local bank attesting to my solvency, a copy of my marriage certificate authorizing my marriage to a Pakistani citizen, and finally, the faxes from my wife's family in Karachi and Lahore stating that I was to be their guest.

The visa office in Washington, D.C., was a small room at the back of the building that houses the Pakistan embassy. I went down a flight of stairs to the basement. Inside the room, with the portraits of the Quaid-e-Azam Muhammad Ali Jinnah and the poet Muhammad Iqbal looking over my shoulder, I handed over my papers to an official standing on the other side of the counter. It was there that I was given the correct application form, and I sat down to fill it out.

One part of the form said, 'I belong/do not belong have previously belonged/have not previously belonged to a MILITARY/SEMI MILITARY/POLICE ORGANIZATION.' It was only when I stepped back into the street outside that I remembered that I had not scratched out the parts of that sentence that did not pertain to me. A fine drizzle had begun to fall. I stood in the middle of the empty street, unable to decide what to do. I thought it didn't matter, I wasn't going to get the visa anyway. Then, the thought came that I wouldn't want it to be denied for such a small reason. I went back into the small room. At the counter, when I told the official about my mistake, he gave me back my application. I was upset at my mistake and tried to correct it quickly. The form lay under the official's gaze. He was a short man wearing a dark suit without a tie. He was not unpleasant but he made it clear that he was busy. In that room, I was very conscious of being Indian. And I did not want to give offence. In my hurry and confusion, I passed my pen over the words that said 'do not belong'. Now, the line read: 'I belong to a MILITARY/SEMI MILITARY/POLICE ORGANIZATION.' I looked up at the official but he remained expressionless. I have made a mistake, I wanted to say. I had no truck with the military, I was only a writer. But, I said nothing because it all seemed silly. The man in his shabby suit, standing on the other side of the counter, watched as I scratched out the whole sentence, making two small check-marks on the parts that said 'do not belong'.

Later, I was describing this experience to a Pakistani acquaintance in New York City who had gone to the Indian consulate to apply for a visa to visit India. Her name is Shabnam and she had wanted to see two friends she had lived and worked with at a non-profit organization in New York City. At the consulate, she was told that Pakistani nationals needed to fill out a different form and then make four copies. She was required to write down not only the names of the places she was going to visit but also the *tehsil* and police station in which those places were located. She had begun to despair then. But there were more demanding questions in store for her. Shabnam was asked to write down the names of two people in India who would be her referees and also write down their 'parentage'. This word was new to her. She spoke at length about it and then said, 'These people have found a strategy. If you stop friends from visiting, you also keep folks hating each other.'

Shabnam's flight for Pakistan was to leave in a week; she was planning to travel to India from Lahore. The woman at the Indian consulate in New York City said that they would need four to five months to process the application. Shabnam was asked to leave her passport which she couldn't because she was travelling soon. It was clear to both Shabnam and the Indian official that this was a futile exercise. Wanting perhaps to make her feel better, the official laughed and said, 'Why are you going to India? You don't even have blood relatives there!' Shabnam said that she was stopped short by this. She had wanted to say something to the woman but didn't. Later, while narrating all this to me, Shabnam wanted to make a point about the Indian official. She said, 'The woman in the embassy was laughing at me for assuming that friendship mattered enough to apply for a visa.'

I thought of what the woman had said to Shabnam— 'You don't even have blood relatives there'—during the days that followed and I sat and waited for news about my visa. I was getting desperate. I wondered if the visa officer from across the border had the same ideas as the official that Shabnam had met. I wanted to say, 'Look, we have been loyal enemies for the whole of my—and my parents'— lifetime. From birth, each country has had the other as a constant foe. We have been spilling each other's blood for more than fifty years. Doesn't that make us blood relatives?'

No word came from the Pakistan embassy for the whole fortnight. I left for India. Then, I heard that my wife's aunt in Karachi had received a visitor from a Pakistani intelligence officer. The aunt was one of the 'sponsors' for my visit. The officer, she said, didn't really ask too many questions; he sat and discussed his diabetes and then left. A day or two later, he contacted her again and said that for my application to go any further, he'd need some money to pay the clerks. The money was given to him. But he was not heard from again. And nothing more happened. I called the embassy in Washington, D.C., from Delhi and was told that there was no record of my having applied for a visa. I did not have much hope. The next morning, however, I went to the Pakistan High Commission to make inquiries. I filed another application although I was told that the process would take at least a few months.

A few days passed. My ticket to Lahore was for 7 December. That day I checked once again, but could find out nothing. The next day, a judge in Pakistan sent a fax that I was to take with me to the Pakistan High

Commission. It was the month of Ramzan, and it was also a Friday. The office was to be open only for a couple of hours. I sought the official whose name had been given to me, and was asked to wait in a room inside the building. There were others in the room, all men, sitting quietly, with the same mingled look of hope and despair that is common to visa applicants everywhere. On a shelf in the far corner, there were coloured pamphlets with titles like 'Days to Remember in Indian Occupied Kashmir' and 'Tell-Tale of 1996 Elections in Indian Occupied Kashmir'.

I might have waited over an hour. Then, the official appeared, his moustache lightly hennaed. He was wearing a grey shalwar-kameez. The official snapped his fingers and asked for our papers. Everyone in the room had a letter from someone. One man in a khaki uniform said that he was a driver of a staff-car in the Prime Minister's Office. He was going to Pakistan to meet his uncle who was close to death. The man in the shalwar-kameez wanted to know why I had not applied for a visa in America. 'It would have been easier,' he said quietly, with a touch of softness. It was the fasting perhaps that had made his breath sour. He said that I could come in the afternoon to pick up my passport. It was as simple as that. When I got out, I saw men and women crowded around the two openings in the wall where inquiries were to be made regarding tourist visas.

I returned in the afternoon. Those I had seen in the morning—or others like them—were now waiting around the windows in the wall marked 'Ladies' and 'Gents'. Most of the applicants were Indian Muslims, wanting to go to Pakistan to meet relatives. This was a very large crowd of people, made up of mainly poor, peasant folk.

Most of them were squatting on the ground. Five men spread their mats in a neat row and began their prayers facing Mecca. Someone said in Urdu, 'It is Friday today, *jumma*, that is why we got our visa.' The religiosity began to affect me; I began to feel I was already in Pakistan.

Everyone was waiting for the windows to open. An older woman was reading the *Qur'an* under the shade of a tree. A blue dupatta covered her head. She was sitting on the ground, her upper body swaying back and forth as she read. All those who stood or sat around me appeared to be fasting. I had some chocolate and bottled water in my bag. I ate the chocolate guiltily, but could not bring myself to drink the water. It was December but still it was hot, and it is possible that no one around me had touched water since dawn. But a small part of my guilt also had to do with something else. That morning, on the visa application that I had handed back to the official inside, next to the box marked 'Religion' I had written: 'Hindu converted to Islam during marriage.' The box was small and all the words would not fit in. I didn't want them to. I wanted them to be noticed by the man examining my papers. This was going to be my ticket across the border.

*

Wagah. Throughout the subcontinent, that single word conjures memories of the Partition, the monumental act that carved Pakistan out of India in 1947. The idea of a separate Muslim state, free from Hindu domination, had first been voiced in 1930 by the poet Muhammad Iqbal. Seventeen years later, when the idea became a reality, the creation of a new country for Indian Muslims was accompanied by an unimaginable violence. The numbers provided by the authorities vary, but it is possible that a million people died. The Partition precipitated the largest exodus in recorded history. How many migrated across the brand new border? Twelve million? Eighteen million?

The British, preparing to grant India its independence, had announced the plan in June of 1947. Three weeks later, they set up a Boundary Commission to separate the Muslim-majority areas from the Hindu-majority ones. In a matter of weeks, the British had created Pakistan. Little thought was given to the millions who lost their homes overnight. People who had just won their freedom from Britain were now told that they were refugees. The principal architect of the Partition, Cyril Radcliffe, had never been to India before. He knew nothing about it, save what he picked up in five weeks in a New Delhi office, studying unreliable maps and outdated census statistics. The day before independence, Radcliffe wrote to his nephew:

Down comes the Union Jack on Friday morning and up goes—for the moment I rather forget what, but it has a spinning wheel or a spider's web in the middle. I am going to see Mountbatten sworn as the first Governor-General of the Indian Union at the Viceroy's House in the morning and then I station myself firmly on the Delhi airport until an aeroplane from England comes along. Nobody in India will love me for the award about the Punjab and Bengal and there will be roughly 80 million people with a grievance who will begin looking for me. I do not want them to find me. I have worked and travelled and sweated—oh I have sweated all the time.

When you go to Wagah and stand near the white line
that divides the two countries, it is impossible not to
think of Radcliffe. Perhaps it's too easy to blame the British.
The writer Khwaja Ahmad Abbas once asked, 'Did the
English whisper in your ears that you may chop off the
head of whichever Hindu you find, or that ·you must
plunge a knife in the stomach of whichever Muslim you
find? Did the English also educate us into the art of
committing atrocities with women of other religions right
in the marketplace? Did they teach us to tattoo Pakistan
and Jai Hind on the breasts and secret organs of women?'
And yet Indian nationalism was a response to British rule.
As a defensive strategy against their rulers, the Indian leaders
opted for a strategy of mobilization which armed the people
with a religiously nationalist zeal. The ideology of
nationalism is an ideology of difference, a return to roots,
a vision of wholeness. That's why so many visitors to
Wagah seem to take comfort in a white line painted on
the ground. The line assures the viewer that the border
exists, clearly defined and zealously protected. The line
returns more than one sixth of the world's inhabitants to
a moment in their history, more than fifty years ago, when
they awoke to freedom.

Those who seek such reassurance are severely tested by
other lines. I'm thinking of lines composed by Urdu and
Hindi writers who write about the Partition. Many of
those visiting Wagah are familiar with Saadat Hasan
Manto's classic short story 'Toba Tek Singh'. It tells of
Bishan Singh, an old inmate of a lunatic asylum, who is
also called by the name of his village in Punjab: Toba Tek
Singh. When he is told about the Partition, Singh exclaims,
'Uper the gur gur the mung the dal of the laltain.' That

is neither Punjabi nor English, nor Hindi nor Urdu—it's just gibberish. In the story, no one seems to know whether Toba Tek Singh belongs in India or Pakistan, and his insanity becomes a mirror that reveals the fundamental absurdity of maps and nations. 'Toba Tek Singh' ends with an aerial view of its eponymous character: 'There, behind barbed wire, on one side, lay India and behind more barbed wire, on the other side, lay Pakistan. In between, on a bit of earth which had no name, lay Toba Tek Singh.'

Where did Toba Tek Singh lie? If the painted line is the border, then where is the 'bit of earth' in between? In Wagah, that's what the young man who'd been asked to extinguish his cigarette wanted to know. He addressed his question to a Pakistani Ranger. At that moment, the guard was showing me the hobnailed soles of his standard-issue sandals. He looked up at the young man and gestured vaguely towards the barbed wire.

A week later, I was at a literary festival in Delhi, listening to Gulzar, the Urdu poet and film-maker from Bombay. Born in a village called Deena in what is now Pakistan, Gulzar crossed into India by train just before the Partition. As he remembers it, 'I was still a child then and I had to step over the corpses.'

At the festival, Gulzar sat on a panel devoted to Partition literature, and he had invited me because he knew that I had just been to Pakistan. The meeting was held in a sunlit brick amphitheatre, with strings of marigold hung from the surrounding trees; mustard plants waved in the fields beyond. Gulzar read a series of works, concluding with a poem entitled 'Toba Tek Singh'. Gulzar's poem is faithful to the details of Manto's story: the poem's narrator wants to go to Wagah in order to tell Bishan Singh that the ordeal of the Partition still continues. There are hearts that have yet to be divided; 1947 was only the first Partition. Bishan's Muslim friends have succeeded in crossing the border, though some only as corpses. Bishan's daughter used to visit him once a year, an inch taller each time; now she is diminished by an inch with every passing year. The poem opens with the narrator hearing the call from Wagah:

I have to go to Wagah and meet Toba Tek Singh's Bishan

I have heard that he is still standing on his swollen legs exactly where Manto had left him.

He still mutters '*Uper the gur gur the mung the dal of the laltain.*'

Listening to Gulzar read his poem, my thoughts returned to the young man in Wagah. The truth is, there is no neutral territory between India and Pakistan. In his travel-book *Amritsar to Lahore*, Stephen Alter writes:

One of the great disappointments of my own journey was to discover that there is no such thing as a no man's land. At both the railway and road crossings, the territory of each country is entirely contiguous. Nothing separates these two nations, except for manmade structures like fences and gates ... .

Pakistan ends precisely where India begins.
So why is the myth of the no-man's land so persistent? I think it has something to do with the power of literature.

Alter himself admits that Toba Tek Singh came to mind when he visited the border. Manto wrote of a no-man's land because, as a writer and also as a man with many friends in India, many of whom were Hindus, he found himself consigned to a non-place between the two countries. And indeed, for many of his readers, Toba Tek Singh has long been the symbol that captures the meaning of the Partition. Bishan is the fool who does not know whether he belongs to India or to Pakistan, and his no-man's land is a limbo of existential doubt and despair. But I think another reading is possible. Maybe Bishan is staking a claim to the 'bit of earth which had no name'. Maybe he is saying yes to both nations. And maybe a no-man's land is the only place he can do that.

*

On 11 May 1998, three explosions rocked the desert wastes of Rajasthan. Hours later, Prime Minister Vajpayee held a press conference, announcing that the world's largest democracy had conducted a test of its nuclear weapons. Of course, this was no mere scientific experiment; the test was a threat, intended to intimidate Pakistan. Newspapers and governments around the world denounced the detonations, but India was unbowed. By the end of the month, Pakistan had exploded its own nukes, realizing the dream of an 'Islamic bomb' and answering India's challenge in kind. When fighting in Kargil erupted the following year, Indian and Pakistani leaders exchanged nuclear threats no fewer than thirteen times. The most remarkable thing about the contest of tests was the rhetoric, a kind of medieval machismo. Bal

Thackeray, leader of the Shiv Sena Party, was positively exuberant: 'We have proved that we are not eunuchs any more.' India had named its missile system Prithvi, Hindi for 'earth'. But Pakistan assumed the Prithvi in question was Prithvi Raj Chauhan, a twelfth century Rajput king who resisted the Afghan invader Shahabuddin Ghori, founder of the first Muslim kingdom in India. Pakistan named one of its missile programs after the aforementioned Afghan invader.

To all appearances, the two countries were more divided than ever. And yet despite all the military posturing, ambivalence about the border runs deep. Indeed, even as they flaunt their nuclear arsenal, the ideologues of India's ultranationalist right-wing harbour fantasies of erasing the border: their dream is to reunite the territories, by force if necessary, in order to create an undivided India. Theirs is a dream of unity—albeit a murderous dream. The dream exists on the other side of the border, too. In Pakistan, militant Islamic groups often express their resolve to wrest Kashmir from Indian control and then use the province as a beachhead for a jihad against the whole of India. No one better embodies this Pakistani dream than Maulana Masood Azhar, leader of the banned Harkat-ul-Mujahideen group, who was released from an Indian jail on New Year's Eve 1999 in exchange for hostages from a hijacked Indian Airlines flight. Azhar has warned India:

Allah has sent me here, and if you cast an evil eye towards my beloved country, I will first of all enter India with 500,000 of my mujahideen, *inshallah*. That is why I am touring almost the whole nation these days. Half a million are ready, and according to the messages I am getting from across the country, I have many more mujahideen than these. The mothers are giving me their sons and asking me to make them like Bin Qasim [the Arab conqueror of Sind in 710 A.D.], not the worshippers of the West. The sisters are handing me their brothers and asking me to convert them into warriors of Islam. The elders are telling me that our beards are white but even today we are ready to take up guns and come with you.

For fundamentalists on either side, the present is just a prelude to the past. Both sides dream of rolling back the clock—and rolling back the border.

These competing fantasies of unity have bred a new kind of affinity on the subcontinent. As the film-maker and peacenik Anand Patwardhan puts it, 'Cross-border solidarity has been the only silver lining in the mushroom cloud.' We were sitting in a makeshift editing room in Patwardhan's Bombay apartment where he was putting the finishing touches on his documentary film *War and Peace*. As we talked, I looked at a freeze-frame on his monitor. It showed a famous Bollywood personality, mouth open, in the midst of uttering a patriotic inanity about how each bit of dirt is sacred to Indians. Patwardhan said, 'Ever since India and Pakistan conducted nuclear tests in 1998, relations between peace activists in India and Pakistan have blossomed.' While much of the country was celebrating the first nuclear blasts, he explained, the Pakistan-India People's Forum for Peace and Democracy had deepened a dialogue between citizens who want to work for peace in both countries. In seven years, the forum has sponsored four successful conferences, and peace activists now gather at every New Year's Eve at Wagah for a candlelight vigil at the border.

Do good fences make good neighbours? The peace activists certainly want better relations between India and Pakistan, but they aren't lobbying for unification. Although they are eager to ease restrictions on travel and trade across the border, they nevertheless want the border itself to remain intact. In a better world, they suggest, borders won't mean so much; indeed, the nuclearization of the subcontinent reveals the arbitrariness of the division. Who needs armed guards and a white line when you can exterminate a city with a push of a button? The white line at Wagah seems almost obsolete, an artefact from an era when fighting a war meant moving troops across a border.

*

In the Hindi film *Gadar*—the story which had so inspired Nazrana Khatoon, the young woman in the remand home in Patna—we see the Atari railway station at the border. The stationmaster, caught among the stampeding feet, people fleeing for their lives, offers his lament: 'The white Englishmen have destroyed India, they have broken it into pieces.'

The writer Bhisham Sahni, who till his recent death had lived in Delhi, crossed that same train station on 13 August 1947. When he reached Meerut, in India, Sahni found out that the trains had stopped. Many years later, in 1971, the writer began work on his novel about the Partition, *Tamas*, which, in the late eighties, was turned into a popular film and screened on national television in India. When I interviewed Sahni two years ago, he spoke of the experience of crossing the border. In his words, I could hear the echo of the stationmaster in *Gadar*, but Sahni also went further. The British misrule as the main cause of the communal strife, he said, was accepted as a consolation by many of those who lived through the riots of the Partition. There was also the feeling that the conflict, horrendous as it was, would not occur again. But, for the past fifty or fifty-five years of independent rule, there hasn't been any peace. Riots have continued to take place. The Babri Masjid was demolished in 1992. Parties like the RSS and the BJP have grown in strength. This was not so then. When India became free, there were leaders in whom the people had great faith. There was Gandhi, there was Nehru. When the riots started, people felt that such leaders, and the parties at whose helm different leaders stood, would be able to control the violence. Now, all such hopes have passed.

Sahni was nearly ninety years old and age had made him frail and given his skin a kind of transparency. He had a beautiful head of white hair and his manners were slow and elegant. His elder brother had been a charismatic film star in Bombay during the years immediately after independence and you could see that kind of handsomeness also on Sahni's face. I asked him to tell me a bit more about his train journey in August 1947, and when he began to give me the details I realized that his remarkable short story, 'The Train Has Reached Amritsar' was an autobiographical one. Sahni had taken the train because he wanted to join in the independence celebrations in Delhi. The riots in his hometown Rawalpindi had taken place in March; but affairs had made a fair return to normality since then. However, when the train began to pass villages and towns where riots were taking place, his fellow passengers grew tense and began to segregate themselves. A frail-looking Babu, a clerk, was being teased by the Muslim Pathans in the compartment. However, upon reaching Amritsar, into the territory controlled by his fellow Hindus, the Babu lost his look of fear and turned upon the Pathans. When the train left the station, the Babu returned to his seat with a metal rod in his hand. The Pathans had by then moved to another part of the train. The Babu, having become strong and menacing, wanted to hurt the Pathans. He got his chance later, however, when he prevented another Muslim man and his wife from boarding the train. The couple was doubtless trying to escape the riots and wanted to get to safety by climbing on to the moving train. The Babu had opened the train's door and struck the man on the head with the metal rod and watched him fall down on the platform in a heap beside his wife. Sahni was the only one among the sleeping passengers to have witnessed the Babu's act.

The motif of the train as the site of violence, so much a part of Partition literature, whether written by Krishan Chander, Manto, Khushwant Singh, Gulzar, or Sahni himself, has acquired a fresh meaning in recent times. When Sahni and I had our meeting in his Sujan Singh Park home in Delhi, only a few months had passed since the killings in Gujarat. The riots there had begun after the burning of a railway compartment which had been packed with Hindu religious workers returning from Ayodhya. Fifty-eight people were roasted to death in that train carriage in Godhra. In the two or three days that immediately followed the burning of the train, as many as 2000 Muslims were killed in a revenge spree all over Gujarat.

Sahni was perhaps thinking along the same lines and he said at the end of the interview, 'This phase is very important for our future—at this time, the secular forces must fight against communal forces. Because this is a very large country— millions live here—we cannot keep fighting each other all the time. We cannot shed each other's blood. This is not a prosperous nation. The people are poor. There is illiteracy and disease. If we keep fighting with each other, what will happen to us? This scenario produces fear. Life for the coming generations will become very difficult here.'

My mind went back to Nazrana Khatoon, the woman who found out that after she married a Hindu, the border had moved to her village, near Benipur in Bihar. However, as I thought about it more, it seemed to me that the border had always been there close to Nazrana's house and *mohalla*. It is just that her marriage had made her conscious, as if through a shock, of the fact that she had crossed the border. Like migrants everywhere, she had suddenly learnt how intransigent borders really are, how intensely patrolled, and how little there is to negotiate in such situations. There are repercussions that follow each transgression and they had fallen down heavily on Nazrana's head. It is impossible to guess to what extent Nazrana would have thought of those consequences as acts of her own choosing. The meaning of her act would not have been clear till it had already been committed. This is because the border's real dimensions appear to you only after you have begun to cross it.

But, Nazrana is only an extreme example. For any ordinary Muslim in India, the difficulty of ever crossing over into a larger community of the nation is a challenge.

It first requires the assertion that he or she has a home and that any border is thousands of miles away. This is how I understand Rahi Masoom Reza's poignant declaration about his sense of belonging in his novel about the Partition, *Aadha Gaon*, which has been published in English under the title *The Village Divided*—and I find it pertinent, too, that it should be addressed to the Jan Sangh, the political party that in its later incarnation emerged as the ruling BJP and spawned growing cadres of zealous rioters:

> The Jan Sangh says that Muslims are outsiders. How can I presume to say they're lying? But I must say that I belong to Ghazipur. My bonds with Gangauli are unbreakable. It's not just a village, it's my home. Home. This word exists in every language and dialect in this world, and is the most beautiful word in every language and dialect. And that is why I repeat my statement— because Gangauli's not just a village, it's my home as well. 'Because'—what a strong word this is. And there are thousands of 'becauses' like it, and no sword is sharp enough to cut this 'because'. And as long as this 'because' is alive, I will remain Saiyid Masoom Reza Abidi of Ghazipur, wherever my grandfather hailed from. And I give no one the right to say to me, 'Rahi! You don't belong to Gangauli, and so get out and go, say, to Rae Bareli.' Why should I go, sahib? I will not go.

*

I grew up in small towns in eastern India and witnessed many riots. Although I had a few Muslim friends, there was never much intimacy among us. I do not remember any Muslim sitting down to eat with me when I was a boy. Under the sink in the kitchen of my parents' home, there could always be found a dirty glass and, beside it, a ceramic plate which was white with small pink flowers. The glass and the plate materialized on our table whenever we had as a guest my maternal uncle who had suffered from tuberculosis in his youth. The only other occasion when the plate and glass were taken out was when a Muslim driver who sometimes ate at our house needed to be fed.

That could not have been an unusual experience, either for the Muslim driver or for me as a Hindu. In his marvellous short story 'Guest is God', Abdul Bismillah writes of the way in which a Brahmin woman shows courtesy to a stranger who turns up at her door looking for her neighbour. Although the neighbour is not at home, the Hindu woman takes on the task of making the unexpected guest feel welcome. The guest has come from a small town; in response to the woman's hospitality, he finds himself full of admiration for the openness of the city. He is even offered dinner, but in the course of the meal, his hosts discover that he is a Muslim. An awkward silence ensues. It is not broken when the gracious hostess picks up the steel tumbler next to the guest's plate and replaces it with a glass one.

It would have been in my late teens that I started telling myself that if the Muslims around me appeared filthy, the real reason for this was that most of them were poor and lived in ghettos. I cannot guess to what extent even this youthful rationalization protected only my bigotry. Although it is true that I grew up in India's poorest state, many Muslim families of great accomplishment had been a part of the region's elite. The Partition had not destroyed them, nor had it put an end to the vibrant Urdu press. My perceptions were clearly ideological in nature. The word in Hindi for a person with a stubbornly insular, closed, uncompromising brand of religious faith is 'kattar'. The English word 'fanatic' would be a close translation. Muslims are fanatics. I have grown up with this idea, almost as an article of faith, although my rationalizations, as well as what I would later learn to call critiques, have put a distance between myself and that belief.

Yet, this distance has been an elastic one. It shrinks, it grows. And among many, if not most, of my fellow Hindus it is akin to a truism. The occurrence of religious riots in the Indian towns and cities, in which the Muslims end up with greater losses of life and property, paradoxically reinforces the popular belief that the Muslims are fanatics. As a result, a good section of the Hindus believe that if the Muslims can't be killed, they ought at least to be sent to Pakistan. One of the cries raised on the streets of Ayodhya after a Hindu mob demolished the Babri mosque was Kamar mein lungi, munha mein paan / Bhaago saalon Pakistan (A lungi tied to your waist, and paan in your mouth/Go away to Pakistan). This feeling loses its oppressive, urgent presence when peace returns to the neighbourhoods, but it lingers like an oil slick on the surface, ready to be set alight whenever conditions take a turn for the worse.

Prejudice, anger and suspicion is also to be found, no doubt, among the Muslims, but, as a part of the Hindu majority, I am more aware of the brutal efficacy of our own powerful hatred. In recent years, with the coming to power of a Hindu nationalist party in New Delhi, anti-Pakistani as well as anti-Muslim sentiments have gained more ready legitimacy. After the September 11 attacks, a leader of an Indian group that practices a militant form of Hindutva had made offensive statements about Muslims. When there were objections in the press, the leader offered what he felt was a useful clarification. He declared, 'I did not say that all Muslims are terrorists. I only said that all terrorists are Muslims.'

When I hear such pronouncements I turn back to the literature of Partition with a sense of longing. This might seem paradoxical because there is rarely any writing about that tumultuous time that is not a document of barbarity. But the truth is that the stories and novels about the Partition recall a sweetness that is precious because it is recalled from a moment in time when it has already become lost. What is precious is the peace and love of neighbours, and the literature of that time seeks to recreate the lost paradise. The consolation that this sweetness offers is undeniably nostalgic in nature, but it also has another aspect to it that is more profound.

The literature of the riots could be called our first national literature, in the sense that it was the first coherent literary response to the birth of the nation. The most striking aspect of this literature is that it is written in praise of community—which, at least in the most powerful examples of this writing, is defined *against the nation and against politics*. It is a cry for people to be recognized as people. This is also the reason why in our murderously hypernationalist times, a reading of this literature touches the reader with its sweetness. It recalls the impossible nation that never was.

In Reza's *Aadha Gaon*, the protest against the nation is
being made in the name of the village. When the fiercely
well-educated Muslim students come to Gangauli to preach
about Partition, and the necessity for the creation of a
new nation of Pakistan, the Muslim villagers are genuinely
bewildered. One of the villagers is a young man called
Tannu who has returned from battle, fighting for the British
in the Second World War. He argues against the urban
visitors in the name of his village: 'I am a Muslim. But I
love this village because I myself am this village. I love the
indigo warehouse, this tank and these mud lanes because
they are different forms of myself. On the battlefield, when
death came very near, I certainly remembered Allah, but
instead of Mecca or Karbala, I remembered Gangauli.'

Tannu's village Gangauli, which he blasphemously pits
against the divine appeal of the Ka'aba, is populated with
both Hindus and Muslims, of course. If the Muslims of
Gangauli voted for the creation of Pakistan, would they
not be betraying their Hindu brethren? Other questions
also bother him. He asks himself whether Indian Muslims
really didn't belong to this land. The Rajput Muslims of
Dildarnagar and Gahmar—with customs and rituals that
were both Hindu and Islamic—pose a greater challenge, in
Tannu's mind, to the separatists who presume separate
identities for both communities. He finds other questions
in his mind. He asks, 'Why were Muslims who had kissed
the sandals of Lord Rama, accepting them as footprints of
the Prophet, making Pakistan?'

That last question stopped me when I read Reza's book
the first time. I still have the same emotional response
when I read those words again. In the image of the Muslim
who is familiar with, and respectful of, Hindu gods I also

see the writer Reza himself, the man who wrote the immensely popular television script of the ancient epic, Mahabharat. This television serial, which was shown in India during 1988-1990, would bring the entire nation to a halt when it was screened on Sunday mornings. I remember how the corpse of a relative of mine could not be burnt—and my family had to wait for an hour at the electric crematorium—till the serial's broadcast was over on television. Many commentators have argued that the telecast of the Hindu epics on national television, most prominently of the Ramayana, beginning in 1987, produced a public which could be mobilized by the Hindutva ideologues of the BJP. The viewing public across the nation was united by television, and the prominence of Hindu gods and symbols were effectively exploited to engender what the BJP called a Hindu awakening. This could only have appeared deeply ironical and tragic to a writer like Reza who, as a Muslim, took pride in the fact that even in the holy city of Varanasi the masks for Lord Ram during the Ramlila festival were traditionally made by Muslim craftsmen.

In March 1992, Reza died in Bombay. Nine months later, the city was torn apart by Hindu-Muslim riots. In the words of the judge who investigated them, these riots were 'unprecedented in magnitude and ferocity, as though the forces of Satan were let loose, destroying all human values and civilized behaviour'. The immediate cause of the riots was the demolition, on December 6 that year, of a sixteenth-century mosque in Ayodhya. The political activists of Hindu groups who destroyed the mosque claimed that it had been built on the site where Lord Ram had been born. The mosque's destruction and the riots that followed in many parts of India were more shocking than what had happened during the Partition many decades ago. These events delivered a body-blow to the Nehruvian ambitions to establish a secular polity in India. Although the rise of Hindutva was clearly evident at that time, the political success of the BJP had seemed very much in question. That can longer be said because the Hindu nationalists were in power in Delhi for more than six years.

The literature of the Partition, in particular, the writing about the riots, no longer has the intimacy of a secret buried in one's past. Instead, it would appear that the hatred has become the story of our times. The sweetness is still there in those pages, but only as a reminder of the difficulty of finding community in the present. The greater meaning of that literature seems to lie in its role as a relic, a broken wall on which are scribbled the words 'It is happening again'.

A short-story Urdu writer in Bihar, Husainul Haq, wrote a story in 1992 about the arrival of a brick—'a consecrated brick'—in a small town. The brick is from the edifice of the destroyed mosque in Ayodhya. The story is told from the point of view of a Muslim clerk, Salamtullah, about whom the author writes: 'All of a sudden he had a bizarre feeling. Is 6 December past and gone? With this another question nagged him—why does 6 December come? Then the fear—will 6 December come again?' It is Salamtullah's Hindu colleague and neighbour, Shivpujan, who has brought the brick back from Ayodhya. The brick is from the rubble of the demolished mosque. For Salamtullah, it must symbolize a terrible catastrophe. When the story opens, a crowd has gathered at Shivpujan's house for a festive ceremony arranged around the brick. But the celebrations cannot go on. The government is cracking down on events which might spark further troubles. This fact provides the story its dramatic turn. Shivpujan has a strange request for Salamtullah. As there are fears of a police raid, Shivpujan wants Salamtullah to keep the brick for a few days. The Hindus in the neighbourhood have refused, as their houses could be raided too. 'Under such circumstances, it occurred to me that they may not raid your house,' Shivpujan says, and adds, 'Moreover ... it's an object of reverence for you, too.'

So this is where we have come from the times of those Muslims in Gangauli about whom Rahi Masoom Reza wrote that they had kissed the sandals of Lord Ram, accepting them as the footprints of the Prophet. Now the Muslims find themselves holding in their hands, like a brick, the unanswerable proposition that the only way for them to show respect for Lord Ram is to accept the destruction of their dargahs and their mosques.

*

There are two borders, one that is never seen as a line in the ground, and the other for a traveller who is turned into a tourist or a spectator.

Consider the first kind. The borders that exist between our communities, between Hindus and Muslims, are often invisible but they are nevertheless pernicious and even devastating. When Nazrana in the remand home was telling me her story, I was reminded of an incident from my boyhood. On the street in Patna where I grew up, there was a house where, when I was still a schoolchild, a young Hindu woman of my caste had jumped off the roof of her house. Her parents had opposed her marriage to a man with whom she was having an affair simply because he was a Muslim. (How easily it is that I say 'simply' ... .) The fathers of the lovers were both government officials; the young man and woman had met at a party and grown close to each other. Her leap from the roof of the two-storey house did not kill the woman. Although she survived, she was paralyzed from the waist down. Her lover left town and then went abroad to England to study. The young woman remained inside her home. When I was in my middle teens, I would see her at weddings, a beautiful, sombre figure moving about on a wheelchair.

Now, the other border. At Zero Point in Wagah, the border is unmistakable, imposing, and even spectacular. The metal gates on both sides at the border are pulled shut at sunset, at the same precise instant, by opposing teams of guards. This evening ceremony is called Beating Retreat, and it's the most popular tourist attraction in Wagah—on the night I saw it, there were visitors from all over the world. I had come to the border from Amritsar on the Indian side. A string of small restaurants line the approach to the border. One of the restaurants, run by a Sikh who has lived in Canada, is called Niagara Falls, and a painted sign shows the Canadian and the US flags intertwined in friendship. There is no such display of Indo-Pakistani friendship anywhere in Wagah. The tourists pass through a metal detector and then climb the stadium-like steps of a viewing gallery. From my seat on the concrete structure, I could see in the distance, across the white line, the place where I had stood some months ago. It seemed so far away.

In the distance, I could see Pakistani viewers sitting on a similar structure on the other side. As I watched them, an energetic man in a cream shalwar-kameez got up and began to lead the Pakistanis in shouting slogans. 'Pakistan ...,' he would say, '*Zindabad!*' the crowd responded. The Indians saw this for a moment and then around me the voices rose in response. '*Bharat Mata ki ... Jai!*' Then, the tone changed and both sides began to shout slogans calling for the death and destruction of the other. It was summer, and it was extremely hot. It required a lot of effort to keep shouting with all one's strength. There was genuine passion present there, but it was also a show. People giggled while all that yelling and waving of arms went on. And then, suddenly, whistles blew and the crowd turned quiet. The ceremony had begun.

During Beating Retreat, soldiers from both India and Pakistan present arms. Then the national flags are lowered amid much blowing of bugles. Commanders from the two border patrols march up to one another and shake hands. The tourists applaud. Before the event is over, spectators on both sides are allowed to rush forward and gaze at each other from across a distance of about fifteen feet. Throughout this ceremony, the guards mirror each other perfectly: their goose-stepping, their aggressive gestures, their shouted commands, all in sync. But the two enemies make sure not to cross the line that holds them apart. So how do they learn to perform this intimate dance? How well do we know each other? How hard do we work to remain enemies?

3

Textbook Enemies

On 6 March 1971, when I was just about to turn eight, the cricketer Sunil Gavaskar played his debut test match against the West Indies at the Queen's Park Oval, Port-of-Spain. India emerged unexpectedly victorious. In the next match in Georgetown, Guyana, Gavaskar scored a century. In fact, he went on to score a total of four test centuries in that successful series, ending the tour with an improbable 774 runs. In India, the twenty-one year-old Gavaskar became a hero. Not too long after he had hit that first century in his second test, I started keeping a scrapbook in which I would paste the photographs that I had cut out of newspapers and magazines—Gavaskar driving through the covers; Gavaskar, all concentration, defending with a straight bat; Gavaskar smiling boyishly as he received the Man of the Match award.

But before the year was over, I had acquired a new scrapbook. Gavaskar was forgotten for a season or two. My heroes now were military generals and pilots. On the last page of my new scrapbook I pasted a black and white photograph that I had cut out from the pages of the *Illustrated Weekly of India*: it showed a military officer, wearing a beret, signing on a white sheet of paper in front of him. Another officer sat next to him, his eyes on the paper. He was a Sikh and his name was Lieutenant-General J.S. Aurora. Military top brass stood behind the two men. The man with the pen in his hand was General A.K. 'Tiger' Niazi of the Pakistan Army, and he was surrendering to the man in command of the Eastern sector of the Indian Army. Aurora and Niazi were sitting in Dhaka, in what was till then East Pakistan. The scene represented the birth of Bangladesh, but in the minds of many Indians this photograph signalled our military invincibility and national greatness.

The war had started on 3 December 1971, when Pakistan aeroplanes bombed Indian airfields in the north. But the fighting had begun even earlier, when India began to support the liberation struggle being carried out by the Mukti Bahini in East Pakistan. With the end of the war, 93,000 Pakistani soldiers came to India as prisoners of war. Thousands of these prisoners were kept in a camp near our town. I saw them sitting in a huge field one winter morning, like sick patients ordered to take the sun for their health. Later I heard the prisoners' voices when they were allowed to speak out their names and addresses on the radio so that their families in Pakistan would know that they were alive and well. All the men in the Pakistani Army appeared to be Muslim. The Indian armed forces, just like our cricket team, were made up of Hindus, Muslims, Sikhs and Christians; the Indian Army Chief was a Parsi, General Sam Maneckshaw, and Lieutenant-General Aurora's Chief of Staff was Major General J.F.R. Jacob, a Jew from Calcutta.

There were large army garrisons in and near Ranchi, the town where my father was the district magistrate. I had gone to rallies where political leaders and commanders addressed the troops headed for the front. My mother, as the district magistrate's wife, had been involved in collecting donations and organizing fund-raising raffles for the war. When the war ended, Lieutenant-General Aurora, the Sikh hero from the photograph with General Niazi, came to our town for a meeting with the victorious troops and I got a chance to shake his hand. But there had been a price to pay. A neighbour's son, who was a pilot in the air force, was doing a practice run on his Soviet-built MiG-21 when the engine faltered and he crashed. For a while, his mother went insane with grief; she accused her husband, who was a judge in our town, of having murdered their child. That is what I overheard my mother telling my father when she came back in the early afternoon from the neighbour's house. My father said in response that the young man had died without fighting in the war, and this would unfortunately rule him out of consideration for any awards for gallantry.

The highest military honour given to a member of the armed forces in India is the Param Vir Chakra, the equivalent of the Victoria Cross. After the war in 1971, one of the PVC medals was awarded posthumously to Lance Naik Albert Ekka, a Christian tribal soldier from a village near the town where I was living. I had cut out a picture of Albert Ekka and pasted it in my scrapbook. He did not look especially brave in the photograph, although his lantern jaw perhaps showed him as a man of determination. There was another picture from a local paper which showed my father giving a shawl and an envelope to Ekka's family. I stuck the cutting in my book and wrote my father's name under it. Ekka had been killed in a place called Gangasagar in the Eastern sector on the day that the war had started. He had bayoneted two Pakistani soldiers who had been firing at his unit with a light machine gun. Then, after advancing for a mile, his company had encountered machine gun fire from a second-floor window. Ekka crawled close to the building, alone, and lobbed a grenade inside. The firing did not stop. He was already wounded. But Ekka scaled a wall and entered the bunker from where the Pakistanis were firing. He bayoneted two soldiers and secured the place for the Indians, but he had lost too much blood and died as a result of his injuries. In the central plaza of Ranchi town, right in front of the store where I was often taken for ice-cream, a statue of Albert Ekka was installed. I would pass it on my way to school every day, a black statue of a soldier with one foot raised determinedly forward, holding in his hands a rifle with a bayonet.

I even received my share of the spoils of war: a Pakistani medal with a crescent and star embossed on it was given to me by someone in my father's office. Every few weeks, I would rub a few drops of Brasso on the medal to make it shine, and it remained among my most cherished possessions for several years. I would show the medal to my friends and make up stories about the Pakistani gunner from whose body it had been plucked by a brave Indian soldier. I would place the body in a destroyed tank, and at other times, in the wreckage of a plane. The medal became my hidden charm. One morning, when my mother took me to see a doctor about a boil on my arm, I put the medal in my shirt pocket, to give myself courage.

My childhood memory of the war between India and Pakistan returned to me when, in February 2000, I read in the newspapers about an attack on an Indian schoolteacher in Goa. The teacher had been attacked by a mob in a town called Marcel because of a question he had posed in a test. The teacher's name was Dharmanand Kholkar and he had been attacked because he had asked his high-school students to state the moral of a story whose outline he had presented as a part of the question. The fictional scenario, according to the newspaper report, involved an Indian soldier who, injured during the Kargil war in 1999, finds himself in a Pakistani hospital. The soldier is surprised to be alive and asks why he has been shown such consideration. A Pakistani soldier replies that they are both soldiers and human beings.

The mob that assaulted Kholkar considered his story and his question for the students anti-national and unpatriotic. Kholkar's attackers belonged to an ultranationalist Hindu group affiliated with the ruling party in power, the BJP. As punishment for showing a Pakistani soldier in a good light, the men beat Kholkar and painted his face black.

I felt bad for Kholkar, but felt worse for his students. I was thinking of myself as the boy with the medal. It seemed to me that as a teacher Kholkar would have encouraged that boy in Ranchi to be curious about the soldier who had been awarded that medal, and to reflect in a more human and perhaps critical way on the circumstances that had forced the medal to now fall in my hands. At the same time, Kholkar would have understood the idea of bravery, and that it is not limited to a single nation. He would even have understood my desire to slip the medal in my pocket when I visited the doctor. The attack on Kholkar must have taught his students an entirely different lesson. It must have taught them that it is morally justified to live in a world where a narrow-minded, zealous pride allows no space for curiosity or compassion.

There was reason to feel despair for Kholkar's students also because Murli Manohar Joshi, minister in the BJP government responsible for education, had given official sanction to ultranationalist demands by saying that Indian textbooks need to be 'enthused with national spirit'. A news report that had appeared a month before the attack on Kholkar mentioned that a group of non-governmental organizations in Gujarat had submitted a petition to the governor to protest against 'the saffron bias' in textbooks. The ninth-grade history textbook of the state education board describes Muslims, Christians and Parsis as 'foreigners'. Similarly, an examination question in the state of Uttar Pradesh, where the Babri mosque was destroyed by Hindu zealots in 1992, asked: 'If it takes four karsevaks to demolish one mosque, how many does it take to demolish twenty?' Back in Gujarat, where books stigmatize women as well as the people belonging to the lower rungs in the Hindu caste-system, one of the social studies books claims that Hitler 'instilled the spirit of adventure in the common people'. The book makes no mention of the Nazi slaughter of the Jews.

The news, unsurprisingly, is similar from the other side of the border. Under General Zia-ul-Haq, a move was made in Pakistan to make an important shift in education. According to one commentator, Ardeshir Cowasjee, this meant that the struggle for Pakistan was 'no longer to be shown as a victorious struggle for a Muslim homeland' but, instead, 'for an Islamic state run according to Islamic law'. Jinnah and his cohorts were now to be seen as Islamic heroes. Even the teaching of science was required to be Islamized. A child passing out of Class V was expected to be able to do the following: '1. Explain the importance of the work of past heroes of Pakistan; 2. Identify the great personalities who contributed to the making of Pakistan; 3. Demonstrate an appreciation for the work of Muslim heroes; 4. Demonstrate respect and reverence for the founder of Pakistan; and 5. Demonstrate respect for the leaders of Pakistan.' How could any adult, let alone a child, be expected to respect, Cowasjee asked rhetorically, 'a group consisting of, inter alia, Ghulam Mohammed, Zulfikar Ali Bhutto, Zia-ul-Haq, Nawaz Sharif and Benazir Bhutto?'

The objectives to be achieved in the education of a twelve-year-old child in Pakistan enshrined in the school curriculum prepared by the federal authorities include the ability to:

1. Understand the Hindu and Muslim differences and the resultant need for Pakistan; 2. Know all about India's evil designs against Pakistan; 3. Acknowledge and identify forces that maybe working against Pakistan; 4. Demonstrate by actions a belief in the fear of Allah; 5. Demonstrate the desire to preserve the ideology, integrity and security of Pakistan; 6. Make speeches on jihad and *shahdat*; 7. Guard against rumour mongers; 8. Understand the Kashmir problem; 9. Collect pictures of policemen, soldiers and National Guards.

In India, as in Pakistan, protest has been voiced against the religious bias in education. A wide variety of progressive groups and individuals in India have been especially critical of the Hinduization of education—the mirror image of Islamization in Pakistan—in the government-owned schools in the BJP-ruled states as well as the more than 20,000 Vidya Bharati schools spread out in the entire country. The disregard for history is carried to such an extreme in the Vidya Bharati schools that the map of India, writes Nalini Taneja, 'is shown as including not only Pakistan and Bangladesh but also the entire region of Bhutan, Nepal, Tibet and even parts of Myanmar'. The students in these schools are taught that Indian culture is Hindu culture and that the members of minority communities are foreigners. This claim is especially absurd in a country where, according to the findings of the Anthropological Survey of India, there are 4635 communities and among whom homogeneity is along the lines of region, not caste or religion. The survey reports that 'popular cultural expression cuts across religion', with social traits widely shared among different groups. The research identified 775 social traits relating to settlement, identity, food, marriage, economy, social organization, and the like. This is what the survey concluded: 'Hindus share 96.77% traits with Muslims, 91.19% with Buddhists, 88.99% with Sikhs, 77.46% with Jains. Muslims share 91.18% with Buddhists, 89.95% with Sikhs. Jains share 81.34% traits with Buddhists. The Scheduled Tribes share 96.61% traits with OBCs [Other Backward Castes], 95.82% with Muslims, 91.69% with Buddhists, 91.29% with Scheduled Castes, 88.20% with Sikhs.' This established culture of sharing means that nobody today can be characterized as an original inhabitant or a foreigner. In fact, the survey says that many settlers professing Islam actually made India their home earlier than those today professing Hinduism.

Heedless of such research, the 'Sanskrit Gyan' texts used in Vidya Bharati schools teach school children that: Homer adapted Valmiki's Ramayana into an epic called the Iliad; the Egyptian faith, according to Plato and Pythagoras, was based on Indian traditions; the cow is the mother of us all and it is in a cow's body that the Gods are believed to reside; and Jesus Christ roamed the Himalayas and drew his ideas from Hinduism. The teachers also tell the children that the languages of the Native American Indians evolved from ancient Indian languages—which must mean that students now accept that Columbus was right after all to come to America thinking that he had arrived in India.

*

In the seventies, I had been a student at a high school built near the Ganges in Patna. Just before my first trip to Pakistan in the winter of 2000, I went to my former school and asked students there to write letters to kids their age across the border. A few days later, I visited the school my wife had attended in Karachi and read out to the students the letters I had brought from India. The Pakistani students then wrote letters back to their Indian counterparts. In both Patna and Karachi, I also visited a second school which catered to a different class of students. In all the schools, I requested permission to meet ninth or tenth grade students. I was struck by the ease with which children in both countries gave assumed names to their correspondents and constructed imaginary lives for each other. When I came across some of the harshly worded letters which accused the ones on the other side of despicable crimes, it seemed to me that this was also important. I am not too disheartened by the fact the many of the kids repeat what they have heard their political leaders saying in the mainstream media about the other nation; the larger truth is that the people in both countries have had very little contact with each other. We haven't even had the opportunity to abuse our enemies, much less to begin to learn to care about them as friends. All we had really had a chance to do, and indeed what we had been taught, was to become textbook enemies. What the students were saying to each other marked for me the beginning of an honest dialogue.

Here are a few of the letters I collected:

To dearest Indian child, Hello! I am also a child like you, from across the border—i.e., from Pakistan. I know that we had a very bad impression for each other between us in the past, but sincerely I really like you people and your country. I also watch Indian channels. The best thing about your dramas is that they show harmony and peace in joint families, which is not here in Pakistan.

We all were once part of the same country, so please, for those past times' sake, if there was some misconception between us it should come to an end.

One thing more! Why do you make movies fighting against Muslims like *Border*? Can't you make films with Hindus and Muslims living with each other?

In the end, I wish that you would also consider that my letter is of right opinion.

Lots of Best Wishes

Dear Sufi,
I would like to ask you about your lifestyle and tell you about our way of living. I think you people are very strict about your lifestyle. Is that so? I believe the girls out there always have to cover their faces all the time. Why is that so? I don't think you all are allowed to go anywhere on your own or interact with a lot of people.

Bye, Rohini

Hi. How are you, hope you are fine. I was feeling really bored, so I decided to write you a letter. We know that Pakistan and India are terrible enemies of each other but don't forget that your government was the one that really irritated us and wanted us to establish a Muslim state. Sorry for that but nowadays whenever we have our cricket matches we become enemies again. I want to clear one thing: that we are thought to be friendly with Muslims and people belonging to other religions.

With love from, Sara

Dear Friend,
I don't know anything about you, but I think that you are very nice. The only difference between us is our religion, but I still think that you are very nice. You people are very friendly, and I sometimes think how good it will be if we live together again without any differences.

Your friend

Hi! How are you? I hope you are fine. I am writing this letter because I was told to write a letter to someone on the other side of the border and to tell the person what we feel about Indian people.

The thought that comes to my mind by hearing the name of India is ruthless killing and hatred in Kashmir. Frankly I don't really like Indian people. Why can't India leave the poor Kashmiris alone and let them decide about their future?

Well, Hindus and Muslims are two different nations. Muslims are not allowed to eat anything with a Hindu, and I don't have any Hindu friends, so I don't know about them, but I don't think the relations of Pakistan with India are very good.

Sareha Rah

Dear Manas,
I am fine. How are you? Here everything is all right now. Few days back there was something wrong that led to an intrusion by some groups of people. I don't know who sent them and what was their motive. Some people said that Pakistan had done it. Some said Pakistan did not. But I think it has been done by Pakistan itself for Kashmir which does not belong to it.

Now I'm ending my letter.

Yours lovingly, Pushpak

Dear Friend,
I have never had any experience with an Indian my age, but recently I downloaded ICQ, I bumped into a guy older than me, Manoj. He's twenty-four, and one of the first questions he asked me was 'Do you mind me being a Hindu?'

Politics—why should they come in our way and prevent normal people from being close to their neighbours?

And Manoj has come so close to me now. He calls me his behna, and for me, he is bhaiya. He gives me love and respect, and I love him, too. I wonder, is every Indian soooo nice?! Why not reach out to our friends and love them and not be fooled by our 'leaders'. After all, is land more important or people? So please, be my friend forever.

Love, A friend

P.S. I used to think of India as a rival, but now I love it as well. It's all so sweet.

Dear Friend,
I am fine here and hope you are also the same. You are a person from the country Pakistan, where people just believe in destruction. India has always wanted to be a friend of yours, but we need two hands to clap.

Hello, whoever is listening or reading this letter of mine. I am a Muslim or the most hateful thing. I am saying this cuz I have never had a feeling of peace & love b/w the two countries that is U & me. I want to come to your country, but U know what stops me—it's Kashmir. I love everyone I meet & I hate everyone I see who is cruel to the people of Allah.

U & I are the same, we have the same colour, creed, culture, etc., but when I see Indian people say bad words to us my blood boils. I feel very sorry for both of us cuz it's not our fault that our elders hate each other. We are all humans & we share the same heart. Can U see a human die? Yeah, I can't see it too. I think our government should read this & should cry on what it is doing.

Dear Student,

I hope you will be fine and enjoying your life in India. The purpose of writing a letter to you is to tell you some drawbacks of Indian culture which we all see in Indian films. These are such bad films with such bad scenes which cannot see with our families and children cannot enjoy such kind of movies. There is always the same topic in these movies which is romance. There should be comedy films also which we can see with our families easily.

Besides drawbacks there are also some good qualities of Indian movies. There are very good songs. I hope that you will respond me soon.

Your friend, Zainah Saleem

Dear Children,

Hi! I don't like Indian culture, but I think that India is a powerful country and has some name in the world. I love to see India-Pakistan match but only in those conditions when Pakistan is winning the match. The world thinks that Indian people are really very beautiful, since last two years India won the title of Miss World, but in my view they are not that much intelligent and beautiful to be Miss World.

Bye.

Dear Indians,

First of all hello!! I am a Pakistani Muslim and I want to inform you that you are liars. You blame Pakistan for every issue. Pakistan wants to establish cordial relations with you, but your government is not ready to do that. I never thought of Indian children, but your government is really ... What can I say? You are always ready to fight. Can't we live in peace? You attacked Pakistan two times in 1965 and then 1971. This is really bad, and are you not ashamed of yourselves?

I know a Hindu girl of college age. She is really nice.

Dear Friend,
The culture which you people have is not at all good. The main reason of huge population of your country is the bad culture you have. I hope that you have understood what I am trying to say. The other thing which I want to say is that your country should stop all the tortures which they are doing on the people of Kashmir and solve that issue with peaceful negotiations.

From your ever loving friend

Dear Mushtaq,
The letter which I am writing please read carefully. Why don't you all change the attitude of your mind? Why don't you all think in a positive way? This is all due to the wrong thinkings of your mind that the both countries are facing trouble. Why don't you utilize your minds in creating something good?

I hope you will change the attitude of your mind and try to become better.

Yours lovingly, Abhishek Khemka

Dear Friends,
I have never been to India but have always imagined how it would be to meet the people living over there. I think that there are lots of things which are common in both of us. Like we speak almost the same language

only their names are different. We also look like as if we are of same country. If we make one man from India and the other man from Pakistan stand together and ask a foreigner to tell who belongs to India and Pakistan, he will not be able to give the answer.

Once I went to the Lahore border where I saw so many Sikhs on the other side. I waved to them and they waved back. They were so friendly.

Hina

The word Pakistan fills me with hatred for all that they are doing to the innocent people in Kashmir. I don't know about Pakistanis but I really hate their cricketers. They always give a sort of being superior look which take them to pigs level.

This all I have gathered and understood of all the articles I have read in newspapers, magazines, and news, nothing like a personal encounter.

Lawleen

Dear Friend,
Pakistan has always extended a hand of friendship and mutual cooperation towards its neighbouring countries, specially towards India. But we don't know why India and Pakistan's relations remained strained. Kashmir is a Muslim majority province, and India promised that they will occupy Kashmir for some period but they betrayed.

Can't they see the Kashmiri mothers bitterly crying before their children's dead bodies? Can't they see little children crying and searching for their mothers? Can't they feel the empty stomachs of the children?

Doesn't Indian government have any kind of heart? I hope in future India and Pakistan will be best friends. Bye.

Yours ever loving friend, Anumali

Dear Aftab,
It seems that we have become very distant from each other because of the relations that the two countries share at present. I only come to know more about Pakistan through the news shown on television and also the news we get from reading the newspapers. We only get the negative side of Pakistan through the news we read. I am sure that might be the case with you even. But I think we should try to cross the barrier and share a more friendly relation.

Utsav Banerji

Hi Friend,
There is one of my cousins in India, she writes to me about her country. She loves India very much. She used to tell me about the studies that the studies there are very tough. Her favourite place in Agra is Taj Mahal. I have just seen it in pictures or on TV. In my opinion it is a real beauty.

Your ever loving friend

Dear friend,
In this letter I will talk to you about 'you', your country, culture, etc. I like you, not your prime minister, president, army. Your old culture is very good & interesting. The old way of dressing and jewellery of women is pretty good. I do not like the Indian Army because they fight

with our Kashmiri friends, and I request you to do
something about the Kashmiri issue.

I like you but not your country.

Please forgive me if I said something wrong.

*

The Hindi film *Border*—the first letter that I have quoted,
above, written by a Pakistani student, complains about
the film—was released in 1997. This was the anniversary
year when India was celebrating fifty years of independence.
The film was built around an important episode from the
war of my childhood, the fifteen-day conflict in 1971
between India and Pakistan. On 4 December 1971, an
armoured column of the Pakistani forces had crossed the
border in the deserts of Rajasthan. A small outpost of the
Indian Army at a place called Longewala was the only
obstruction in its path. The soldiers at the Longewala
post, helped by Hunters flown by Indian pilots stationed
at Jaisalmer to the north, stopped the Pakistani attack.
Border pays tribute to that military triumph, albeit in
worrisome ways. The film's closing demand for peace
appears bogus after it has spent three hours defending
jingoism. In much of the film, nationalist pride finds
expression mainly as majoritarian or Hindu assertiveness.
Not surprisingly, the film found a receptive ground when
it was released and again, two years later, when the Kargil
War broke out and the BJP gave nationalism its hard edge
as resurgent Hindu identity.

In my meetings with the students in India and Pakistan—
after the letters had been written and we would begin to
talk—I made it a point to bring up *Border* for discussion.

The film was well-known in both countries. I would tell the students about Dharmanand Kholkar, the teacher in Goa whose face had been painted black by a mob which was angry that he spoke of the enemy soldiers in human terms. Then, I would ask the students to recall a sequence from the film when the soldiers at the Longewala post have just received letters from home. A soldier looks at a letter that his comrade is reading and says, 'What does your son write? His handwriting seems to be good.' His friend replies, 'He writes good things too. Writes that our teacher tells us that the people across the border are just like us. They dress like us and speak a language similar to ours. If that is true, why is it then that they fight a war with us? Return home soon, when the war is over.' I would ask my audience if the teacher was right. Did they feel that we had a shared culture or a shared history? In Pakistan, when I asked the question at my wife's former school, some girls whispered among themselves and then one of them got up and, surrounded by giggles, answered, 'What we have in common is Hrithik Roshan'. Hrithik, Shahrukh, Aishwarya, Kareena, Amitabh Bachchan ... the stars of Bollywood films surprise the visitor from India by appearing in the enemy's homes, the workplaces, even in the first words used in greeting.

In other words, the strongest intimations of history and culture seem to come only from Bombay films. And it is the fascination with these films that explain why the school-children, at my slightest bidding, began to sing a popular song from *Border*. In the film, the song *Ke Ghar Kab Aaoge* (When will you be coming home?) is sung by the soldiers when the postman brings mail. It wasn't so only with the kids in India. The school-children in Pakistan also tapped their fingers and sang in one voice, their bodies swaying, that one song that they had heard the enemy soldiers singing in the film. *Ki chitthi aati hai/To poochhi jaati hai/Ke ghar kab aaoge* (When the letters come, they ask the same question, when will you be coming home)? In the plastic wallet of one of the Pakistani soldiers killed in the Kargil War, men from the Indian Army had found a picture of the Bollywood actress, Kajol. How many faces were the fanatics on either side of the border going to rub black paint on?

The song *Ke Ghar Kab Aaoge* pays homage to the home, especially the village, and those left behind, namely the aged mother and the young wife or beloved. This view of reality is both simple-minded and conservative; it is rooted in a nostalgia for a world where wars have little to do with political manoeuvering, arms sales and naked ambition. All that seems to be involved is patriotism, sacrifice, pain and glory. We can critique the film's fraudulent sentimentalism, but, at the same time, how does one deny the suffering of women in the overwhelming male economy of murderous wars? I told the children whom I met in India and Pakistan about the dispatches from Kargil by a journalist named Srinjoy Chowdhury. A major in the Indian Army had shown the visiting reporter a letter from his wife. Their son was only twenty-one days old. The letter said, 'You have another one to look after now ... . This is a prayer, an appeal and a request. Come back in one piece. Life is so difficult. It was bearable with you around.' The letter had made the reporter reflective. He had added: 'I had seen a similar letter once. A young woman had written to a captain in the Pakistani Army. She remembered his smile; she wanted to see him smile after he came back. The letter was found beside his dead body.'

I was affected by such sentiment, and that is why a year after my visit to the classrooms, I went looking for the widows of Kargil. There was another reason. On May 28 1999 I had been on my way to Toronto from New York City by plane. I was going to meet the parents of the woman I was in love with; as it happened, it was during this visit that my girlfriend Mona and I decided to get married. The plane might have been in air for only five minutes when, looking at the Canadian newspaper on the empty seat beside me, I learned that Pakistani forces had shot down two Indian fighter jets. One pilot had been killed, and the second captured. I did not know—and neither did many in India—that the Kargil War had begun. My distress at the troubles at the border was, I should confess, tied to a smaller issue. I was going to a Pakistani household for the first time in my life and, to make it worse, this wasn't just any anonymous family but the parents and brothers of the woman I might soon marry. Over the next few days, the news grew worse. Everyone, including Mona's parents, spoke of the war in grim tones when they met me. I felt uncomfortable about the war, and about being in that house during such a time, and I made awkward jokes about it. And over the next several days, as hurried preparations were made for the marriage which would be held a fortnight later, I thought more than once of those women in India and Pakistan who were being turned by the war machine into young widows.

In a village called Kukurwar, about three hours' drive away from Patna, I met Munni Devi, the widow of Sepoy Hardeo Prasad who was killed in Batalik during the Kargil War. Hardeo was a soldier in the 1 Bihar Regiment and his wife showed me his large, framed picture taken when he was a part of the UN Peacekeeping Force in Somalia. He was a tall, well-built man with dark skin and a light moustache, and in the photograph he wore the blue UN cap and a blue turtleneck under his camouflage jacket. Behind him was the Somalian photo studio's painted backdrop. It showed a garden and a house with a TV aerial and, further in the distance, a row of mountain peaks on which the artist had added a layer of white snow. Next to this picture was another glass frame with a one-dollar bill pasted inside it. Hardeo had brought the dollar note back with him from Somalia in 1994. Munni and I were sitting in the small brick house that was built with the compensation money that the government had given her. The room was not very large; it had just enough space for four chairs. There was a doorway to my right and we could hear Hindi songs being played on a loudspeaker in the distance. Now and then, I would glimpse a hen walking outside with five or six tiny chicks that had been coloured a bright green by their owner. It was a winter morning and Munni, slight and barefoot, with only a thin shawl wrapped around her sari, continued to shiver as she spoke to me. When her hand shook, I would look away, concentrating my gaze at the picture of a smiling child in the Magadh Automobile calendar hanging on the wall behind her head.

Munni was twenty-eight years old. She had three children, two daughters, and also a little son who was six months old when his father died. Munni's education had stopped at high school. In response to a question I had asked, she began to tell me about the different places where her husband had served with the army. At first it was north-east India, mostly Assam, and then Somalia, before he was sent to Kashmir from where he had returned with some saffron and dreamed of trading in it. (Hardeo had begun to say to Munni, 'Money is the only VIP.' Munni looked up at me when she used the English term 'VIP'.) Hardeo had left home for Kargil on 21 May at the conclusion of a two-month leave. He was dead less than a month later. While he had been home, Munni said, he didn't do much. She said, 'He would listen to the radio.' I suddenly remembered that the 1 Bihar Regiment had been involved in the war from the start: the first army casualty from the Indian side had been Major Saravanan who had been killed on 29 May at Point 4268—and his body was among the last to be recovered in the war when his regiment captured the hill, on the night of 6 July, where he had died months earlier. While Munni and I talked, Hardeo's old father came into the room and sat down. He didn't say anything to me, and several minutes later, when I looked at him, I couldn't decide if his eyes were old and watery or if indeed he was crying. Munni said that they would listen to the radio all the time to get news of the war going on in Kargil, and it was through the news bulletin that they first heard of Hardeo's death. There was some confusion, however, because the radio had mentioned the wrong village, even though it had got the name and the regiment right. Then, the subdivisional magistrate came and spoken to Munni. She had been sitting outside her hut. The brick house, she reminded me, had not yet been built. The officer said in formal Hindi, 'Is this Hardeo Prasad's dwelling-place? He has been martyred.'

Munni said, 'I had been unhappy for the previous day or two. I had been crying for an hour. I wasn't surprised when the man came. I did not move from where I had been sitting outside the house.' At night, at two in the morning, soldiers in an army truck brought Hardeo's corpse wrapped in the national flag. The body, Munni said, had turned completely black, and, as if putting a half-question to me, she said that the enemy had used some poisonous substance. Munni said that the district officials had told her that they would have to wait till Bihar's chief minister, Rabri Devi, came to the funeral with her husband. The dignitaries arrived by helicopter and the Chief Minister offered a few words of support to Munni. She also gave her a cheque. Months later, Munni said, women in the village would comment that she had got a house and a television after her husband died. This hurt her, Munni said. She would rather have her husband back.

Munni said that her husband had been hiding near a hill with an officer when the shooting began. Hardeo was hurt in the right arm. The officer said to him that they should get medical aid but Hardeo said that he was okay. Munni said, 'After two-three hours, he began to suffer a bit.' Four men from his regiment carried Hardeo to the place where medical aid was available. He asked them for a drink of water and told them about his family. Then, he said that he would not live.

When Munni had finished speaking, she kept her head bent down. The parting in her hair was bare. As is customary for a widow, there was no sindoor in the parting. When I asked her what was it that Hardeo wrote most often to her in his letters, she quietly got up and fetched a few letters from the next room. The first letter I read was actually written not by Hardeo but by Munni herself. It was in broken Hindi, and began 'My dear husband ...' The other two letters had been written by Hardeo and they were dated about eight-nine months before his death.

They inquired about Munni's health and then instructed her to take care of the children. Both were addressed to 'Dear Mother of Manisha ...' Manisha was their elder daughter. Hardeo signed his name in English with some flourish. That signature and the address were the only words he wrote in English. And when I looked at the address, I realized that he was perhaps dyslexic, because he had transposed several letters of the name of the village as well in his father's name which appeared on the top.

I reopened Munni's letter. I was embarrassed to read it in front of her, but I went ahead anyway. I thought that her way of addressing Hardeo was much more playful. 'Priya Patiji, Namaste, Namaste' (Dear Husband, my greetings, my greetings). Her letter mentioned that Hardeo had been a more regular correspondent; she had simply not had the time to write to him more frequently. Manisha was staying at her maternal uncle's house; she was attending school in Jehanabad town. Munni wanted Hardeo to come home for the chatth festival, and if he was given leave, she wanted him to inform her in advance. Munni had also written, 'What else can I write? You know what a family is like. And for a wife it is the husband who gives happiness. The wife's happiness is not there without you. What can I do when this is written in my fate?' She had noted that the potatoes had been harvested, and the rice threshed. There was mention of loneliness in another brief sentence and also a hint about some tension in the wider family. I thought of one of Hardeo's letter, in which he had scribbled in the postscript, 'Don't fret too much and whatever people might say or do in the house, you shouldn't utter a word in response. Okay. Ta-ta.'

Hardeo's younger brother, Vinod, a pleasant, unemployed man, had come and sat down on the ground near me. He was holding a yellow sheet of printed paper in his hand. It was a rather bombastically worded tribute to Hardeo on his first death anniversary which had been observed only a few months earlier. The tribute ended with a declaration in Hindi: 'By being a soldier and by assuming command, you have taught the young men of your village that it is not only Kargil and Kashmir but also Lahore and Islamabad where the Indian tricolour will fly. For the peace of your soul, the District Development Forum takes this solemn oath.'

Tea and sweets had been brought for me on a small stainless steel tray. Munni also brought an album of photographs. There were only a handful of pictures in the book. A few of them showed Hardeo in Somalia, and in one picture he was standing in front of a temple in Bhutan. There were photographs from the funeral, including one of the dead body, washed and laid out on the ground with a brown cloth wrapped around the torso. The hands of the villagers were propping up the head and shoulders for the photograph. There was a picture of Hardeo and Munni which had been taken during happier times. It said 'Prabhat Studio' in the bottom corner. Munni was difficult to recognize in the photograph: she wore her hair loose over her shoulder, and her clothes were new and bright. She appeared amused as she looked at the camera. I asked Munni if I could take a picture of her. She took down the framed photograph of Hardeo in Somalia, and holding it solemnly in front of her, posed for me with her eyes fixed on the ground between us.

A few minutes later, I stepped out of the house. The sun was covered with clouds. I still had the camera in my hand and Vinod remarked that his brother Hardeo had said to him, 'Whenever you have your picture taken, make sure that one foot is ahead of the other, as if you were marching.' A little distance away was the narrow road that connected the village to the broken-up highway that I had taken from Patna. The village road had now been named after Hardeo. A tractor loaded with sand was driving away from us. I thanked Munni for talking to me, but there was something else I wanted to find out before I left. I asked her if she would have anything to say to a woman in Pakistan who was also a war widow like her.

Munni said, 'Why should I say anything to the one who took away my husband?'

'But the women, the widows, they were not fighting. They did not take away Hardeo,' I said.

But Munni shook her head. She would not relent. Maybe she was right, maybe she was not.

Maybe the fault lay in my fantasies. I was dreaming of a dialogue between all those who had suffered from war's injustice. There are many on both sides of the border who still hold on to that dream. It could be argued that Munni was the war's double victim. She had not only lost her husband in the war, she had also lost a link to the broader world which shared her suffering.

*

So, in a way, Munni refused to write a letter that I could take to the other side of the border. And yet, if I had a chance to return to the schools, I would have told the students in Patna as well as Karachi about Munni's experience and her reaction to my questions. I would have liked to share with them Munni's words and also my sense of confusion at her refusal to my last demand. There was a lesson in all this for the students, but also for the likes of Dharmanand Kholkar and myself.

I had thought that perhaps women who had lost their husbands would come together in solidarity, but I had been naïve and motivated by a somewhat academic sense of rationality and politics. And it wasn't Munni alone— I met other Kargil widows in the weeks that followed and I got similar responses. It was only the grief that was real, little else mattered. I do not know what it would have been like in Pakistan. During my second visit there, I contacted an army commander and requested permission to meet the war widows of Kargil. The officer straightened his back and said, 'Those widows would be the wives of the freedom fighters. I don't know about them. The Pakistani Army was not involved in the war.' This claim was laughable. Pakistan had initially denied that its army had any role in the infiltration into Kargil in the summer of 1999; later, the official position had been changed and the government admitted that it was providing assistance to the invaders. The Kargil conflict had led to hundreds of casualties on both sides. It was even accepted that the man who later emerged as Pakistan's dictator, General Musharraf, was the architect of Kargil. Yet, the Pakistani officer that I spoke to gave me a stiff smile and dismissed my suggestion that there were Kargil widows in his army. I did not ask him to explain to me why his government had awarded sixty-four gallantry medals to its soldiers and officers for their heroism and sacrifice in Kargil.

Three years after the Kargil War, the *Indian Express* published a string of brief interviews with the families of men killed in the fighting. In each interview, you got a sense of the emptiness that the war had left amidst those one could call the survivors. But what struck me more strongly was that in every interview that was published, there was a call for a conclusive war with Pakistan. The father of one officer who had been awarded the Param Vir Chakra said, 'All parents feel proud of their sons if they sacrifice their lives to protect the motherland. But the battle should be a decisive one ... .' Another parent said, 'We should not give Pakistan the benefit of time. We should strike immediately. It has already been identified as a terrorist country. Pakistan has to be crushed.' This position appeared a bit of a sham to me. Like the Pakistani officer I had spoken to, the parents of the slain soldiers were also indulging in denial. Another war would undoubtedly result in more men getting killed while trying to kill others. The war might or might not end, but their lives would. In fact, it is quite likely that the war would end, but the grief of the others would not. Perhaps I should not say these things, for unlike Munni and the parents I have quoted above, I have lost no one in a war. But, on the other hand, our political leaders who appear the most belligerent when they speak of the enemy and of our need to annihilate it do not have among them anyone whose son was killed in Kargil. Perhaps there is another question that Dharmanand Kholkar could ask the kids in his classroom: 'Why not build a memorial to the deserter in the war? Is he not brave who, when death seems near, turns away from battle because he has the courage to declare his love for his family?'

Those who call for a war to end all wars forget that, as nuclear nations, both India and Pakistan can destroy the world. According to the journalist Praful Bidwai, the two countries exchanged no fewer than thirteen nuclear threats during the Kargil crisis. Bidwai outlined other costs of the war in India: the whipping up of communal hysteria, a belligerent intolerance of internal dissent, as well as the censorship and rigging of the media. In the face of the threat of nuclear annihilation, we have to teach children about peace not only because our leaders are hypocritical—a total sum of 13.7 billion dollars was spent on defence in India during the year following the Kargil War; was there no self-interest involved in the patriotic cries being raised by the politicians and the arms lobby?—but because the apocalyptic vision on both sides damns all our futures. Late in 2001, around the same time that I was talking to the children in the schools, a brigadier in Islamabad told a reporter for the *Atlantic Monthly* that Pakistan should not hesitate to use the nuclear bomb preemptively against India. The brigadier's rationale was so stunning and, at the same time, strangely believable that it bears quoting at length:

> We should fire at them and take out a few of their cities—Delhi, Bombay, Calcutta ... . They should fire back and take Karachi and Lahore. Kill off a hundred or two hundred million people. They should fire at us and it would all be over. They have acted so badly towards us; they have been so mean. We should teach them a lesson. It would teach all of us a lesson. There is no future here, and we need to start over. So many people think this. Have you been to the villages of Pakistan, the interior? There is nothing but dire poverty and pain. The children have no education; there is nothing to look forward to. Go into the villages, see the poverty. There is no drinking water. Small children without shoes walk

miles for a drink of water. I go to the villages and I want to cry. My children have no future. None of the children of Pakistan have a future. We are surrounded by nothing but war and suffering. Millions have to die away.

These sentiments are only a step away from being presented as wisdom to children in the classrooms. In India, for example, the nuclear explosions in Pokhran found approval in the minds of the educators. A conversation-and-essay-writing assignment in the state of Rajasthan where the explosions had taken place asked students to comment on the following exchange: 'Student: "Teacher, what has India achieved by doing the nuclear tests? Was it a right step?" Teacher: "Undoubtedly it was correct. India has achieved a huge success." Student: "What success? Economic sanctions have been slapped on." Teacher: "Economic sanctions do not matter. The country should first become powerful. Only the powerful are listened to. Now we can talk about world peace aggressively."'

In April 2002, the US signed an agreement with India to sell eight long-range weapon-locating radars for about 146 million dollars. The previous year, France sold to Pakistan the Agosta submarine as well as the technology to build; and then, it made a bid to sell six Scorpene submarines, allegedly a generation ahead of the Agosta, to India at a higher price. According to a May 2002 report in the *Guardian*, Britain had made a successful bid to sell sixty Hawk jets to India, a deal which was worth over a billion pounds, equal to about ten years of UK bilateral aid to India. BAE Systems, the manufacturer of the Hawk aircraft, was making efforts to sell Jaguar combat aircrafts to India. According to the Stockholm International Peace Research Institute, the agreement was for 126 Jaguars. The

Guardian had quoted the director of an activist group called Saferworld, 'It is alarming that, under license from a UK company, India is building Jaguar aircrafts that are capable of delivering nuclear weapons.' Later, the news from Aero India 2003 was that military aircraft-makers from Britain, Russia and the US were competing over a multibillion-dollar order to supply sixty-six advanced jet-trainers to the Indian military. In the next decade, another news report said, India was likely to emerge as the biggest importer of arms in the world.

Such transactions also raise the spectre of corruption. It is not only that the Kargil War cost 2.3–3.5 billion dollars; what was also disturbing was that the aftermath of the war brought to light shocking accounts of financial scandal. In December 2001, a government audit in India revealed that 'highly inflated' prices had been paid for the metal coffins used to bring back the bodies of the soldiers who had died. The coffins, bought from a company in the US that was the sole bidder for the contract, cost 2,500 dollars each. But while the auditor's report on the expenditure of 1.5 million dollars for the coffins received a lot of attention in the press and the Indian parliament, the real criticism of the report was levelled against the expenditure of 500 million dollars on urgent supplies for the soldiers who had been hurriedly sent to the mountains to fight. The auditor's report had concluded that almost half the money 'was spent fruitlessly, breaching established principles of propriety'. A story published in the *New York Times* said that the auditor's report seemed to confirm press accounts of soldiers sent off to fight in sub zero temperatures at high altitudes without proper equipment: 'Thousands of pairs of boots turned out to be too small for any adult to wear, the audit report said. Wool socks, sleeping bags and bulletproof jackets materialized months after the fighting was already over. The army urgently ordered 46,554 pairs of Italian gloves, but the delivery was slowed when the company proposed a different colour fabric.'

The Defence Minister, George Fernandes, was under attack in the press. He had been forced to resign earlier in the year because his party chief as well as defence personnel were caught on video accepting bribes from journalists posing as defence contractors. Later, while a commission of inquiry was still investigating the scandal, the prime minister had reappointed Fernandes to his former post. Now, faced with a new charge, Fernandes explained to the Indian parliament that the coffins were essential because he had wanted the bodies to be returned to the families rather than have them cremated where they had fallen. Indeed, the BJP government had made sure that high officials of the state were present at the funerals for the soldiers back at their homes. In many ways, the government was putting all available pomp and dignity at the service of the dead soldier—and also at the service of the ideology of aggressive patriotism which was used to prop up the nation-state. Each funeral was an occasion for rousing nationalist feeling as well as support for the government which wreathed itself in gallantry. Back in the year of the Kargil War, a month after Hardeo's death, Fernandes had come and visited Munni. She had been pleased by his visit, but I could not see how Fernandes would bring to her the news of the coffin scandal or the accusations that the soldiers in Kargil were missing shoes and other supplies. Munni had said to me that she wasn't a well-educated woman, but she would have quite easily understood, I think, the complicit links between patriotism and profits.

*

A day after the news of the coffin scandal came out in the press, I returned to Delhi from Patna. My Delhi flight was delayed because the Indian parliament had been attacked by five terrorists suspected to be members of the Pakistan-based Lashkar-e-Taiba group. Delhi was full of talk about the attack—the terrorists had been killed, but six security personnel and a gardener had also died—and the daring plan to reach into the very centre of India's political class.

After arriving late in the city, I went to sleep at a friend's house and, early the next morning, went to meet Sharmila Pundhir. She was the widow of a young pilot, Squadron Leader Rajiv Pundhir, who had been killed on 28 May 1999 at the start of the Kargil conflict. Pundhir had been flying an MI-17 helicopter gunship when he took a hit from a shoulder-held Stinger missile. All four crew members died. Two Pakistani soldiers, Havildar Major Nasir Ali Shah and Gunner Mohammed Kamal, had been given medals for shooting down the Indian helicopter, even though the Pakistanis had first claimed that the shooting had been the work of mujahideen rebels. Pundhir's craft was hit a day after the first two Indian planes had gone down—and about whom I had read, without knowing that a war had started, as I made my way from New York City to Toronto to meet my future in-laws.

I had contacted Sharmila by phone several months earlier from the US and learned from her that she was a school teacher. When I met her, she told me that she had recently given up that job. The government had provided her a licence to operate a gas station and she was trying to get the shop built. Sharmila was probably in her early thirties.

She was dressed in a white-and-black-print churidar-kurta. I was struck by how attractive she was and, very soon into our conversation, when Sharmila began to cry inconsolably, I was touched by how little she tried to hide her love for the man she had married, and whose pictures, from his postings in different parts of the country and in Sri Lanka, hung on the walls of the room in which we were sitting. Her husband's career, which Sharmila proudly described to me, had been an impressive one from the standpoint of the armed forces: he had served in India's disastrously interventionist war in Sri Lanka, he had also been an instructor in nuclear-biological-chemical warfare at the College of Military Engineering in Pune, and, in addition, he had flown missions in the troubled areas of Kashmir. The violence of a retributive military power could not possibly have been foreign to his milieu. And yet, when Sharmila, crying freely by now, said that she didn't have the strength to pretend that she was full of fortitude and that, nevertheless, she did precisely that because she had two children, and everyone else expected her to keep a brave front because otherwise it became difficult for all of them to handle the situation—when she said all this, wiping her tears on her dupatta, her voice hoarse from crying, it was impossible not to feel the suffocating weight of a deep and terrible destruction.

Several months later, I was passing through Delhi after I had spent time in Gujarat, and I called Sharmila. I said to her that I had often wondered how she was doing and if the gas station was running by now. We decided quickly that I should stop by her house the next day, and she would drive me to the city's outskirts where her shop was located. We made our trip to the gas station the next morning. There was a large sign in Hindi, past a row of eucalyptus trees, saying '*Kargil shaheed Hero of Tololing, Squadron Leader Rajiv Pundhir Ko Pranam*' (Greetings to the Kargil martyr Hero of Tololing, Squadron Leader Rajiv Pundhir). The station had several Z-shaped machines for pumping gas. It was a very modern set-up, still uncommon in most parts of India, and the machines were all manned by uniformed attendants. Music was being played on the sound system. I felt happy for Sharmila and I said this to her. She only said, 'I find myself a misfit in this field. You have got to have the temperament for this.' Then, she added, 'I have one mission. I want to educate my kids. I don't even bring them here. I do not want them to develop an interest in this kind of work.'

Sharmila skimmed the ledger in her office and then began to describe the plans for future construction at the gas station. A convenience store with an ATM, an automated teller machine, was to be built and on top of its roof a garden would be laid out. Sharmila revealed that before her husband died, she had merely been interested in wearing beautiful clothes. That was no longer true, she said. Now, she didn't even go to any social gatherings. Her own brother had got married recently but she had stayed away. When she said this, I remembered how the widows in my Hindu family would not go near the *mandap* where the wedding ceremony was being performed. No one wanted the shadow of their bad luck to fall on the couple getting married. I looked at Sharmila and it was difficult to see her as a widow whose life was now behind her. Unlike a traditional widow in a white sari, she was wearing a bright lemon churidar-kurta, and I was aware once again of the beauty that her pain could not hide. I asked Sharmila whether her friends wanted her to get married again. She replied in English, 'Yes. But the concept of remarriage is not acceptable to me ... I don't think I'll ever get over what happened.'

In the car, when Sharmila was driving me back to her house, she said, 'I always ask myself why all this happened. I know I will never understand it.' The previous year she had told me that her faith in religion and prayer was lost with her husband's death. And I thought she had returned to that same theme because we had just passed the saffron-clad pilgrims on the road carrying water from the Ganges to the Shiva temple in Haridwar. But, Sharmila was thinking of more secular matters because, a moment later, she said, 'Life in India is very cheap. Every day there are more casualties on the border. There should be a permanent solution to the problem.' I asked her if she meant that we should have a war, and I could see that the question caused her anguish. Not simply because it returned her to the memory of her husband's death, but because she did not know if there was a simple answer to that question. She said, 'When I hear of incidents with the terrorists coming and killing people, my blood boils. I feel we should just either do or die ... . But I also know that the personal loss is such that it is not worth it. Time is not the healer.' And even as Sharmila was replying to my question, something else clicked in place for me. I remembered the reports from earlier that summer when the parents of the soldiers killed in Kargil had demanded a war to end all wars. The demand for violence had puzzled me. Now, however, while Sharmila was talking to me, it suddenly made sense. Sharmila did not want to think that her husband had died in vain. She wanted his death to matter. Her husband's death would have been meaningless if the war in which he had sacrificed his life had not led to peace. It would have been as if he had died without any consequence. His life would then appear to be as without meaning as his death.

*

A professor of education, Krishna Kumar, has written that 'as a topic of study, Pakistan is taboo in Indian schools, and the same applies to India in Pakistan'. The children in Indian and Pakistani schools 'do not hear about each others' country as part of their formal learning'. But, what is equally significant, Kumar writes, is that in both countries the students' 'everyday reality is steeped in the consciousness of the "other"'. We know very little about the enemy, and yet, the enemy provides the frame for our every thought.

My first real acquaintance with Pakistani faces and names took place in 1978—I was already finishing high school—when the Indian cricket team went to Pakistan. The two sides were playing with each other after a gap of eighteen years. Whenever the Indians played a series abroad, for example in England or Australia, it meant that we had to listen to the cricket commentary, often furtively, at odd hours of the day or night, with the radio hidden under a quilt to escape detection by our parents. But not in Pakistan. The time zones were only half an hour apart. Also, television had come to my town and other parts of small-town India. There was a tantalizing closeness in the encounter. Yet, that did not dim the rivalry between the two teams. If anything, the competition was even greater. Pakistan was the enemy. For me, our foes had faces and there were eleven names to go with them—Imran Khan, the stylish pace bowler, the master batsman Zaheer Abbas, the dependable all-rounder Mudassar Nazar, the wild, lusty competitor, Javed Miandad ... . Sadly, in that series of 1978–79, the Indians were beaten 2-0. The only one who really shone from the Indian side was my boyhood hero, Sunil Gavaskar. In the final test that was played at Karachi— the city which I would visit more than two decades later, the same city where my wife was born—Gavaskar scored superb centuries in both innings but was unable to prevent Pakistan from taking the match and the series.

I did not learn anything about Pakistan at school, or at least nothing more significant than the dubious lesson that Muhammad Ali Jinnah was the cause of the Partition of India. But, in the field of sports, which is what mattered to me as a boy, my obsessions were focussed on Pakistan. No victory tasted sweet unless it was wrested from those who lived across the border. Nor did a defeat feel as devastating as one inflicted by the hated Pakistanis. The strange thing is that when I reflect on my boyhood, it appears almost idyllic in comparison to the situation today. I say this because schoolchildren in both India and Pakistan these days are not only kept ignorant about each other, they are also, in ever larger numbers, brought up on systematic misinformation and lies. This situation is made worse by the fact that the contemporary obsession with the enemy is not limited to sports or to one or two localized aspects of life. Instead, the emergence of terrorism as an ever-present threat, one that is often also manipulated by the nation-state, has made the idea of the enemy an omnipresent danger. The enemy is not limited to those who live on the other side of the border; instead, it is now identified as the enemy precisely because it crosses the dividing line.

Nuclear bombs on both sides have granted our obsessions greater legitimacy and also allowed the hysteria to be turned to an unprecedented pitch. The technological threat by itself would not be so immense were it not for the volatility of the emergent fundamentalist movements in both countries. The fundamentalist turn is primarily responsible for the youth, especially in non-elite schools, being served a staple diet of poisonous prejudice.

According to a liberal group in Pakistan, the textbooks used in schools run by Jamaat-ud-Daawa teach that 'Muslims alone have the right to rule the world and are allowed to kill infidels that stand in the way of Islam.' The Jamaat-ud-Daawa, in its earlier incarnation, was known as the Lashkar-e-Taiba. The report states that 'probably fictitious letters from jihadis killed in battle are strewn across textbooks. "If I am killed in battle, celebrate," reads a letter from one Abdul Nasir to his mother and sister which can be found in the seventh grade textbook. "Make sure you conceal your body and never wear perfume"'. The report also states: 'India is presented as Pakistan's sworn enemy and Saudi Arabia as its best friend. Kashmir is presented as Pakistani territory forcibly snatched by Hindus and Pakistan as a country created only for Muslims.' The second-grade textbook exhorts the students to become holy warriors: 'We should all be willing to lay down our lives for the great nuclear power that is Pakistan.' The teachers are particularly intent, according to the report, on informing the students of Islam's glorious past.

The mirror image of this benighted pedagogy is to be found among the Hindu fundamentalists on this side of the border. Over the past few years, the BJP government has gone about systematically doctoring the school history books. Among its chief passions is the deletion of all references to beef-eating practices in ancient India as well as all remarks critical of the *varna* or caste system that allowed the oppressive dominance of the elite groups over the rest of the society. More dangerous are the over 6000 RSS-run Vidya Bharati schools about which the National Steering Committee on Textbook Evaluation reported that much that was taught there was 'designed to promote bigotry and religious fanaticism in the name of inculcating knowledge of culture in the young generation'. The textbooks seek to refashion the past by wilfully denigrating Islam or destroying its historical claims. The evaluation committee had objected to the assertions like the following where the Black Stone in Mecca is falsely requisitioned as Shiva's phallic symbol for the greater glory of Hinduism: 'Thousands of opponents of idol worship, the followers of Islam, go to the pilgrimage centre of Islamic community at Kaaba to worship "Shivlinga". In Muslim society, the greatest wish is to have a *darshan* of that black stone (Shivlinga).'

This is a provocative rumour being taught as history.

One writer named P.N. Oak has been claiming for some years that the Taj Mahal is in reality an ancient Shiva temple called Tejo Mahalya—'more magnificent and majestic before it was reduced to a sombre Islamic cemetery'—which was not built by the Mughal emperor Shah Jahan but only commandeered from the Hindu king of Jaipur. Against such prejudice parading as knowledge, I am appealing for the use of the 'testimony' as a way of experiencing or living in history. Munni and Sharmila offer accounts that are a part of the contemporary history of India and Pakistan, but stories like theirs have not found entry in the textbooks used in our schools. The aims of testimony and rumour diverge radically from each other. I am borrowing the terms from a book on India's partition by the historian Gyanendra Pandey in which he refers to Lawrence Langer's contention that testimony is 'a form of remembering' while rumour 'is a form of doing—of making happen—by telling'. Against the malice of rumour, against also the indifference of a nationalist history, the testimonies of the widows push into the frames of our consciousness a record of suffering and even an uncelebrated strength that has nothing to do with prowess on the battlefield.

The riots between Hindus and Muslims in India are spread through rumours. An efficient administration in a democracy ought to take steps to inform its citizens of the lies that are being spread and the dangers they pose. My interest in presenting testimonies and letters is not so much a corrective for rumours as it is a tool for the classroom. It is primarily aimed at promoting thoughtfulness and curiosity among students. This goal is not the result of some abstract, civic impulse. It arises from the observation that even amidst violence it is the children who remain the most open-minded and willing to learn. They are willing to share with you the reasons which have shaped their beliefs; the masking of prejudice or the kind of dissembling that adults routinely practise in polite conversation is still far off in their future. These are reasons for hope.

In testimonies and letters written by victims of violence, what is most surprising, although there is no reason that it should be so, is the evidence of dignity and even patience. In his extraordinary book about the violence in Rwanda, Philip Gourevitch has written about his meeting with 'a preacher who had been accused of presiding over the slaughter of hundreds of his congregation'. The preacher, Pastor Elizaphan Ntakirutimana, had fled Rwanda and was living with his son, a cardiac anaesthesiologist, in the suburbs of Laredo, Texas. The United Nations' International Criminal Tribunal for Rwanda, sitting in Arusha, Tanzania, had issued an indictment against the pastor, charging him with three counts of genocide and three counts of crimes against humanity. When Gourevitch tracked down Pastor Ntakirutimana in Texas, he asked him if he remembered 'the precise language of the letter addressed to him' by seven Tutsi pastors—the men who had been killed in the town where Ntakirutimana headed the Mugonero Adventist church. This is the letter written by the doomed men:

Our dear leader, Pastor Elizaphan Ntakirutimana,
How are you! We wish you to be strong in all these problems we are facing. We wish to inform you that tomorrow we will be killed with our families. We therefore request you to intervene on our behalf and talk with the Mayor. We believe that, with the help of God who entrusted you the leadership of this flock, which is going to be destroyed, your intervention will be highly appreciated, the same way as the Jews were saved by Esther.
We give honor to you.

It was this remarkable letter written by the Tutsi pastors, a letter from another place and another time, that I often thought about when I was visiting Gujarat.

In a school that I visited in the Muslim area of Juhapura in Ahmedabad, almost all the students had witnessed violence during the riots. The principal, Mr Maru, a tall, bearded man in a white polyester suit, took me around and in each classroom I heard accounts of students having to prepare for their exams with bombs exploding outside their windows. I was moved by the undisguised pain with which the students spoke of their experiences, but I was also startled by the fact that, perhaps because I was the first visitor to their school, the Muslim youth there turned our conversation into a touching appeal to the dominant Hindu majority in the city. A fourteen-year-old girl named Reshma said that she didn't understand why the Hindus called the area in which she lived and went to school 'mini-Pakistan'. She switched to English and said, 'We are also Indians.' Her voice faltered as she added, 'We are not foreigners. We should have rights as Indian citizens.'

The problem was that the people to whom I was to carry Reshma's appeal included the teachers. Who would educate the educators? Consider Mr Jani whom I had met that very morning at the Little Flowers School in another area of the city. I had arrived during the recess and the gate to the school was mobbed by the students buying sweets and savouries from a man with a cart. Mr Jani had been told to expect a visitor, and he asked me to wait in the corner of the school office. Mr Jani was in his sixties and he was the deputy principal. He was a tall, grey-haired man. He was wearing grey trousers, a half-sleeved white shirt and a tie. I told Mr Jani that I was interested in talking to students about what was happening in Gujarat.

'What is your good name, please?' he began.

When I told him my name, Mr Jani said, 'I am hard of hearing.'

I had a feeling that Mr Jani wanted me to repeat my name so that he could be absolutely sure of my religious identity. I gave him my business card which had my name on it and the information that I was a professor in the US.

Mr Jani nodded with satisfaction.

He had a story to tell me. A Muslim boy was on the school's cricket team. There was some talk of the boy being given the captaincy, but Mr Jani had put his foot down. He had felt that there would be problems if the boy was given that responsibility. Some years later, in 1996, there were Hindu-Muslim riots in the city. The Muslim boy had long passed out of the school but he appeared at Mr Jani's office door with a gun.

Mr Jani told me that his former student said to him, 'I am going to shoot you.'

After a pause, during which I watched the students milling about in the field outside, Mr Jani said, 'These matters are very sensitive ... And in particular, the Muslim community is a little bit aggressive, a little bit fanatic.'

I waited for Mr Jani to go on. He said, 'The world still believes that it is the minority that is being wronged. Not true. The poor Hindu cannot even use a penknife. It is not in our blood.'

The bell rang. The noise of the playground came closer as the kids began to run back to their classes. The line of students filing past the open door was apparently endless. Yet, looking out of the window, I could see that the crowd of kids outside had thinned by now. I asked Mr Jani if we shouldn't maybe make our way to the classroom and he said that we would leave in a few minutes. A minute or two passed. Mr Jani had something on his mind. He clicked his jaws. After a long pause, he looked at me meaningfully, and said, 'You see, we Hindus are passive. Some organization in America needs to take up our cause.'

4

Please Prove Your Identity

A dog was licking me on the side of the face, and when it drew back, my wet skin felt cool in the breeze. That image from my dream stayed with me after I woke up in the middle of the afternoon in my hotel room. There was a slit in the curtains covering the glass windows and a straight line of white glare divided the darkness.

The room was air-conditioned. I hadn't had this comfort in Delhi, where I had been staying in a friend's *barsati*, and I immediately wanted to take a nap. A short flight earlier that morning had brought me to Jammu. The previous week, I had been in my parents' home, in Patna. My little nephews, who were visiting one evening, had brought a puppy with them. The small animal was happy to meet anyone new, but it was suffering in the heat and I saw that its pink tongue hung out, dry. I had cupped water in my hands in the bathroom and sat down on the floor. My nephews watched as the puppy lapped the water dripping from my palms. I did this several times and the puppy kept licking the water. But, the boys were growing impatient. The younger one said, 'It thinks that's milk.'

I lay in bed for a few minutes, thinking about my dream, thinking about the dog in Patna, even though he didn't resemble the one I had seen in my dream. The comfort of the hotel room had taken me back to the few days I had spent in my home town with my family. When I thought of the dog in my dream, I began to wonder what it had stood for. My nephews had decided, mistakenly, that the puppy had confused water for milk. The mistakes preyed on my mind, a traveller in a strange city, looking for clues to a story of violence.

After a while, I got up and forced myself to step outside the hotel. The wide street, nearly empty at this hour, burned in the heat. I had been told to wait for a bus going to Ramgarh. The tar on the road melted under my sneakers. I wished I was carrying bottled water. The bus was not long in coming. It took me past a statue of a Sikh military officer in the middle of a roundabout and dropped me off at Jewel Chowk where I needed to wait for another bus headed for a town called Akhnoor. That bus would drop me off at the Mishriwala camp.

Five thousand Kashmiri Hindus, commonly called Pandits, lived in Mishriwala. It was a refugee camp for the Hindu families that had fled the Kashmir Valley out of fear of the Islamic militants at the start of the insurgency in 1990. The bus dropped me at the side of the road and I could see rows of one-room tenements stretching into the distance on the other side. There was a brick kiln close to where I stood, and, a couple of hundred yards away, a small group of men sat quietly under a canvas shamiana with a banner behind them. The tenements were to the right and I walked down the road to an area where a group of teenagers were huddled around a transistor. India and England were playing the final one-day cricket match in the NatWest Series at Lord's. I had checked the score at Jewel Chowk and had learned that England had scored a hundred runs and so far lost only one wicket. At the camp, the sad expressions on the faces of the young men said it all. The English side was well on its way to a very big total. I learned that their opener Marcus Trescothick had scored a century.

Satish Kumar, whom I met that day, had arrived in the camp exactly thirteen years ago on 13 July 1990. The camp had been in existence only for six days when he first came there. Kumar's hair was light brown in colour and his eyes had the kind of lightness that people like me, folks from the plains, associate with Kashmiris. Lifting his gaze above my head every time he spoke to me, Kumar said that the 'Pakistani fundamentalists' had begun by putting up intimidating posters in Urdu. There were threats made against the Hindus, he said, especially against the Pandit womenfolk. Then, the trees in his apple and almond orchards—in Pattan village, in Baramullah district—had been cut down in the night. In the Mishriwala camp for the Hindu refugees, Satish Kumar was now as rootless as his trees.

Kashmir's entire population is nearly ten million. The Hindu Pandit population that migrated from the Valley is said to be around 135,000. The number of Hindus remaining in the Valley is not more than a few thousand. It is tempting to see the decline in the numbers being compensated for by the presence of soldiers from the Indian Army. As much as half a million Indian troops, mostly from other parts of the country, make an aggressive, anxious army of occupation in an area that is often alien to them. In this conflict that started in earnest in 1990, as many as 80,000 Kashmiris have died, although the state's estimates are closer to half that number.

The tenement in which I had been invited to sit belonged to Ramesh Pandita. He was a large man and moved around us in shorts and a vest pulled over his paunch. Pandita had worked as a quality controls inspector in Srinagar. When he fled south to Jammu in 1990, he had to look for a new job like everyone else. He was now a sales officer for a processed food company. We were all sitting on the bed which took up most of the room. I could see that the space meant for the kitchen was being used as a tiny room. Against the outside wall, with a corrugated roof for cover, a cooking stove had been placed and there were stainless steel utensils arranged neatly beside it on a wooden board. Ramesh told me that five people, including his wife and mother, lived in this space. When Pandita went away to make tea, the men sitting on the bed explained that his wife was away, and then they began to complain that because of the power outage, they were unable to watch the cricket match telecast.

Kumar began to tell me about an attack on the Khir Bhavani temple in Tula Mula, Srinagar. When the separatist guerrillas had used rocket launchers, the deity's power was such that the rockets were blocked by the chinar trees. 'Pakistan is giving huge temptations to the young,' he said. More men walked into the room and sat on the bed around us. Kumar began to talk about the Afghani, Lebanese and Sudanese jihadis who had infiltrated into the Valley. The other men in the room nodded. One of them said that there were many people in India who did not know what the Pandits had suffered in Kashmir and the torture that they were still undergoing in refugee camps in various cities of the country. Kumar said in English, 'Our birth rate is zero per cent. Our death rate is hundred per cent.' This statement appealed to a young man, Pintooji, who had introduced himself to me as the president of the youth association in the camp. He was a college student working towards a degree in English. Pintooji wanted to add to what Kumar had just finished saying. He spoke up now. 'Human right. What does it mean? That I should have privacy. My brother is married, he has no privacy. Why should I marry? One marries for enjoyment. Here ...' He pointed to the bed on which we were sitting and became silent. No one said anything after that.

The tea had been drunk. I thanked our host and said that I wanted to walk through the camp. When I got up I noticed that pasted on the wardrobe were RSS decals, saying, '*Hamari Sanskriti, Hamara Dharm, Dharmantaran Paap Hai*' (Our culture, our religion, religious conversion is a sin). I knew that the ultranationalism of the BJP had great support in Jammu, but I couldn't but find that zeal incongruous in the camp. Here were people complaining of not having toilets and having power outages that lasted for several hours each day. They needed civic comforts, not rhetoric; they also needed homes, not lessons in hate. As I went from one tenement to another, people pointed out the cracks in their ceiling and the clogged gutters. The Pandits of Mishriwala appeared to me like lower-middle-class people who had arranged the details of their lives around the small pictures of gods and goddesses hanging from nails on their cramped walls. As I walked through the camp, several men and women stepped out of their doors and asked me, with great courtesy and warmth, to come in for tea. A thin, young man, who said he was a final-year student in a Bachelor of Arts correspondence course, complained of the suffocating heat in the rooms that lacked any ventilation. The young man had a slight stutter and it seemed, as he spoke to me, that the heat was sucking the air out of him.

As the young man talked, I was reminded of the writer and activist Sonia Jabbar's conversation with an old Pandit woman in a camp in Delhi. The old woman had said to Jabbar that she would survive Delhi's hot summers by sitting in front of the cheap coolers with her eyes shut. She told herself that it was the cool Kashmiri rain and not drops of water from the fans of the cooler caressing her face.

There must be disappointment, and also rage, in such exercises in false, cheating nostalgia. Jabbar has written of the pathos of the Kashmiri Pandits who must have realized that it was not 'a question of a few weeks or months but perhaps forever' that Kashmir was now lost to its former inhabitants. Taking measure of the pain, the anger and the bitterness of the refugee felt towards all those 'who were fortunate enough to remain in the Valley, be they Muslims or Hindu', Jabbar wonders what is the worst form of loss: 'to lose a beloved, to lose a father or a son, or to lose one's entire universe'.

*

The news was not good. The boys with the thin faces, gathered around a transistor in the doorway of a tenement in the Mishriwala camp, said that England had built up an unbeatable total in the match at Lord's. The English captain, the India-born Nasser Hussain, had also scored a century. I wanted to get back to my hotel to watch the match. The people I had met in the camp were inviting me to stay back for dinner. But I said no. I could suddenly see myself sitting in front of the television set in my hotel room. The thought made me feel guilty. An old woman, wearing Kashmiri jewellery—with long, delicate tracery of gold called *athooru* hanging from the ears—was telling me that people lived in the camp like 'chicken in a coop'. She was sitting on a culvert, fanning her face with a newspaper. I lingered before leaving, but then I began to hurriedly say goodbye to everyone.

The men walked back with me to the road where I would wait for the bus. Pintooji, the youth who had earlier spoken of the impossibility of a conjugal life in the camp, now fell in beside me. We exchanged addresses. As he was a student of literature, I asked Pintooji to name the book that he liked best. He answered me as if he were a character in a novel about Kashmiri Pandits written by an English graduate. 'I like Samuel Beckett's *Waiting for Godot*,' he said. 'We are waiting for the government to come to our help.'

The journey back, in the gathering dusk, took longer than an hour. A large part of Jammu was in darkness. I had paid for my room at an expensive hotel that morning because I had been assured that they had a generator which would be switched on during power outages. I wanted to watch the cricket match very badly; I did not get to do this in the town where I lived in America. At the hotel, I found out that the English side had amassed 325 runs. But, the Indians had started impressively. They had scored almost a hundred runs without losing a wicket. I asked room service to send me a Punjabi meal of paratha and butter chicken, and sat down to enjoy the rest of the match.

By the time my food arrived fifteen or twenty minutes later, the Indians had lost both their opening batsmen. I called room service again, and ordered a beer. Sachin Tendulkar, the star, was still to play. There was great excitement on the field, or maybe it was only inside me, and in order to calm myself I sat holding my elbows in the palms of my hand. Then, without warning, the electric supply failed and I was in the dark. There was no sound to be heard and I might have sat like that for two or three minutes before I heard the roar of the generator outside. The power returned, bringing the voices of the cricket commentators back into the room. Another wicket had fallen. Although Tendulkar was still at the crease, he was not to stay there for too long. When he was out, my euphoria vanished. I had eaten too much, and my stomach felt bloated.

There was no point in switching off the television. If I had changed the channel, it is likely that I would have learned about the massacre that had just taken place a few miles from where I was sitting. But, I didn't. I sat watching morosely while the game continued. There was a knock at the door. It was a bearer who had come to collect the plates. I said to him that India was going to lose. He said about the Indian cricketers, '*Saara mazaa kharaab kar diya*' (They have spoiled all the fun). He had not heard about the shootings either. The hotel staff had been watching the match on the television in the foyer on the first floor. Even the police had arrived at the scene of the killings late because they had been watching the match.

All this I discovered only the next morning. That night, however, after the bearer had left with the dirty plates, I began to look at my notes from the Mishriwala camp. I had the volume on the television turned low. Among my notes was a phone number that Pintooji had given me and I began to wonder whether the whole camp only had a single phone. I had seen an STD booth at the mouth of the camp. Then the idea came to me that I might call my nephews in Patna and commiserate with them about the match that wasn't going our way. But I didn't want to step outside and hunt for a phone booth. There was something else that was happening. It began to become clear that the match was not over at all. Two young players in the Indian team, Yuvraj Singh and Mohammed Kaif, seemed determined to rescue their team from the mess it was in. More than thirty runs had been scored while I had been perusing my notes and scribbling words in the margins. Both the batsmen were striking the ball with great confidence. By the time an hour had passed, a win for India seemed tantalizingly within reach. Even when Singh's wicket fell, Kaif was undaunted and kept hitting the ball to different parts of the field. I was standing up now, unable to sit, and in the last over of the game, when Kaif went for a single that got victory for India, I cheered and pumped my arms in the air.

In the morning, the newspaper that had been slipped under my door didn't have the headline I expected. Instead of the Indian victory, it said, '25 killed, over 35 injured as militants strike in Jammu.' As I found out more details, I discovered that around the same time that the Indian openers had begun building their impressive partnership, a group of unidentified men had opened fire with automatic weapons and thrown grenades in a poor settlement called Rajiv Nagar. There was no electricity in that area. There were some among those killed who had been listening to

the cricket commentary outside their shacks. The attackers
had started by lobbing grenades, guided in the dark only
by the sound of the transistor radio.

No one responded to what was going on in Rajiv Nagar
because they were following the game on radio or
television. When Sachin Tendulkar's wicket fell, some people
gave up on the game, changed the channel, and learned
that the killings had just taken place in their town. A few
persons in Jammu's posh Gandhinagar locality, oblivious
of any other event, burst into loud celebrations when the
winning run was scored. It was close to midnight, but
they exploded firecrackers. A television journalist thought
this was a second terrorist attack and went on the air to
transmit to the nation this bit of spurious news.

In the hotel lobby, I learned that the home minister
was expected in an hour. He was going to Rajiv Nagar
and then he was to visit the hospital where some of the
injured had been brought. The chief minister of Jammu
and Kashmir was flying in from Srinagar and so was the
governor. It was Sunday and I took a bus to a border
town—suddenly more aware of the sign in the buses saying
'Chek Your Seat Before Siting'—but later caught the mass
funerals on television. The dead from Rajiv Nagar were
being cremated at Jogi Gate. The camera stayed on the
row of funeral pyres and then passed over the sweating,
tearful faces of the relatives crowded in the smoke. The
television station was also running a ticker-tape of
other news from around the nation at the bottom. Again
and again, running in circles, the following words appeared
under the scenes from the funeral—'Prime Minister
Vajpayee Congratulates Victorious Indian Cricket
Team.'

The next morning, I went to Rajiv Nagar. It was an illegal settlement—a colony of makeshift shelters—built on a dry and stony river basin. The river bed was made up of smooth, round stones. The houses were flimsy structures of wood from discarded apple crates that had been patched together with plastic sheets. There were several plain brick structures too, and rising behind them, on a hill, spread the dense Raika forest. It was in this forest that the killers had vanished. The people who lived in the settlement were migrant labourers from Rajasthan, Uttar Pradesh and Bihar. A Sikh gentleman with a thick bundle of notes in his hand was counting out free cash for a group of wailing women. One of them had seen her daughter shot dead. The daughter had asked for food, but her mother had asked her to wait for her father. The mother was now full of sorrow that her daughter had died hungry. I asked the Sikh man who he was. He said he was from the Congress Party and was paying everyone who had lost a family member one thousand rupees.

The woman who was sitting closest to me, Maya Devi, had already received Rs 100,000 from the government as compensation. An older woman sitting next to her showed me the black ink on Maya's right thumb. She had had to mark a piece of paper saying that she had received the money. One man who said that he was a balloon-seller picked up a bullet shell from the ground and gave it to me. He said he lived there in Rajiv Nagar. I asked him about the money that was being given out by the Sikh gentleman. The balloon-seller smiled slightly and said that they were workers, they didn't have money to buy land, but they could vote and that is why they were given money by politicians.

There was a grimy brick room, about six feet by six feet and decorated with two calendar-pictures of Lord Hanuman, which served as a gymnasium for the settlement's youth. Dumb-bells made from small rods—stuck in the cement that had been poured into tins of the sort in which milk-powder for infants was sold—seemed to have been the only equipment used there. As the room had a door, some of the young men had rushed inside when the shooting started, and remained hidden there. But the killers had shot the latch from the hinges and come inside. There was still blood on the floor and on a pair of white rubber slippers from which the bloodied feet had been withdrawn. I was surprised at the absence of any smell. There were only flies in the room. The balloon-seller said that two of the men who had been killed in that room had been blind. Both of them were beggars.

*

On the morning after the massacre in Rajiv Nagar, I had taken a bus to the border. It was still early morning and the bus passed the army station at Kaluchak where, some months earlier, three terrorists had killed thirty-one people. Eleven army children had died in that attack. A man who owned a cosmetics shop in Jammu was on the bus with me and said that in the early 1980s he had lived in Punjab. During those days, everyone would keep in their pockets a slip of paper with their name and address on it. They could then be sure that their bodies would be returned to their families if they were killed. The man said that he had fled to Jammu to have a better life but the killings had followed him to this place. I asked him where the problem lay and he said, *'Yeh to kudrati daraar hai, Hinduon aur Musalmanon ke beech mein'* (This is a natural division that exists between Hindus and Muslims).

The bus came to a stop in a small busy town called Vijaypur. Rows of buses were parked on the main road. Sweetmeats and fried snacks were stacked in jars on roadside stalls but the rising heat made everything unappetizing to me. A couple of shops had television sets in them and I noticed the previous night's cricket match was being rebroadcast. I stopped to watch Mohammed Kaif hit a boundary. Kaif was a Muslim. He was a hero in the whole of India that day. The man in the bus who had spoken against Muslims was all praise for Kaif, smiling and applauding the youth's courageous play on the cricket field. He saw no 'natural division' between himself and the Muslim cricketer.

The bus that I took was headed for a village called Dagh and it was very close to the DCB—the letters stood for the military term 'ditch-cum-bundh'—where the army had dug its trenches and artillery shelters. The border with Pakistan was only a hundred metres away from there.

The bus got crowded with all kinds of passengers, women in gaudy shalwar-kameezes holding the hands of their children and Sikh farmers carrying cans and tractor parts. We had not travelled even for a few minutes before the first checkpoint arrived and a soldier came inside to look under the seats and inside the petrol jerricans and the aluminium containers for milk. Every five minutes, there were further checks and questions. I was going to the border because I wanted to see evidence of the new mines that had been laid on both sides by the Indian and Pakistani armies. This was a new development. Earlier,

villagers with land next to the international border were
able to farm their land. But the mines had changed all
that. The Delhi papers had reported that the army had
been moving the villagers out of their homes. They were
no longer able to farm on their land. I was nervous,
however, about the soldiers who were asking questions
when the bus stopped at the checkpoint. All the passengers
seemed to be locals. I was the only outsider. Whenever a
soldier climbed into the bus, I removed my sunglasses so
that I would look more familiar. I had already put my
passport in my pocket so that it wouldn't be found in my
bag when searched. If the soldiers looked at my passport,
they would have found out that I had travelled to
Pakistan. The trip would suddenly become very
inconvenient. I had prepared my excuse if questioned. I
was going to the shrine of Baba Chamliyal at the border.
This shrine was maintained by the soldiers of the Border
Security Force, but people went there to ask favours of
the Baba who had been a Sufi saint. The Baba was said
to be especially effective if you had skin ailments. The
journalist in Jammu, who had told me about the shrine,
had blown smoke from his cigarette, and said, 'In India
and in Pakistan, you are allowed to do anything in the
name of religion. So, if you tell the soldiers that you are
going to the Baba's shrine to pay your respects, no one is
going to stop you.'

So that is what I did. Just a few days earlier, I had made
several phone calls to the press officer of the external
affairs ministry. The female bureaucrat had been dismissive
of my request for a pass to visit the border in Jammu and
Kashmir. But the journalist had been correct. In Dagh,
when I asked a soldier to point the way to the shrine, he

told me to walk west for a little less than two miles. Then, as an afterthought, the soldier asked me whether I had come from Jammu. I said in Hindi that I had come from a much farther place in search of the Baba's blessings. The soldier nodded and repeated that I should take the left fork and after a while I'd arrive at the army post where the shrine stood. There were fields on both sides of the village road and cattle were tied to small posts. Two boys joined me after I had been walking for ten minutes. One of them, shaven-headed and barefoot, asked me gently, 'Sir, what is your problem?' It took me a moment to understand his question. He was asking me to tell him about the skin ailment that I was suffering from. I replied that I had heard about Baba from my friends and had made up my mind to press my forehead on his shrine. The boy nodded and lifted his shirt to show me his afflicted skin. His stomach as well as his back was covered with sores that looked like the spots that the first drops of rain make in the sand.

The boy who had spoken to me was named Parveen. His companion, whose name was Ankush, must have been in his early teens. The soles of his feet were cracked and would not heal. The boys wanted me to know that the Baba's head was buried in India but the rest of his body was in Pakistan. He was worshipped on both sides, by both Hindus and Muslims. They also said that the water from the well at the shrine was called 'sherbet' and the clay in the fields around it was called 'shakkar' or sugar. Both the boys were going to stay at the shrine for twenty-one days; each day they would rub the clay on their body and then wash it with the water that had been drawn from the well.

I spent several hours at the shrine, but every now and then, I would glance at the guards facing away from us. They sat with guns and binoculars next to thin, horizontal openings in a mud wall about fifty metres away. A large sign painted in Hindi said 'Alert' although it could also have meant 'Danger'. There was a path that led to them. Beyond them lay Pakistan. The priest at the shrine was an old BSF soldier from a village near my own hometown. When he spoke to me he called me 'bachcha'. I asked him if I could go up to the guards and sneak a peek at Pakistan, and he said, 'You first pray at Baba's shrine, tell him what you want, and later, around sunset, I will take you to the guards.'

The old man suggested that I spend the night at the camp along with the others who were there because of their ailments. Then, he asked one of the men there to give me 'sherbet' to drink. The man unhesitatingly dropped a bucket in the water. His right ear seemed to have been eaten away by some disease and the skin on parts of his arm had faded into grey blotches. When the man pulled the pail up, he touched the surface of the water with the tips of his fingers and flicked the drops behind his head while murmuring a prayer. I took the glass of water and gulped it down nervously without tasting it.

The priest had a small bedroom with a ceiling fan in it. The room had a small attached kitchen where two women were cooking lunch for everyone at the shrine. There were about a dozen people there that day. Most of them were near the barbed wire on the far side of the shrine, brown male bodies covered in mud, resting under the trees or lying on the ground beside small pits. Only one man, who was very sick, stayed outside the priest's room. He was a

Sikh truck driver with only his eyes visible under a grey blanket. The sores on his body, he said, could not be exposed to the sun. While the man spoke to me, a radio played Hindi film songs. It was a Sunday and the show was a special one for soldiers. It used to be a favourite of mine during my youth. I began to sing aloud when I heard Mukesh singing, 'Phool tumhe bheja hai khat mein, phool nahin mera dil hai.' The man with the blanket was amused by my singing, and when he laughed and lowered his blanket, I saw the lesions on his body and decided that what I had just seen were signs of Kaposi's sarcoma. I asked him if he had seen a doctor. He had been to many doctors in the towns and cities, he said, and he had found no relief except there at the shrine.

The man with the blanket watched me as I ate while sitting on a sheet on the ground. The priest sat beside me and he ate too. We could hear the afternoon news being read on the television, and we learned that the death toll from the killings the previous night had now gone up to twenty-seven. After the simple, vegetarian meal, the priest stretched out under the fan. He pointed at the rolled-up mats in the corner and invited me to lie down wherever I wished. I wanted to return to my hotel in Jammu. But I also wanted to see the mines that the two armies had planted at the border. I told the old man, who had been very kind to me, that I would go and sit in the shrine. The tiles in the small courtyard were burning hot. But it was cooler inside the structure. Baba Chamliyal's grave was covered with a green cloth in the manner of Sufi saints but the decorative tiles all around showed Hindu gods and goddesses. I put some money under the green *chaadar*. And then, as if following the priest's instructions, I told Baba

Chamliyal that I wanted to go up to the guards and see where the mines had been laid.

Then, I touched the feet of the grave with both hands. I turned around and, barefoot and without my notebook, I started walking to the post at the border. A bird was calling in a tree nearby. I stepped over a low barbed wire fence and was surprised when, as I kept walking towards the post, no voice was suddenly raised to stop me.

*

A bullet-proof vest hung beside the soldier at the nearest post. Apparently, it was too hot to go for that kind of protection. The post itself was a thatched shelter with a cot for sitting under the hole in the mud wall. The soldier had two rifles next to him. I expressed some curiosity about his guns. Lance Naik Vineet Kumar pointed to one gun and said that it was a self-loading rifle. The other one, which had a belt of cartridges falling out of it, was a medium-machine gun. The militants, the Lance Naik said, used AK-47s. He spoke with a degree of longing about the AK-47. It was a smaller gun, and also much lighter. It was easy to hide and easy to use.

A phone rang. Vineet Kumar removed a piece of cloth covering what looked like two metal receivers, military green in colour, and said, 'Jaidev Chamliyal, sir.' I immediately thought that a superior had seen me and wanted me removed from there. But it was a routine call. When Lance Naik Kumar kept the phone down I asked him if I could look through his binoculars. At first, I could see nothing. Then, I saw the green and white Pakistani flag fluttering in the breeze. A structure like a tree-house was built beneath it, and Vineet Kumar said that there was an armed Pakistani soldier there. I began to search the ground between the two posts. Wheat was rotting in the fields. Those were the fields where the mines had been laid. There was nothing else to see.

Lance Naik Kumar was an amiable young man and he spoke freely about the hard work done by the army jawan, the stress during the patrols every day and night, and also the boredom. There was a logbook lying open next to him and I asked him if I could look at it. There was an entry for the previous day. The soldier on duty had fired forty-five rounds at 16:40 hours after noticing some movement on the other side. The enemy, he had written, fired sixty rounds in return. The soldier had also noted that all the men he had seen were wearing khaki. This meant that they were probably soldiers; the terrorists coming from the other side rarely wore uniforms. Although mostly Hindi words had been used in the entry, they had been transcribed into English. 'Humne harkat dekhi.' Kumar said, 'Army mein angrezi bahut use hoti hai, sir. Sub kuch Roman mein hai' (English gets used a lot in the army, sir. Everything is put in Roman).

I sat there a little longer, talking about war and Hindi films, but our conversation was interrupted. A man in a loose white shirt and khaki trousers appeared from the direction of the camp, and Vineet Kumar snapped to attention. I stood up. The man looked as if he had just been woken up. He was authoritative and brusque. If there was firing from the other side, he said to the Lance Naik, and they were left with a dead body, a government inquiry would be instituted. Then, he turned to me. As the BSF commander of the post, he said, he had enough worries.

He wanted me to leave immediately. I wasn't going to get away without an interrogation, however. The commander would ask a question and then, two or three questions later, attempt to trip me by repeating an earlier query. I began to notice other details about him. He was a fairly thin man in his fifties, and his hair and moustache had been dyed an inky black. The dye had made small maps near his temple. He looked a bit like the men at the shrine seeking cures for their skin ailments.

My wallet was in my pocket. I gave the man my business card. That seemed to put us on a professional footing. He saw that I taught at an American university. One of the questions he asked me was whether rice was expensive in the US. Then, he began to probe my interest in Baba Chamliyal. I remembered the journalist in Jammu. I said that I had come to Baba with a wish. The commander waited for me to tell him more. I offered the piece of information that my wife had told me that I should pay my respects to Baba. This led to the question about my wife's place of birth. I lied again and said that she was from Delhi. He asked me if we had children. I looked down and said that we hadn't been lucky. The commander asked me how long we had been married. I doubled the number of years of our marriage and said five. That also explained, I added, why I was there that day. The commander nodded, satisfied, and then returned my business card to me as if it were my identity papers.

We walked back to the gate of the camp. The officer watched me as I piously struck the bell at the temple gate, and then, he gave me a thin sheet of paper that he wanted me to keep. The sheet was titled 'Brief History of Religious

Place Chamliyal'. It offered sketchy details of the Baba's life and ended with the following words:

People from all over country (mostly) those who suffer from skin disease visit this place. Those suffering from skin disease stay hear for 21 day's and most of go back absolucely cured. The devotees staying hear are provided all facilities like boarding and lodging free of cost by the BSF. The mela is celebrated by Indians and Pakistanies but because of securty reasons Pakistanies are not permitted to cross the international border. How ever Sarbat & Sakker are placed at border & same is distributed to Pakistanies devotees 'after the pooja ceremony' the mela is attended by about 8 to 10 thousand people from India.

The walk back to Dagh was difficult in the searing heat. I wet my handkerchief in the water gushing out of a tubewell and spread the cloth over the half of my face that faced the sun. The hand that held the cloth to my head was began to feel as if it were on fire. There was no other sign of life anywhere around, except for a small bird, which sat on a telephone wire, its beaks parted.

In Dagh, there were two soldiers getting a haircut. In a small store next to the barber's shop, I bought a soft drink. Quickly, I gulped down three bottles and immediately felt sick. I no longer felt that someone was about to snatch off my scalp but now I had a painful headache and my cheeks twitched when sweat rolled down my face.

The bus came and this time it was less crowded. Once again, there were farmers with small tools and one or two lower-middle-class families from the nearby towns, in their

Sunday best, returning after paying a visit to a relative in the village. A man sitting next to me began to extol the Baba's power. I could not participate in the conversation. It seemed to me very much like a part of a peasant belief in holy miracles. The men I had seen in the camp had encouraged each other by saying that there had been an improvement in their condition. To me, they had all appeared sick and in need of serious attention. I could allow that the clay in the camp had medicinal properties; the baths and the simple diet must also have been beneficial. But the rest was bogus, and I was irritated by the piety. While sitting in the priest's room in Chamliyal earlier, I had kept thinking that the poor had been left with very little beside their faith.

There was another reason for my impatience. The newly laid mines made a mockery of the platitudes about the shared shrines at the border. The effect of the new mines was evident in a small town called Samba which was about a thirty-minute bus-ride away from Jammu. The region's newest migrants were there for all to see, housed in a building on temporary loan from a corporate body and also in rows of canvas tents pitched on open land. They were the displaced people from the border. They were all farmers, and now they were unemployed. Their fields had been laid with mines. Half of their homes, built over a lifetime or more in their villages, had been destroyed by shelling, and were now abandoned along with the rest of the houses that still stood unharmed. Over 120,000 villagers have been displaced since 2001 in India alone; according to Indian official figures Pakistani shelling has killed seventy-two persons and injured over 200. Nearly fifty schools have been shut down and thirty-seven health centres closed. The story is likely to be similar on the other side of the border.

Near Chamliyal, I had seen fields where the wheat that had been planted in the last season had not been harvested. The yellow of the wheat was slowly turning grey. Weeds had come up in places. Bright red pennants, so much like the flags atop temples, signalled the freshly planted mines. Two lines of barbed wire were drawn on the sides of the fields that had mines, but there was space between the wires, enough for a dog or a calf to step through. A fortnight before my visit, a boy had gone to pick up a mango that had fallen from its tree, and lost a leg. There were several such stories to be heard from the villagers who had now come to Samba. Eight to nine hundred families had been uprooted as a result of the mining; the people from five villages numbered around 5000. There had been no money given for the cattle killed. Although promises had been made for providing compensation for the crops left to die in the fields, no actual payment had been made to any of the villagers. The men and women in the SIDCO complex in Samba, sitting in the open field as a storm threatened to break over us, said that the government provided them eleven kilos of grain and two hundred rupees in cash every month. There was nothing else to do but pass each day with the little that had been given to them.

It began to rain as I walked from one tent to another, talking to the inhabitants there who were pulling inside their tents, the cots, the clothes set out to dry, a bicycle, and even a goat. One man, Joginder Pal, tall and heavy-set with a glass right eye, asked me to take shelter in his tent. He began to tell me that even the children in his village understood what it meant to live on the border in the state of Jammu and Kashmir. He pointed to his five-year-old son, Surinder, and said, 'He would be able to go to school only two or three times a week. On the way to school, he would often hear the firing overhead.' Joginder Pal smiled and asked his son to show me what they had been taught to do at school when there was shelling. In the cramped tent, the boy quickly threw himself flat on the ground and waited for his father to tell him to get up.

*

It was several weeks later that I returned to Jammu and caught a plane going north to the Kashmir Valley. In Srinagar the border was never far away. You saw it in the tense faces of the Indian Army soldiers, with their bullet-proof vests and light-machine guns, as they stood at regular intervals by the roadside. Whenever there was a shooting or a bomb blast, the Kashmiris that I was with appeared calmer than me, and they would show great care in protecting me from my own sense of curiosity. But even the calmness of my friends and their leaning towards extreme caution only exposed the violence. To a visitor's eyes, the signs of fear seemed as pervasive as the dust choking the busy streets or clinging to the dark wooden houses covered with corrugated iron. The imagination of the outsider is prone to exaggeration, but not much remains to be imagined when you see police posts on the highways equipped with steel planks that have eight-inch spikes protruding from them.

For the Kashmiris, the soldiers are seen as a part of an occupying army. Abdul Ghani Bhat, one of the leaders of the Kashmiri resistance, told me that the presence of the army means that the disputed border between India and Pakistan exists as a dividing line in Kashmir 'in every room, in every office, in every street, at all levels'. The actual international border, over six hundred miles long, is only a little distance away from Srinagar. It is crossed only by militants who come with arms from Pakistan. The ordinary Kashmiri, often with family on the other side, has to take a long trip to the plains in the south and, with the right papers, cross the border at Wagah. In places like Uri, in the north of Kashmir, people stand on a rooftop so that they can watch while across the border another part of the family participates in a wedding. There is little to do from a rooftop but stand and wave while the wedding procession passes in front of you. The megaphones on the mosques are used to tell people on the other side the names of those getting married or, for that matter, the identity of the one who has just died.

I heard the story of the families at the border one night from a clerk sitting in a dark government building. The man had a story of his own. His uncle had migrated to Rawalpindi in Pakistan during the Partition and had not been permitted to come back for his sister's funeral. The clerk was the woman's son, and his voice began to quaver as he told me of his uncle's recent trip, when he finally visited his sister's grave, the sister who, after their mother's death, had provided him food and milk. The man who was talking to me in the office had been born exactly fifty years ago and he had seen his uncle for the first time only a year earlier. Now, a nephew was going to get married in Srinagar in another ten days. The clerk wanted his uncle to visit from Pakistan but knew that this would be impossible because the two neighbouring countries had cancelled diplomatic relations. 'We are suffering,' he said, 'May Allah bring the two countries together.'

When I repeated this story to Rasheed, a Kashmiri journalist, he nodded his head and then looked away. Then, he began to talk. He wanted me to understand that the violence in Kashmir was bad not only for the people who had been born there. It was devastating even for outsiders. The next morning, as if to prove his point, he took me to the Government Hospital for Psychiatric Diseases. The partially burnt-down structure of the hospital is set away from the street in Srinagar. The fort that the Mughal emperor Akbar built in the sixteenth century can be seen atop the hill nearby, the military bunker there sharply outlined against the blue. I asked Rasheed about a possible visit to the fort and he said that he had gone there a few years ago and come back convinced that it was being used by the army for torture.

In the male psychiatry wards of the hospital, Dr Sadaqat Rahman, who said that she was the only clinical psychologist in Srinagar, was making her rounds. The doctor wore a long gown and her head was covered with a scarf. We stood talking for a few minutes in the corridor. In front of us, there was a garden with small trees and varieties of flowers in bloom. The garden's fence was made up of the hospital's discarded metal cots set on their side. Then, the doctor walked into a section of the ward marked 'Hamam' or Bath. There were three small cells in that section with gates that were made of metal bars. Large stone slabs had been laid on the floor but they were broken near the mouth of the cells. A man was squatting at the gate of the first cell and he quietly asked for a cigarette. The second cell was empty. In the third cell a man hung upside down, like a parrot in its cage, his hands gripping the metal bar in the window. A red towel was knotted to the metal gate. Dr Rahman said softly, 'Mushtaq, Mushtaq.' The figure unfurled itself with great agility and stood at attention. He demanded water in a hoarse voice and then saluted. Mushtaq was short and well-built. Dr Rahman called out to a guard for water and said that her patient suffered from bipolar mood disorder.

I began to ask the doctor if the violence in the Valley had changed the number of patients that she treated. She said that separatist militancy in Kashmir had begun in the late 1980s. Till only a few years ago, there were about eight to ten patients visiting the hospital each day. Now the number had grown. These days the hospital treated anywhere from 100 to 150 patients daily. Yet, Dr Rahman was reluctant to relate the increased problems simply to the violence in Kashmir. According to her, the malady was worldwide. She said that by the year 2008 there would only be psychiatry, no medicine. She smiled slightly, as if she were providing me gentle assurance, as I contemplated the fact that in a few years the whole world would go mad.

In the corridor, men in grimy white uniforms striped with blue sat on the floor, rocking their bodies against the wall. Dr Rahman had an easy, affectionate manner towards her patients, many of whom had gathered at the windows of the wards in which they were locked. They shouted out appeals to the doctor in Kashmiri. They all wanted to go back home. A little distance away was the women's ward but Rasheed and I were not permitted to go there. But we could see the women in the one-storey building. They sat in groups in what was a large hall with a corrugated tin roof, listening to the Kashmiri folk music that tumbled out of the windows.

We left the doctor and came to the section where the daily patients were standing in long lines. An ambulance of the armed forces was parked there. This is what Rasheed had wanted to show to me. Sitting inside the vehicle were soldiers from the BSF. I decided to speak to the soldiers but Rasheed wandered away by himself. There were four soldiers in the truck. The other patients, Kashmiri men and women, moved around them in the hospital yard, but the soldiers sat by themselves in the ambulance. They had come to the hospital because they were suffering from the effects of trauma. Many Kashmiris had complained of the aggression of the armed forces; in the hospital, it was clear that violence does not spare the perpetrator either.

Dr Rahman told me later that when the soldiers went in to see her, these patients, who were in uniform, carried their rifles with them. She explained that the soldiers do not trust even the doctors. After our meeting, the doctor was going to attend a board meeting to deal with the cases of the soldiers, taking decisions on advising the military superiors that the soldiers not be given access to arms and ammunition. In the BSF truck, I had met a soldier who was from a village in the plains near Allahabad. One of the first things that he told me was that he was a Brahmin, and his name was Pandey. He asked me if I had seen the graffiti on a wall outside saying 'Indian Forces Go Back'. It is only when I said yes that he began to talk about the deep-seated suspicion experienced both by the Kashmiris and by the Indian soldiers. He said he suffered from stress and depression. He felt okay, the man said, when he was back in his village but he felt disoriented outside.

The local papers that day had carried reports of a BSF commander having been shot dead by an army soldier in Kupwara to the north. The men in the ambulance knew about that piece of news, but none of them wanted to comment on it. Pandey, the soldier from Allahabad, told me that it was his first visit to the hospital—but it was also true, he said, that soldiers are brought here every day. It struck me that for people like Pandey the move from the village to the places outside was also an entry into the ideology of nationalism. The army which sent him to a distant place—on which he could still lay claim—was an institution of the nation-state. Without the idea of the nation, a person like Pandey was lost. The militant from across the border, who carried the idea of the Islamic nation like a gun, was a figure that the soldier recognized. Oddly enough, it was the armed militant who confirmed for the soldier everything he believed in. But what the soldier found more disturbing, and even incomprehensible, was the ordinary Kashmiri who, unarmed, vulnerable, and in no way committed to Pakistan, would still not grant him the gift of inviolable nationhood. The anonymous, painted sign on the road, asking the forces to go back, signified for the soldier a loss of the self. In the resulting incomprehension, nationalism survived only as a neurosis. The only way out of this neurosis was for the soldier to identify each Kashmiri as a potential Pakistani. This act, full of the violence of negation, filled him with despair.

The greater despair is of a Kashmiri woman like Parveena Ahangar whose son Javed has been missing since 1990 when the soldiers had picked him up. Parveena is in her forties and the mother of five children. I had read that although she had had very little education, she had founded the Association of Parents of Disappeared Persons in 1996. I went to meet her one afternoon in Srinagar. But Parveena had gone out to a wedding celebration. I returned the next morning and found her in her front yard. She was hanging clothes on a line that stretched beside a pomegranate tree. Small, purple eggplants, sliced in four parts, had also been stuck into the clothesline to dry in the sun. When we were inside, Parveena said, 'I was told last night that you had come. Today I saw a dream. I saw a man. I told him the story of my son. This is the truth. In my dream, the place where I was sitting had the same green walls.'

Parveena took a photograph down from her wall and placed it on the carpet in front of me. It showed a youth with large eyes and the fresh unshaven moustache of an adolescent. A small label beneath the photograph said 'Javed Ahmad Ahangar Missing 18 August 1990.' Even before Javed disappeared, Parveena's fourteen-year-old son, Mohammed, had been taken away by the security forces in June 1990. (He was released a year later.) A few months after Mohammed's arrest, it was the sixteen-year-old Javed who was picked up during a raid. He was never seen again. Parveen believes that the army was looking for her neighbour's son, who is also called Javed, and who was a militant. Instead, they arrested her boy.

Parveena said that Javed had a bad stammer and when he was disturbed and could not speak he would strike his foot against the ground. She was afraid to think about how her son would have fared during interrogation. That is her nightmare. Her son is being tortured but finds himself—out of fear or anger—unable to do anything other than hitting the floor of the cell with his foot. In that terrible silence, Javed disappears into darkness.

For years, Parveena waited outside jails and interrogation centres. She also filed petitions in the courts. But nothing came of her efforts. She was asked to approach the district administration and claim compensation. Parveena said to me, 'I do not want money. I want my son.' Today there are more than 3000 young men who are believed to have disappeared in Kashmir after the armed forces took them away. Their families have been consigned to the hell of waiting. Parveena's group has 300 members and they meet at each other's houses to give much-needed physical and emotional support. In July 2001, the group got together to build a memorial to the men who did not return after the army took them away. The foundation stone was set in place by three children whose fathers had been taken away before their birth. The establishment of the monument was disrupted by the police, however, and all those who had gathered there were forced to disperse.

While Parveena had been talking to me, a young woman with light skin and thin, beautiful features, arrived at the door. Parveena greeted her and told me that the visitor was the wife of a youth who had disappeared. The woman was barely out of her teens. Her name was Shafiqa and her husband, Abdul Hamid Badyari, had disappeared after being arrested in January 2000. Shafiqa was holding a jute bag with the words 'Say No to Plastic' in English printed on it. From the bag, she took out photographs of her husband, a young man with curly hair, wearing a colourful parka. Badyari was the driver of a three-wheeler. He had been arrested by special operations forces from his rented home. After waiting a few months, Shafiqa had begun working because she had to take care of three small children, aged three to eight. She washed dishes in a few homes and earned Rs 150 each month (a little more than three dollars). Most of her time was given to wrapping ten kilograms of small sugar candy in plastic wrappers. This job, which took eight to ten hours each day, got Shafiqa a monthly income of Rs 300.

In the new language that violence always gives rise to, Shafiqa was now what was called in Kashmir a 'half-widow', the wife of someone who had disappeared. As the disappeared persons are Muslims, they are governed by the Indian Muslim Personal Law; this law does not allow the wife of a disappeared person to remarry for seven years. In fact, after seven years, she has to move court to get her disappeared husband declared dead. All of that was far from Shafiqa's calculations. She was hoping her husband would return. Her father-in-law had filed a case, however, requesting that he be given any compensation that the government would provide for wrongful death or disappearance of his son. Shafiqa was living alone with her children in a shack she had rented in a slum. I couldn't even look at Shafiqa for long without feeling a pain in my chest; she was half my age and was bringing up her kids by herself. The money that she earned through so much labour each month was less than one fourth of what I was paying for my hotel room in Srinagar that night. That her husband had disappeared after being taken into custody was a brutal crime committed in the name of the nation but, all the while I was with Shafiqa, I felt that what exposed even more starkly the myth of democracy was this young woman's forlorn poverty and the fate of her children. Her only help was the unlettered but brave and compassionate Parveena Ahangar, the chairperson of the Association of the Parents of Disappeared Persons, who can be reached at Dhobi Mohalla, Batmaloo, Srinagar, 190 009, India.

*

It was my last morning in Srinagar. I was looking for Hotel Leeward on the Dal Lake where V.S. Naipaul had stayed for four months when he had first come to India in 1962. Writing three decades later about Kashmir and the hotel, Naipaul had noted that the time and the place 'remained a glow, a memory of a season when everything had gone well'. The hotel had made its first appearance in Naipaul's *An Area of Darkness*.

All around me were the empty houseboats on the lake, waiting for tourists who now came in smaller and smaller numbers. One houseboat was called 'Freedom' and it had a 'To Let' sign hanging beneath its name. There were others with names striving for beauty or grandeur, names like 'Gulfaam', 'Meena Palace', 'Floating Castle' and 'Highland Queen'. When I suddenly caught sight of Hotel Leeward, I experienced it as a discovery: the white building with blue trimmings on the edge of the water. The *shikara* I was sitting in passed a few shops and a public-call booth on the lake, and then, gliding along a waterway, drew close to the hotel's concrete steps. A dragonfly whirred above the lowest step, the morning sun lighting its wings. But, I was not allowed to step off the boat. A soldier with a Sten gun waved me away. He told me that the hotel was not open to outsiders. The Border Security Force used it as a bunker now.

My trip to Srinagar ended with what it had started: the sight of soldiers in bunkers and on the streets. What stayed in my memory was the image of the painted sign outside a police station: 'Please Prove Your Identity'. This was the demand, or threat, under which Kashmiris lived. The people I had met there had spoken so desperately of their need for peace. When they called for peace they often had in mind a Kashmir independent of the two countries that have turned it into a battlefield. Sitting in sight of his lovely pomegranate orchard, a well-known writer named Rahman Rahi said to me, 'We are not happy with India. We are not even concerned with Pakistan. Autonomy is *our* issue. India and Pakistan treat it as their issue.' In other parts of India, such talk is met with rage. As Indians we repeat what we have learnt in school: Kashmir is a part of our identity as a nation. The Pakistanis, it is obvious, have the same belief. They think that the land under Indian occupation has to be freed from the oppression of the kafirs, the unbelievers. President Musharraf, in Islamabad, had been the architect of the Kargil war and he continues to send armed infiltrators into India across the border. Indeed, most of the foreign militants present in the Valley are Pakistanis, the majority of them from western Punjab. But the land that they want to liberate is for the Pakistanis a cipher, forcibly evacuated of its real inhabitants and their distinctive culture, and populated instead by figures of their fantasy. For the militants of the Pakistan-supported jihadi units like the Hizb-ul-Mujahideen, Kashmir is nothing more than a piece of political real estate that has to be painted green in the established colour of Islamic fundamentalism.

The reality of Kashmir's past, which the foreign militants ignore, is that both Hindu and Islamic influences have shaped its culture and beliefs. This lesson was brought to me when I sat with the poet Farooq Nazki in his garden in a part of Srinagar called Sheopura. Nazki looks a bit like a Kashmiri Pablo Neruda: in his eyes there was a look that could be described as a mix of dolorousness and sensuality. That afternoon, Nazki recited to me a poem he had written when the troubles started. It was a short poem, addressed to a dead Hindu comrade, and it mourned the mass migration of the Hindus from the Valley. It told the dead man that his mother, Kamli, has left Kashmir. She has taken with her the plate in which she used to serve food to the two friends. The short poem ended with these words about the mother: '*Aiy, tu jaanta hai,* / *Woh mere dar se Kashmir se bhaag gayi hai*' (Hey, do you know? / It is because she is afraid of me that she has fled Kashmir).

Nazki pointed to the homes beyond his walls that belonged to Kashmiri Pandits—one, two, three, he counted till six—and I realized that the Hizb militant from the other side of the border had no such memories of a shared life. He has known only sameness. He has not experienced the force, or the grace, of religious difference as a vital part of his society. What the Kashmiri poet was lamenting that day was the killing of a syncretic culture that is the larger story of that land.

Naipaul, travelling in Srinagar in the 1960s, had felt that he was in a medieval city, a world that 'had not developed a sense of history, which is a sense of loss'. But each Kashmiri is a keeper of another kind of history, one not of loss but of a distinctive achievement. Under the fourteenth century mystic poet Lal Ded, who was born in a Brahmin family but was very much influenced by Islam, and also under saints like Hazrat Sheikh Nuruddin who followed Lal Ded and was revered as Nund Rishi, there had flourished in the Valley a religious movement that had brought Hindus and Muslims together in a unique way. The sense of loss that Naipaul had found missing in the 1960s, and which now pervades every street and every home in Srinagar, is also in part about what a recent documentary film about the horrors in Kashmir calls 'the memories of days when we were so proudly human'.

The documentary I have just quoted from is Ajay Raina's *Tell Them the Tree They Had Planted Has Now Grown*. The film's title comes from a statement that the wife of an old family servant makes when the film-maker returns to the home in which he had lived with his parents, the home where they had planted pine trees and from where they had fled after the violence began. Raina is a Hindu and in the film he returns to Kashmir after more than a decade and talks to people about the region's recent past. The film is beautifully made, its poetic texture mirroring, in many ways, the film-maker's sensitivity and anguish. There are moments, however, when Raina cannot escape the prison of his own subjectivity. He sees the struggle in Kashmir, like many other displaced Kashmiri Pandits, as a fight between democracy and fundamentalism. At one point in the film Raina makes the simple minded and inaccurate claim that 'the soldier representing secular India is locked in a mortal combat with the jihadi from across the border'. But other voices in the film nudge into view alternative claims and understanding of the situation in Kashmir. In fact, rather early in the film, the Kashmiri writer Akhtar Mohiuddin tells Raina about the way in which the dominant Pandit minority was seen as oppressive and in complicity with the distant rulers of the Indian

nation-state. Mohiuddin, who had returned the Padma
Shri awarded to him by the Indian government to protest
its actions in Kashmir, tells Raina on camera, 'India betrayed
us and the Pandits supported them during every betrayal.'
The Kashmiri Muslims, 96 per cent of the population in
the Valley, had a literacy rate of only 0.8 per cent. Hindus
formed about 4 per cent of the entire population of the
Valley but it was they who occupied many of the
administrative and political positions of power. If 63.4 per
cent of the population in the Valley is today unemployed,
then these new resentments feed into and distort a very
old rage.

Raina's film is more successful in showing in a series of
images from Charar-e-Sharif shrine, the agony and the
faith of the Kashmiri people. The Charar is the shrine of
Sheikh Nuruddin and was gutted in 1995; the security
forces as well as the separatist guerrillas blamed each other
for the fire. In Raina's film, we see ordinary men and
women weeping at the shrine, their hands held open in
ardent prayer, tears flowing down their faces. *I'll give you
my life, dear beloved, of all universe.* In this gesture of
prayer, at a shrine which had traditionally been shared by
both faiths, what is expressed in the chant is contrition
and love. It is easy and tempting to find only innocence
there.

There *is* innocence, but it takes a more surprising form.
In the film, we watch as Akhtar Mohiuddin tells Raina of
a 'mini short-story' he has written. This is a story that I
heard repeated many times when I was in Kashmir. Its
popularity might be explained by the fact that it outlines
a situation where the loss of innocence is represented not
through assault but by the seduction of violence. The story

is titled 'Terrorist'. A woman named Farz Ded is walking down a narrow street. From the opposite end of the street, a police patrol approaches her. Farz Ded's young son starts crying. The commander thinks that the kid is scared and he reassures him. Farz Ded says to the man, 'This rogue is not afraid of you. He sees the soldiers and cries, "I want a gun ... I want a gun."'

5

The Long-Distance Nationalists

Professor Dalmiya had sent a message asking me to wait for him in an Indian restaurant which was close to the university in New Jersey where he teaches engineering. Till recently, he was the head of the group that calls itself 'Overseas Friends of the BJP'. The professor came in from the rain, shaking the drops of water from his umbrella. He was a short, trim man with square, gold-rimmed spectacles. His manner was friendly, and once we were seated, he began to answer my questions directly, even if a little too loudly. 'Give me the name of one Hindu text in which it is written that we should kill the unbeliever,' he would say, and add, 'We don't have any, while Islam has many ... .'

Dalmiya made statements like this and did not seem to care that other customers in the restaurant, mostly students and professors from the university, were probably able to hear every word he was saying. There was no pretence of modesty in Professor Dalmiya's speech, nor did he seem to find any use for polite, academic forms of doubt.

We began to talk about our childhood in India. Dalmiya was born in a small town called Sambhal in Uttar Pradesh. His brother was a leader of the Hindu Mahasabha and all the boys in the family attended the *shakha*, or the branch, of the RSS. Each evening, he would go to the shakha grounds and play games that built his 'physical and mental character'. His family runs a business selling peppermint oil. He said that Sambhal is today the biggest producer of menthol oil in India. It was his elder bother, Dalmiya said, who had introduced menthol oil to Sambhal in 1985. Many people in his town who own land have switched from rice, wheat and sugarcane to the cultivation of the menthol plant. The Muslims of Sambhal have also joined the same business, even though, Dalmiya pointed out, they have only introduced corrupt means into the profession. He said, 'Do *number ka dhandha karte hain.*'

Sambhal was a 'one hundred per cent' Hindu town till Babur, the sixteenth century Mughal emperor, came and converted a large part of the population. Now nearly 90 per cent of the town's population was Muslim. Sambhal had been famous for a Shiva temple. According to Dalmiya, there were three Hindu temples that Babur had turned into mosques. The first was in Ayodhya, the second in Panipat, and the third in his hometown, Sambhal. The temple in Sambhal was on a hillock and it was called Harihar Mandir. Although the Muslims know it as Jama Masjid, he said, the Hindus still call it by the earlier name.

How did he know that the mosque had indeed been a temple?

'In my town, every child knows this,' Dalmiya said. 'Each child is taught this from his childhood.'

On the night of Shivratri, that is, on the night of Lord Shiva's birthday, one should pour milk or, alternatively, water taken from the Ganges, on the linga inside one of the locked rooms in the temple. If this was done, Dalmiya said, an avatar of God Kalki will be born who will slay all those who defy religion. The only reason no one has attempted this is because on that night a thousand police constables guard the structure. Professor Dalmiya also wanted me to know that most of the people in Sambhal who were converted by Babur were Brahmins. They were deliberately given the job of butchers by the Muslim ruler. And yet, those Brahmins even today continued to hold on to traditions that had been a part of their lives when they had not departed from the fold. There were some books, Dalmiya suggested, which showed that these assertions were based on real evidence.

In Sambhal, the Muslims were so numerous because each couple often had ten offspring. The Muslims, he said, were 'illiterate, uneducated and with a ghetto mentality'. The prejudice that the professor was repeating could be heard anywhere in India. It was just that his words carried an American inflection. He continued, 'They are sleeping like dogs and cats in a room, one in a corner, another under a cot. Like dogs and cats, literally, I am telling you, this is how they live. After the Partition, only 40 per cent of the population was Muslim. Now, in Sambhal, they are 83 per cent of the total population. Everything will be destroyed. Wherever there is such a high population of Muslims, there is a decrease in employment opportunities, an increase in crime, you have to accept that. Where are you going to send your kids to study?'

I paused in my eating and said to Professor Dalmiya that I was married to a Muslim. He stopped for a moment, and then, began to smile. He asked, 'How did you get trapped into doing this?' I smiled too but said nothing. Dalmiya said, 'Usually it is the other way around. They take our girls. Muslim men marry Hindu women. Hindu women convert. You know the actress Sharmila Tagore.

She is now Ayesha Begum ... . You need to be congratulated.'

Dalmiya had studied at Hind Intermediate College in Sambhal, and then gone on to graduate in physics from the Benares Hindu University. After he had finished at the top of his class there, he had then been admitted to the Indian Institute of Technology in Kanpur. His doctoral work had been done in America, under another Indian professor, in the field of materials science engineering. Dalmiya's current expertise was in microwave processing of materials. When I asked him what that term meant, he put a finger on a ring he was wearing. He said, 'This ruby crystal was made in nature by a process that took ten million years. I can make it through microwave processing in ten minutes. And it will look better.' The next day he was leaving for Japan to give a talk at a conference near Osaka on this subject.

Later, I asked the professor if his scientific work and his religious activism were at odds. 'I don't see any contradiction,' he said, and began to talk about Einstein. Would Einstein find virtues in cow urine the way the RSS seems to do? Dalmiya saw this as a serious question and said, 'Even scientists from the United States are today finding out so many qualities in cow urine. We have known this for millions of years.' In March 2002, a government body in Dalmiya's home state ordered the purchase of cow urine at the price of Rs 5 per litre for use in the manufacture of medicines which would then be sold through government-owned outlets throughout the country.

Professor Dalmiya's words reminded me powerfully of another aspect of Hindu fundamentalism in India. The mobilization of support for Hindutva had relied, on the one hand, on religious icons, most prominently the image of Lord Ram and his rath, but the VHP had also employed technology, as in the use of the adorned DCM Toyota van as the chariot which was also equipped with audiovisual equipment for addressing rallies. When I asked Dalmiya about it, he said, 'This is a very important question. We are now dealing with new challenges. The biggest publicity for the Hindutva movement was achieved through the Internet. My organization was the first to convince the BJP of the need to use cyber technology. I was personally responsible for launching the web page for the BJP.'

The professor began to speak of the struggles in Internet activism. A group of Hindutva cadre settled in the US had got together and begun to put out their views on the Web. It was a difficult process because he and his friends were not skilled in the use of English. In contrast, he said, the Indian leftists were very much at home in English and this made it terribly hard to engage in debate. But, eventually, the Overseas Friends of the BJP had begun to win the hearts and minds of the people. During the height of the movement to build a temple in Ayodhya, he claimed, more than 80 per cent of Indian Americans could be counted as their supporters.

Dalmiya said that the intellectual arrogance of the leftists, particularly their belief that they were always correct and the others always wrong, are essentially characteristics of a fascist group. His work on the Internet had successfully exposed the weaknesses of his opponents. I asked him if his description of the left applied to the people in India, or whether he meant to criticize the global left as such. He laughed at the question. He said, 'Where else do you find

communists? Only in India! I was in China recently. I did
not find any communists there.' Despite the rant, I had
become interested in what Dalmiya had been saying earlier
about feeling that he did not have enough English. It led
me to think that perhaps where the Indian brand of
secularism had failed was that it was essentially a provision
of the state, and spoke the language of the law. It did not,
in other words, speak in the language of the people and,
as a result, remained elitist and therefore profoundly
undemocratic. Instead of an engagement with this question,
all that Professor Dalmiya was willing to do was hold up
another enemy for attack. Speaking of Nehru, he said, 'It
started with him. He was an atheist. His education
minister ... what was his name? Something Haq? In any
case, his education minister was a Muslim and a
communist. Half of Nehru's cabinet was made up of
communists.' No doubt, the man that Professor Dalmiya
had in mind was Maulana Abul Kalam Azad, a
sophisticated scholar and poet, a man who was at once a
widely respected Muslim theologian and a committed
secular nationalist, a leader who had presided over the
Congress prior to Independence and was, along with Nehru
and Patel, one of the main lieutenants of Mahatma Gandhi.
Azad was free India's first education minister. One cannot,
despite his many other achievements, call Azad a
communist. It is possible, of course, that Professor Dalmiya
was using the term loosely, a bit like, say, a bigot in the
American south calling Reverend Martin Luther King Jr. a
communist because King was black and demanded equal
rights.

Professor Dalmiya and I were at the end of our meal.
I asked him, rather lamely, whether he had any Muslim

friends. 'Yes, yes,' Dalmiya said hotly, adding that his room-mate in college was a Muslim. He said that there was no question of there being a personal animosity with any Muslim. Then, he added, 'You see, it is a question of our survival. Hindus are fighting for survival; their culture, their life, their civilization is threatened. Otherwise, Hindus are not violent at all.' Dalmiya did not lower his voice as we crossed the length of the restaurant on our way out. As we stepped out of the restaurant into the drizzle, Dalmiya stood under his umbrella and delivered his final words. What he was saying could have been said by any Hindutva-sympathizer in India, but there was once again the American angle in his words. He said, 'Islam has been threatening us for the past 1500 years. Since then, the Muslims have been trying to convert India into *darul Islam*. India was the only country they were not able to convert. In the last few years, ever since the Iranian revolution, this jihadi movement has come up. It has caused serious concern. After the events of September 11, you must understand that anything can happen anywhere. What people like you need to grasp is the scientific equation. Communism plus Allah equals Islam.'

*

But, Professor Dalmiya is not the first person who comes to mind when I think of the long-distance nationalist.

Let us consider the Indian past.

It is the end of May 1893. A young Indian barrister-at-law lands in Port Durban, South Africa, to help with an important lawsuit that is pending in the courts there. One of the parties involved is a trading firm whose owner is a

Muslim man from the lawyer's hometown in Gujarat. At the Maritzburg station, on his way to Pretoria, the young and well-dressed lawyer is pushed out of the train by a police constable and left shivering in the cold. The night passes in the waiting room which does not have a light. There is an overcoat in his luggage thrown out of the train but he dare not ask for it out of fear that he will be insulted again. The next morning he sends a cable to his employers as well as the general manager of the Railways. The Indian traders of Maritzburg come to see him at the station and tell him that Indians travelling by first or second class were routinely harassed by railway staff and the white passengers. That same night, our lawyer resumes his journey by train to Pretoria and receives further insults and beatings on the way. The events of this journey set into motion a process of political discovery that will allow the young Indian to develop the doctrine of *satyagraha* or non-violent resistance which he will use successfully in South Africa and then, upon his return after two decades, in British-ruled India.

Our traveller, of course, is Mohandas Karamchand Gandhi.

A thumbnail sketch of his life as an Indian nationalist abroad would provide the following outline. Gandhi had been hired by the Gujarati Muslim businessman in Pretoria for a fixed period of one year. In his book, *Satyagraha in South Africa*, much of which he wrote while in Yeravda Jail in India several years later, Gandhi describes how he came to learn—over the course of the year he spent in South Africa—about the conditions under which Indians lived in that country. The ruling white minority was in need of Indian labour but it was also anxious about their growing number—in Natal province alone, there were 60,000 indentured labourers, 10,000 ex-indentured and 10,000 free Indians. In 1894, just as Gandhi was about to leave for India, he learnt that the Natal government was about to introduce legislation that would disenfranchise Indians and rob them 'of what little rights they were then enjoying'. Gandhi proposed that the Indians resist this legislation and, on the insistence of the local Indians, he prolonged his stay by another month. Meetings were organized and a petition with 10,000 signatures was sent to the Colonial Secretary. These efforts were not successful but, as Gandhi himself writes, this was the South African Indians' first experience of political agitation and 'a new thrill of enthusiasm passed through the community'. Gandhi did not return to India and, despite opposition from some racist whites, he took up the job of a barrister at the Natal Supreme Court. By May 1894, he had helped found the Natal Indian Congress, whose members 'included Hindus, Musalmans, Parsis and Christians, and came from all Indian States that were represented in Natal'.

After two and half years in Natal, Gandhi returned to India to fetch his wife and two children. It was during this trip to India that he met the Indian Congress leaders—Sir Pherozeshah Mehta, Justice Badruddin Tyebji, Mahadev Govind Ranade, Lokamanya Tilak, Gopal Krishna Gokhale—and spoke to them about the struggles of the Indians in South Africa. He wrote reports for the Indian newspapers, and these dispatches were also picked up by Reuters and sent to England. This news made its way back to South Africa, and when Gandhi returned there, an angry mob did not allow him to get off the ship. There were actually two steamers that had come from India; there were about 800 passengers in all. It was after a lengthy quarantine lasting twenty-three days that the vessels were allowed into the harbour. Gandhi, on his way home from the waterfront, was attacked by the mob, but managed to escape with minor injuries. Pressure had been put on the Indian owners of the steamers to return the passengers to India, but they had not given in to either inducements or threat. There was no doubt now in Gandhi's mind that the Indian community had found its strength as well as self-confidence. He had also reached a personal conclusion at the end of the stand-off at Port Natal. God was preparing him, Gandhi was to write later, for the lifelong practice of satyagraha.

The second Boer War started in 1899. Despite arguments to the contrary, Gandhi decided that Indians should side with the British during the war, and he himself served as a nurse in an Ambulance Corps made up of nearly 1100 Indians from Durban. When the war was over, Gandhi returned to India after having stayed in South Africa for six years. But soon, in 1902, he was once again summoned back to Durban by the Indian community which was now facing new assaults in the Transvaal. The newly opened Asiatic Department in that region had begun to function as 'a frightful engine of oppression for the Indians'. While permits were no longer required from Europeans, they continued to be demanded from Indians. Gandhi resolved to fight against the injustice of racial laws. This time, he took up residence in Johannesburg, which was home to the majority of Transvaal Indians, and applied for permission to be enrolled as a barrister at the court.

In 1904, a journal called *Indian Opinion* was launched and Gandhi was the main force behind it; it was in its pages that he began to develop and communicate to others around him the principles and practice of satyagraha. One of the tasks that Gandhi performed in Johannesburg was to represent indentured Indian labourers from Bihar and South India who were being displaced by the municipality from the land on which they lived—land which had been made inhospitable and unhygienic due to negligence and overcrowding. There was further trouble. Pneumonic plague broke out in those settlements where the impoverished labourers lived, and they were moved to another location and the whole settlement burnt down to prevent the spread of the disease. When the Zulu 'rebellion' broke out, Gandhi offered to raise a Stretcher-bearer Corps of Indians and worked for a month, often carrying wounded Zulus to places where they could find aid. On occasion, Gandhi and his companions would march as much as forty miles in a single day. But, very soon after this, a draft Ordinance was put forward by the Transvaal government which, Gandhi feared, 'would spell absolute ruin for the Indians in South Africa'. The ordinance demanded that every Indian would need to register with the registrar and take out a certificate of registration; without doing this, Indians would forfeit their right to remain in Transvaal; every Indian would be required to carry the certificate on his or her person and produce it on demand. Refusal to comply would lead to a fine or a prison term.

In the pages of *Indian Opinion*, the government's proposal came to be called the Black Ordinance, and meetings began to be held where members of the community pledged resistance. As the struggle gathered strength, the problem arose of finding a name for it. 'None of us knew what name to give to our movement,' Gandhi wrote nearly two decades later. The name 'passive resistance' was also confusing, and there was dissatisfaction that the name was in English. A small prize was announced in the pages of *Indian Opinion* for the reader who sent in the best suggestion. A friend of Gandhi's, Maganlal, to whom *Satyagraha in South Africa* is dedicated, came up with the word 'sadagraha' meaning 'firmness in a good cause'. Gandhi changed it to 'satyagraha' because, as he explained it, 'Truth (*satya*) implies love, and firmness (*agraha*) engenders and therefore serves as a synonym for force. I thus began to call the Indian movement "satyagraha", that is to say, the Force which is born of Truth and Love or non-violence ...'

The above sketch of the events that brought Gandhi to the discovery of his political and spiritual truth is accurate enough, but it misses out on a very important aspect of his struggle. The experience of reading *Satyagraha in South Africa* makes it clear that political awareness was an acutely personal matter for Gandhi: it was shaped by hurt and built on a profound, spiritual quest for truth. And what becomes apparent, more so in the pages of Gandhi's autobiography *My Experiments with Truth*, is the fact that Gandhi's battle with an oppressive enemy was also, in no less significant a way, a struggle with his own self. The enemy, although that might not be the most appropriate word in this context, was not only outside but also inside oneself. This quality distinguishes Gandhi from all latter-day long-distance nationalists for whom not only belief but also the self is beyond scrutiny. It also explains why satyagraha, while viewed by its practitioners as an expression of strength, establishes itself as a sign of humility.

Gandhi's political practice was built on a foundation of self-questioning and critique, and this meant that his sole fidelity was to his principle of truth. This allowed for a host of eccentricities and often baffling, even inconsistent, decisions on Gandhi's part, but, at the same time, it provided the basis for a radical openness of thought and action. This openness, perhaps surprising in a person so religious, is nowhere more evident than in his religious practice itself.

On his very first morning in Pretoria, back in 1893, Gandhi had woken up and gone to meet Mr Baker, the attorney who was the counsel for his employers. After they had discussed professional matters, Gandhi found out that Baker was also a Christian preacher who was of the firm belief that salvation lay only with Christ. When asked by Baker to explain his religious views, Gandhi replied, 'I am a Hindu by birth. And yet I do not know much of Hinduism and I know less of other religions. In fact I do not know where I am, and what is and what should be my belief. I intend to make a careful study of my own religion and, as far as I can, of other religions as well.' The next day, Gandhi attended a prayer meeting run by Mr Baker. That night, he went to sleep pondering questions like 'How far should I undertake the study of Christianity? How was I to obtain literature about Hinduism? And how was I to understand Christianity in its proper perspective without thoroughly knowing my own religion?' The missionary zeal of his new-found Christian friends did not prevent Gandhi from returning to the prayer meeting at one o'clock each day. He read several books about Christianity that were given to him, and even attended a convention of Protestant Christians that lasted three days. Gandhi shocked his Christian friends by telling them that it was impossible for him to believe that he could 'go to heaven or attain salvation only by becoming a Christian'. His own attitude towards their own beliefs, and even towards what one could argue was their zealotry, remained remarkably benign. He was delighted at their faith. He liked the fact that the good Christians were praying for him, and reported that he found the hymns that they were singing very sweet.

Gandhi did not change his faith because he could not accept that Christianity was the perfect or the greatest religion. But, at the same time, he was also at pains to clarify to himself and others that he was no chauvinist when it came to his own religion. 'Hindu defects were pressingly visible to me,' he wrote. He was especially critical of Hinduism's sanction of untouchability and its elaborate caste hierarchy. This is another trait that distinguishes him from our contemporary long-distance nationalists. The latter would never espouse Gandhi's egalitarian sense of organization within a faith, nor his belief that no system of belief was inherently inferior or superior. They can never be expected to echo Gandhi's words: 'What was the meaning of saying that the Vedas were the inspired Word of God? If they were inspired, why not also the Bible and the Koran?'

The birth of the concept of satyagraha is indebted not only to fervent belief in the sanctity of truth but also a commitment to the equality of religions. On 11 September 1906, a meeting had been called to discuss the Transvaal Indians' response to the 'Black Act'. At the meeting, Gandhi was 'perplexed' when an elderly Muslim by the name of Sheth Haji Habib went on to 'solemnly declare in the name of God that he would never submit to that law'. As the meeting wore on, however, Gandhi's perplexity was turned to 'enthusiasm' about what Habib had proposed, and he requested the man presiding over the meeting for permission to speak. In his speech, Gandhi told the men gathered in front of him about the sanctity of an oath taken in the name of God. To violate an oath with God as witness, he added, was also to forfeit one's manhood. But what was equally important, to my mind, was Gandhi's insistence that the Indians were united when they took God's name. At the beginning of his remarks, Gandhi said, 'We all believe in one and the same God, the differences of nomenclature in Hinduism and Islam notwithstanding.' The Hindu ultranationalists who killed Gandhi, and have today sidelined his memory, have also erased the fact that Gandhi's early successes in South Africa were won as a result of the assistance and faith of his Muslim supporters. The experiment in satyagraha, which was instrumental in winning Indian independence, owed its inception to a Muslim man's invocation of his God. The battle for the Indian nation was not fought by men and women of one religion alone.

*

South Africa is the place where Gandhi became Indian.

Over the past few years, I have made trips to South Africa in search of material for a documentary film. Gandhi is the starting point for my discovery of my relationship with that distant country. But there are also other points of interest in the story. When I was a student, the struggle against apartheid had been going on for decades, and it didn't appear that its end was near. As a schoolboy, I would read also about white South African cricketing greats like Graeme Pollock, Barry Richards and Mike Procter; these were talented white cricketers who were not able to play test matches because of the international sporting ban against South Africa. In the classroom, I had learned about Gandhi's experience in the train in South Africa, but the knowledge of the lives of the descendants of the Indians whom Gandhi had met remained remote.

The fact that people of Indian origin in South Africa were participating in the struggle against apartheid came to me very late, when I was in my early twenties. I was reading Winnie Mandela's *Part of My Soul Went with Him*, and I came across the mention of a fellow-prisoner of Mandela's on Robben Island, a man with an Indian last name, Maharaj. I learned that it was Mac Maharaj who had smuggled Nelson Mandela's prison writings out of Robben Island. Years later, when Mandela's autobiography was published, he acknowledged the help of two other Indian fellow-prisoners, Ahmed Kathrada and Laloo Chiba. When I went to South Africa, I would meet these men. Kathrada was one of the accused in the Rivonia Trial in 1963, and, along with Mandela, Walter Sisulu and Govan Mbeki, sentenced to life imprisonment. Like Kathrada, Chiba was a political prisoner in the same wing of the Robben Island Prison, the B-Section. During the time of his arrest, Chiba was a part of National High Command of the Umkhonto we Sizwe, the military wing of the African National Congress, and he was handed an eighteen-year term of imprisonment for sabotage. In *Long Walk to Freedom*, Mandela's autobiography, there is mention of a scheme that Maharaj, Kathrada and Chiba hatched in prison. In order to open lines of communication with the prisoners in other sections, these comrades secretly collected the matchboxes thrown by the warders. Maharaj had the idea of constructing a false bottom in the matchbox and slipping a message in it. And, writes Mandela, it was Chiba, who had once trained as a tailor, who wrote minuscule coded messages and slipped them inside the converted matchboxes. These were then dropped off at strategic places on the paths where other prisoners would later walk. When the matchboxes were picked up by the political prisoners a day or two later, they contained hidden messages written in response.

I have been watching the footage of the film we are trying to make on the involvement of the people of Indian origin in the South African struggle. Chiba, standing in the lime quarry on Robben Island, his own handsome face craggy like the hills around him, talks of the hard labour of the political prisoners. His arms sweep over the mountain of lime in front of the camera and then extend to the emptiness where, he says, the rest of the mountain used to be, the huge mound that was cleared by the twenty odd men over several years. Lime which was broken down into small stones and mixed with seashells so that the roads of the prison-island could be resurfaced and parts of the prison rebuilt. It was easier to pull dirty seaweed out of the cold sea and the prisoners preferred it to the rigours of working in the quarry. The glare from the walls of lime destroyed the men's eyesight. (When I was about to take pictures of Mandela during my first visit, his aide whispered in my ear that the flash hurt the leader's eyes. I was to use only the available natural light.) The lime also affected the skin and caused a variety of diseases. The prisoners found out that even a few minutes of work left their hands bleeding. Chiba worked in the lime quarry for nearly fourteen years. He wanted to write letters. In the initial period of his imprisonment, he was allowed to write and receive only one letter every six months, and the length of the letter was limited to 500 words. Later, when the opportunity came, he would rewrite the pages that Mandela had written in his cell down the corridor; the thick, voluminous manuscript reduced to fifty pages and then slipped into the artificial cover he had made for a photo album. When Mac Maharaj left the prison after his release, he walked out with a copy of Mandela's manuscript hidden in the album.

When I was in Johannesburg, I had met a young woman named Meena. She was Chiba's niece and after some cajoling she showed me the letters that her uncle had written to her from prison. A letter written to Meena when she was in her teens showed the stamp of the Robben Island Censor Office; I remember the letter chiefly because Chiba had noted that when he had last seen Meena she had been only two years old. Meena's parents had a shop. Her father, Mr Parbhoo, was a tailor. Before Chiba was arrested, he had often taken shelter in the Parbhoo house. In the earlier years, Mr Parbhoo and Chiba had been room-mates. Mr Parbhoo didn't have his own shop then, he had worked for another Indian. A young Laloo Chiba used to work with a milk-delivery agency. Then, Chiba went to prison.

When he came out nearly two decades later, Chiba was elected to parliament in the first democratic elections to be held in South Africa. It was Meena, a thin, nervous woman with great political passion, who had first introduced me to her revered uncle. When I met Chiba, I had been reading about him in a memoir written by another political prisoner of Indian origin on Robben Island. In Indres Naidoo's book, *Island in Chains*, this is what is written about Chiba and the first visit in prison from his wife: 'Laloo had suffered because the warders had insisted that he speak only English or Afrikaans and his wife knew only Gujarati so that the two of them had simply had to stare at each other for the whole visiting period with tears in their eyes and saying nothing.' When I met Chiba, I found him an exceedingly modest person, and I remember his telling me, while taking me to the plot of land where Gandhi's ashram had once stood, that his own sacrifices in prison were nothing compared to the price his ordinary compatriots had to pay as supposedly free citizens of a South Africa governed by apartheid.

A few days after my first meeting with Chiba, I had travelled to the coastal city of Durban. One evening I was listening to a local radio station which was playing Indian film songs—I had already been excited by my discovery that the South Indian last name 'Naidoo' took up fifteen pages in the phone directory, with the name 'Pillay' coming second with ten pages devoted to it—when a call-in programme started at the same station. It was a programme devoted to debating Indian identity in South Africa. A man called in to say that he was Indian because he prayed every day. The show's host, an intelligent, acerbic man named Ashwin Desai, asked the caller if, for example, Jewish people prayed every day, would that make them Indians. The caller insisted that he was Indian because India, the land from where his forefathers came, is, as we all know, the greatest country in the world. I made a call to the radio station from my hotel room. On the air, I invoked Chiba's name. I asked why the radio caller was proud of his Indianness because he prayed each day—and not because an Indian like Laloo Chiba had fought for freedom from apartheid. I also mentioned other leaders, like Yusuf Dadoo who had laid the foundation for Indian and African liberation earlier in the century, or, later under apartheid, people like Ahmed Timol who had been tortured in prison for their resistance to racism and paid for it with their lives.

I was roundly abused by the show's listeners who called in that evening and again, the next night, when I was asked to appear on the show. One caller even said that the Indians in the subcontinent were 'a bitter lot' envious of all that the Indians in South Africa had accomplished. I admitted on air that I was indeed envious of Indian South Africans, saying that I envied the fact that so many of them had fought against apartheid. I was speaking more as an Indian living in the US. Here, we take pride in acts of jingoistic muscle-flexing in the subcontinent or worship the gods of Bollywood. I have encountered very few instances where our sense of community, and our pride in it, emerges from our acts of cross-cultural activism and achievement. We'd rather go on about yet another Indian child who has won the spelling-bee contest!

And yet, I had made a mistake on the radio that evening. In reminding the listeners of heroes like Dadoo, or Kathrada, or Chiba, and Timol, I had overlooked what the ordinary, less-celebrated people had done during the long struggle against apartheid. I am thinking now of someone like the Parbhoos. A slightly built, quiet, unassuming man, focussed on running his tailor shop during the worst years of repression, Mr Parbhoo seemed to have no truck with politics. Yet, he had often been called upon to do his bit for the struggle. His car would be used by the activists; a few times, he would have to drive strangers to secret destinations. A message would come that a clandestine meeting would be held at his house. His wife would be asked to cook for a certain number of people. Mrs Parbhoo, feeding me food in her kitchen, spoke of her experience. She would be scared, of course, but she was also very pleased to be cooking for Chiba and his comrades. These men are now the leaders of a new South Africa, but back in those days, when they were on the run, Mrs Parbhoo enjoyed giving them food because often they had not eaten for days. The men who came to her house, she said, were from all races, black, white, Indian and coloured.

Among the Parbhoos, however, there is no exaggerated sense of their involvement in their country's fight for justice. If anything, there is only self-effacement. Meena, the daughter of the Parbhoos, saw her uncle, Laloo Chiba, for the first time when she went to visit him on Robben Island on her eighteenth birthday. She discounts any attribution of pride for the unnoticed but courageous acts of her parents. Meena's sense of the past is focussed only on the outrage of the imprisonment of all the leaders whom she reveres. 'It's not fair to us. It makes us angry,' she said, her voice catching as she spoke, her thin fingers pressing into her black hair. 'They kept them in for so long, so that when they came out they were so old.'

*

Professor Dalmiya in New Jersey, despite his talk of micro-wave processing, had been more interested in telling me about the religion that was anathema to him and its holy book, the *Qur'an*. You'd think he had learned it at school. And, in a way, he had. It was at the RSS shakha that he had picked up his beliefs as a kid and now, as an adult, he saw himself as a part of a fraternity of Hindutva warriors. The shakha, which he had visited daily as a boy, provided him with a bond which tied him to other Hindus, and to the memories of his childhood, and also to Bharat Mata.

An Indian film-maker, Lalit Vachani, has documented the role of the shakhas in his two films, *The Boy in the Branch* (1993) and *The Men in the Tree* (2002). In October 1992, Vachani went with his team to Nagpur, the city which is home to the RSS, and began work on filming the process through which boys were indoctrinated in the Hindutva ideology. The film that resulted, *The Boy in the Branch*, centred on Kali, a nine-year-old boy who went to the shakha each evening because that was a place where boys went to play after school. There was a simplicity about this fact, and Vachani was surprised by it. When he went to the shakha in Nagpur, he had expected to see fascist symbols of indoctrination, reminiscent of Nazi Germany. Instead, what Vachani discovered was more ingenious and unsettling, cheerful boys in a circle playing games. The subtle attraction of fundamentalism was something as innocent as the lure of a playground. But the games were not innocent at all. In one of the games, for instance, a man asks: 'Who owns Kashmir?' 'We do, we do,' the children shout enthusiastically in response.

Six weeks after Vachani had finished shooting his film
in Nagpur, many hundred miles to the north, in the town
of Ayodhya, the Babri mosque was demolished by zealots
belonging to the RSS and allied organizations. This event,
which challenged any safe assumption one could have made
so far about Indian democracy and its secular credentials,
posed a slightly different question for the film-maker. He
wanted to know what the boy Kali thought of the mosque
being destroyed. He also wanted to know where the young
men, whom he had seen instructing the boys in games and
martial arts, had been when the mosque's dome and walls
were brought down. Eight years later Vachani returned to
Nagpur with his camera.

The film-maker wanted to find out what they thought
of the fact that 1500 Indians (mostly Muslims) were killed
in the riots that followed the mosque's demolition. The
film that Vachani shot as a sequel to *The Boy in the
Branch* is entitled *The Men in the Tree*. It is a record of the
shifts in the lives of his individual subjects, but the greater
shift that the film documents is the movement of the RSS
and Hindu nationalism from its somewhat peripheral place
in the Indian polity to a position of dominance at its very
centre.

The young men, who had been in their teens when
Vachani made *The Boy in the Branch*, were now mature
professionals. Sripad was only eighteen when the first film
was made; he played the role of the physical instructor at
the shakha. When Vachani returned to make the sequel,
Sripad, stocky and heavier, had begun working as a building
contractor. We watch him explain that he had also been
helping with an RSS project involving the construction of
thirty houses. He says that the facilities will be used to do

research on cows, including the use of cow urine in medicines. Later, he tells the camera that he was up on the dome of the Babri mosque when it was brought down. He used rods and sticks. 'It was a lifetime achievement,' he says.

Sripad and also the others admit that there was a great deal of planning involved in sending a fixed number of people from different towns and cities to Ayodhya. The demolition of the mosque was a triumph of diabolical organization. And then, without added emphasis, as if he were sharing information about the weather, Sripad states, 'The Muslim society will come to our way of thinking ... . An environment will be created gradually ... . If the Muslims want to live in this country, they'll have to listen to the big brother.' There, in a nutshell and without fanfare, is the truth that Vachani had gone to Nagpur to find out, the truth about the terror of ethnic cleansing that the youth he had earlier met were calmly contemplating in their fascist hearts.

And yet this is not all that Vachani learns and shares with the viewer. The boy Kali who had been the focus of the first film has grown up, and in the second film we see him managing a small shop. He does not go to the shakha any more. He used to go there to play and has now outgrown that need. When asked about the events in Ayodhya, he says, 'They shouldn't have broken the Babri mosque. It is the ordinary people who get killed.' In *The Boy in the Branch* we had seen Kali as someone who had been a bad learner, a member of the shakha who had simply been unable to pick up the propaganda lessons in history. Then, eight years later, Kali shows us that he has not changed. The film-maker asks him a question about a nationalist icon and Kali makes one or two valiant attempts to add a detail or two to the name, and then breaks into a smile and gives up in frustration. He is there to remind the viewer, I think, that not everyone has lost their sense of humanity.

In fact, in exploring the individualities of each of the members of the shakha, Vachani has succeeded in showing us that the Hindutva cadre is not only human but also impossible to stereotype. And, in the case of someone like Kali, even likeable. There is a challenge that such a film poses. It reminds us all that our enemies often look a lot like us. Take the case of Sandeep. In *The Boy in the Branch*, he was a wispy youth with a talent for playing the flute. In the later film, he is older but his smile still has its sweetness. We learn that he now works as a salesman for Ayurvedic medicine. Sandeep tells the film-maker that he had liked being an RSS worker and later became an RSS preacher. He gave six years to the RSS, staying away from home, and he wanted to give more, but couldn't. It is easy to believe that we are watching a lower middle-class young man revealing as best as he can the ideals that he had discovered at young age and how he worked hard to live up to them.

As Vachani understands this attitude well, we also see the pleasant-faced Sandeep shaving and singing, doing ordinary things that ordinary people do. Sandeep and Vachani visit the old shakha building which is being torn down. That is where they had met during the making of the first film, and Sandeep, who had spent four and a half years there, speaks of his memories which are bound to that place. When I now reflect on Sandeep's nostalgia, and his affection for a place where his life was shaped in the company of his comrades, I am reminded of Professor Dalmiya talking of his warm memories of the time spent in the RSS shakha. It is tempting, in this state of mind, to forget that murder and mayhem are also plotted at the shakha. A former member of the RSS, D.R. Goyal, tells Vachani in *The Men in the Tree* that he and his fellow RSS volunteers would fabricate letters and posters ostensibly written by Muslims. These texts would suggest that Muslims were planning an attack on Hindus. The RSS would produce such posters in order to incite riots. Goyal recounts one instance when he had helped prepare a fake flier that was seemingly written by a Muslim and it urged fellow Muslims to kill Hindus during the month of holy month of Ramzan. As a result of the flyer, there were several clashes between the Hindus and Muslims, and a man in Goyal's household was also killed as a result. This man was a servant whose name was Gama. And although Gama was a Muslim, Goyal said, he used to take care of the cows with a devotion that would equal any Hindu's. Such incidents would, in time, take Goyal away from the RSS.

I do not really know why someone who is a fundamentalist at any one point stops being one. Nor can I explain the process that is its opposite. Those questions cannot really be answered satisfactorily. It seems to me more accurate and important to contend that one is never wholly or only a fundamentalist. And vice versa.

Right in front of my parents' house in Patna, in the park where I had grown up playing cricket, I saw an RSS shakha meeting in progress during a recent visit. I could see the saffron flag and the trademark khaki shorts. I had not seen these young men there before during all my previous visits, so I went over to chat with them. I waited while the dozen or so youth, most of them I'd imagine in their late teens or early twenties, performed some drills. Their marching was quite clumsy and their attempt at calisthenics was lacking in rigour and rather shabby. But, here they were—the Hindu right's barefoot foot-soldiers— and I was curious.

The wait grew a little longer. After the drills, the youth stood in a circle and played a game in which they ran in circles and giggled a lot while chasing each other. The saffron flag flapped in the breeze. When the game was over, I approached the youth for the first time. I told them that I used to live in that house over there, just across the street, and now I had come home for a few days. Could I talk to them? They all nodded. Their leader, a serious, spectacled fellow, said to me, 'Please wait so that we can pray.'

The prayer was a chant that began with the words: '*Hindu rashtra ki anant shakti jag rahi/Arya desh ki swadesh bhakti jag rahi* ... . (The Hindu nation's endless strength is rising/The nationalist devotion of the Aryan nation is rising). I asked the youth in khaki what it was that they aimed to do at their shakha and what was it that they liked about what they were doing there. I was speaking to them in Hindi. The answers I got were simple, and, what was also surprising to me, the answers were given with an air of what I can only call unimpeachable innocence. 'Our aim is that in our Hindu nation each person becomes a *shreshta nagrik* (good citizen). Whatever it is that we do, we try to do it together. The biggest thing among us is discipline.' To enforce this fraternal feeling and also the discipline, these young men met every day for an hour. To me they were the upper-caste, but not affluent, part of Bihari society that felt marginalized by the rise of the so-called backward castes. A dominant leader like Laloo Yadav, who led an alliance of backward castes and minorities, was the enemy for them. These young men, with little economic potential and decreasing political clout, had reached out for a right-wing nationalist ideology that granted them morality and masculinity—at the expense of the minorities and others who, till yesterday, they had been able to dismiss as inferior. This feeling was present also among my own impoverished relatives who had not had the good fortune that had taken me away from home.

I wanted to press the youth to tell me a bit more about what they thought of their social enemies. So, I asked them if in what they were doing there was any place for Muslims or the Dalits. The young men were unfazed by my question. Their answer was automatic, and a little chilling. 'He who has been born on this soil is a Hindu,' the man with the spectacles said. Another added, 'We do not demand that the Muslim be separate in India. We dream of an *akhand Bharat*, an undivided India.' A dream nourished by a sense of primordial Hinduism, an undivided India stretching far beyond its current political boundaries, all its inhabitants united by allegiance to a single faith.

I went away after this conversation. A parliamentary by-election was being held in Patna that day. Long lines of men and women waited patiently in the sun to exercise their democratic right. There was the drama of violence, even shootings, at some polling stations. But I kept thinking of the youth in the park near the house where I had grown up. As far as I could tell, they were all decent youth. They looked cheerful and harmless as they chased each other and, in an attempt, not without its own pathos, to acquire and give respect, they incessantly greeted each other with a formal namaste. Of course, I was disappointed that they were drawing back into a narrower identity, one that relied on an idea of India as unitary and insular. They were perhaps susceptible to the further corruptions of right-wing ideologies through which piety would rationalize genocide, patriotic fervour would disguise cupidity, and a desiccated and moralizing ideology of discipline would choke any sign of non-conformity. Nevertheless, I couldn't help feeling that the youth were not wholly to be blamed for not knowing otherwise. Corporate ideologies had swept across the country in the past ten or twenty years, but no reality could have been more alien to these provincial, ill-equipped youth. The mindless consumerism of mainstream television had offered them impossible dreams and also the realization that impossible things were not for them. With the education system in shambles and the prospect of employment getting dimmer each day, it was likely that almost no meaningful issue in their lives had been addressed or resolved—except in this retreat into the unexamined embrace of a familiar, regressive ideology on the rise.

It is impossible for me to dismiss the youth with their saffron flag and their khaki shorts even though I see them as my enemies. I am not about to sympathize with their beliefs, but it will be stupid of me to laugh at them. Because those youth are as modern as I am. We are both products of the same forces. I left my small town and went abroad. I learned to speak the language of the world. They caught hold of the idea of nationalism and of citizenship which are powerful, modern ideas and they are now using it in a narrow way for their own ends in the small space left open to them. The market, especially the global market, has come to them with the mantra of sameness. The youth have accepted that too. They believe in homogeneity and are going to erase, they believe, all signs of difference from their land. It is frightening and wrong, but it is as real and as contemporary as that which had made me who I am.

*

Professor Dalmiya of the Overseas Friends of the BJP had provided me names and numbers of his party members in London. I went to England to meet them. But it wasn't any different from meeting Professor Dalmiya. They all said the same things. While I attended more meetings in London, I asked around for names of those who had written about long-distance nationalism, and that is how it came to be that one evening I was waiting for Chetan Bhatt in a pub opposite the British Library in London. Bhatt is a political scientist who has written a book on Hindu nationalism. For Professor Dalmiya and his London friends, Bhatt is the enemy, a leftist academic who has used his scholarship to discredit the RSS and the VHP.

The pub where I was waiting for Bhatt was showing a soccer match on its television screen. The game was being played between Arsenal and Manchester United. I was extremely conscious of being an outsider and wondered what the men in the pub thought of me, an Indian sitting by himself in the corner, his face turned away from what was filled with fascination for them. This was not a narcissistic concern on my part; instead, I was thinking of minority consciousness and the emergence of fundamentalism. It is possible, I thought, that secular critiques of religious ideologies have proven ineffective because, especially in the diaspora, the left has been unable to organize vibrant festivals or, for that matter, a football match. (Let's hear it for the two teams playing each other today, the Netaji Reds against the Nehru Blues.) Then, Bhatt arrived. A tall man in his thirties, with a serious, academic air, he immediately got down to the business of explaining the mechanics of Hindutva organizing in the UK. It was in the late 1980s and early 1990s, he said, that the RSS presence became very explicit. It was certainly very marked when, in 1989, 55,000 Hindus turned out for the Viraat Hindu Sammelan in Milton Keynes near London. The souvenir volume had dedications from the Queen, among others, and Margaret Thatcher went to the Finchley shakha to put a garland on the bust of the RSS founder. By the early 1990s, there were about forty shakhas meeting regularly in the country. Bhatt said that he had read a report of a shakha meeting where the leader asked the people assembled there where they had come from. A few hands were raised when the speaker asked if there were those who had been born in India, and a few went up again when asked if there were any who had been born in Britain, but the largest number of hands that went up were of those Hindus, mostly Gujaratis, who had come from Kenya. After the Rushdie affair, and especially after the demolition of the mosque in Ayodhya in 1992, the mood among the diasporic Hindutva crowd had altered. 'There was an increasing desecularization of community affect. There was a change even in the language being used. After years of anti-racist campaigning, there was this sudden shift—you were no longer Asian, people were talking of Hindus and Muslims.'

When Bhatt was telling me about the ways in which the VHP had gone about its task of converting people to its cause, I asked Bhatt to explain why identity politics is of great appeal to the migrant. He said, 'The diaspora Hindu, trapped in "the castle of his skin", develops a consciousness of persecution.' Then, he said that he had heard the historian Romila Thapar remark that, in India, the language of the majority Hindu—that 80 per cent of the population in threatened by 20 per cent of the rest—is actually the language of the minority. Where does it come from? According to Thapar, this language is a consequence of diaspora. In other words, the Hindu abroad, responding in different degrees to the reality of racism, is responsible for giving to the Hindus in India the entirely bogus claim to being persecuted. Bhatt's reserve cracked when he said this, and he smiled, showing that he did not wholly accept this argument. But he clearly found the theory attractive. I did too. Bhatt said, 'It is significant that the VHP started its organization as international. They never forgot the diaspora.' Even during the struggle for independence, and certainly in the period after, mainstream India had pretty much ignored the diaspora and now, he seemed to be saying, we were all paying the price.

Bhatt had attended some of the meetings that had been organized in the Asian community after the riots in Gujarat. He found that when the Hindutva activists spoke, the people in the audience were turned off. Bhatt said, 'Their orientation was so inhuman, people were getting more and more angry at them.' I felt that Bhatt was underlining hope when he said this, but then he said, 'In the ordinary

Hindu's mind, Hinduism is now associated with Islam. This is the VHP's contribution to Hinduism.' This was a darker statement, emphasizing that in the Indian context any perception of one's faith was cast only in a narrow and antagonistic relation to the other. If there was reason for hope, there was also enough evidence to make one pessimistic. This was also borne out by the fact, Bhatt said, that in the diaspora not a single Hindu organization had spoken out against Hindutva.

Where did things go wrong? When I asked this question, Bhatt was unsparing in his criticism also of the dominant white majority in countries like Britain. They practised what he called an 'unethical multiculturalism'. There were several members of parliament and mayors who, in the name of multiculturalism, provided support to the most reactionary immigrant groups. At the same time, Bhatt was critical of the role of the secular or progressive forces that had ignored civil society. In contrast, the right had been active and sought its support among the people. 'If you don't attend a shakha, the shakha will come to you,' Bhatt said. But, wasn't there also something about the left having ignored religion per se? When I asked this question, Bhatt's responded quickly, 'The secular left has failed to deal with enchanted civil societies.' I liked that phrase at the end but also wondered if Bhatt would give a more personal response. I asked him to tell me about the terms on which he accepted or rejected religion. But Bhatt would not offer me anything, and he repeated the argument, dear to secularists, that religion for each citizen was a matter that should remain in the private sphere.

An hour later, Bhatt said goodbye to me near the tube station. I had to wait long for my connecting train because a strike by the British firemen had led to cancellations and detours. There was much to think about while I waited at the underground station. I had enjoyed meeting Bhatt that evening; our academic backgrounds and our politics were similar. We stood outside our own enchanted society, looking in, comprehending various things but unable to do much more. I was aware of our failure. I hardly had any friends who were *both* religious and progressive. There was maybe one. I could not easily imagine the conditions under which this divide would be breached. I was suspicious of myself and believed that I had been trained to be suspicious of religion; at the same time, as I stood on the platform at Baker Street, I could not see how it could be otherwise. Then I remembered Jameel.

I had met Jameel Chand one night in Johannesburg during my last trip to South Africa. Jameel was now in his early thirties but when he was only twelve, in apartheid South Africa, he had joined in the school boycotts. When Jameel turned nineteen, he joined the ANC; then, he became a part of the armed struggle and was sent to Botswana to receive military training. He had two South African Indian comrades. One of them was Prakash Napier, a radical working-class Hindu who was a little older than Jameel. The other was Yusuf Akhalwaya, a religious Muslim youth with a strong commitment to racial and economic justice. Together, the three of them formed the first—and only—Indian guerrilla cell of the South African struggle. They called themselves the Gandhi unit. Later they renamed themselves the Ahmed Timol unit in honour of the South African Indian teacher who had been killed by the security forces for his role in the resistance. They travelled to Angola to learn to be better guerilla fighters. After their return, the trio carried out thirty-five successful bombing operations. Jameel deposed to this effect in front of the South African Truth and Reconciliation Commission. All attacks had been carried out within a relatively short period, 1987–89. These were the last, and arguably the most brutal, years of the apartheid rule. Unknown to Jameel and his friends, the day of Mandela's release from prison loomed on the other side of the darkness.

In the late hours of 11 December 1989, the members of the Ahmed Timol unit had planned two sabotage operations in Johannesburg: the bombing of the Hillbrow police station and the Park railway station. A major union had declared a strike and, in support of the workers, they were going to carry out two attacks in the course of a single night. The group had carried surveillance at the sites for a month and they were confident of success because they had sufficient training as well as experience. They followed a pattern during these ventures. The person in the vanguard walked about fifty-sixty metres ahead of the one in the middle who carried the explosives. The third person walked an equal distance at the back. At the Hillbrow station that morning, the man in the middle, the one with the bomb, was Prakash Napier. Yusuf Akhalwaya was in the forefront, and Jameel brought up the rear.

The three men had planted the first bomb at the Hillbrow police station and were at the Park railway station when the bomb exploded prematurely. Although he was a full fifty or sixty metres behind Prakash, Jameel was thrown off his feet and knocked back by the blast. Soldiers were running, rushing past him, with rifles on their way to the blast. No one noticed Jameel even though he lay there with a large Soviet gun in his hands.

Jameel was telling me this story in his home. He sat on his sofa, his right hand resting on his wife's thigh. Their daughters were playing in an adjoining room. We could hear their laughter. Jameel kept providing the details in a low, unwavering voice. 'I walked for a couple of hours with the gun in my hand,' he said. 'I knew that Yusuf and Prakash had been killed.' Because he was in shock, it was not till a long time later that night, while still walking down a street that Jameel realized that he should throw the gun away. He put the weapon in a garbage can. The three friends had discussed various scenarios while they planned their activities, what they would do if one of them was arrested, but there had been no talk among them about what they would do if one of them died. Jameel said to me, 'I don't recall us ever speaking about death.'

Soon after the accident, Jameel left for Lusaka. After a debriefing with the ANC, he was given various options, including offers of scholarships to study abroad. But, Jameel chose to stay in the struggle. He was sent to Moscow for further training. One day, Jameel was in his room when Russian friends came rushing to give him the news that the ban had been lifted from the ANC. His initial reaction was of shock and sorrow. His first thought was: 'The struggle was in vain, my brothers were killed, and six months later, the ANC was unbanned.' In hindsight, Jameel said, he felt otherwise. He began to think that it was 'because Yusuf and Prakash were killed that Mandela walked free'.

Earlier, in Lenasia, the prominently Indian part of Johannesburg, I had passed a stadium with the sign that said 'Yusuf Akhalwaya and Prakash Napier Sports Complex'. I was with Meena, Mr Parbhoo's daughter, and she told me their story. That is how I had ended up going to meet Jameel.

Meena had also told me that Yusuf Akhalwaya had been a married man. His two comrades were unmarried. Yusuf's widow, Meena said, had later married Jameel. Her name was Firhana. She had interrupted Jameel's story only once—after he had given me the number of sabotage operations that the Timol unit had carried out—to clarify that not a single civilian had been killed in their attacks. I had learned from Firhana that she was a radio journalist. I asked her whether she had known that Yusuf was an armed militant when she had married him. She hadn't. She had learned of Yusuf's involvement in the movement only on the day he died. In fact, he would tell her that he was going for a political meeting and that she should not tell his mother or sisters anything about it. She never did. She had not been aware that he was an armed combatant in the underground. But, when her husband didn't come back that last night, and she heard the news about the blasts on the radio, Firhana knew immediately that it had something to do with Yusuf. It was not till much later, when South Africa became free and Jameel had returned to the country, that she saw him. Firhana knew Jameel, she had seen him in college. Yusuf would greet Jameel and sometimes exchange a word or two, but neither Firhana nor anyone would have suspected that the two were members of a closely-knit armed unit. When Firhana saw Jameel for the first time after her husband had been killed, she was filled with rage. Although there was also anger in her heart for Yusuf—because he had chosen the revolution over her and their little daughter—her rage was also directed at his friend who survived. When she saw Jameel at meetings, Firhana said, she asked herself why God hadn't taken him away instead of her husband.

But Firhana also wanted to talk to Jameel. There were several unresolved issues for her. She wanted to understand what had happened. She felt that she had been so very alienated from Yusuf's life that she wanted to learn all its details. Firhana said, 'Jameel and I would meet, we would talk.' She would ask Jameel what Yusuf would say. Firhana told me that Jameel was extremely supportive and they became close friends. At this point, Jameel took up the story. He said, 'In those meetings, I fell in love with Firhana.' His friends were a bit wary of this development. They suggested in different ways that he might be feeling some guilt, and was falling in love out of some sense of obligation. Jameel, however, was clear in his mind. 'It wasn't that I needed to be with her,' he said, 'I *wanted* to be with her.' Firhana, smiling, said that Jameel 'wasn't even my type'. He was very different from Yusuf. But she was also in love with him. The two of them got married. Firhana already had a daughter from her marriage with Yusuf. She had two more daughters with Jameel. It was the laughter of the girls that rang out intermittently from another part of the house while we talked.

At one point, Firhana had said to me that soon after Yusuf Akhalwaya and Prakash Napier were killed, the ANC office in Lusaka had released a statement. The statement had made mention of the last report by Yusuf which had described the character of the relationship between the members of the Timol unit. 'Although they came from different religions,' the report had said, 'the love they had for each other was the highest form of brotherly love.'

It was this memory that returned to me as I stood on the platform of the London tube station. The struggle in which the Ahmed Timol unit was involved brought together Hindus and Muslims; in a fight for social justice it had united the religious-minded and the secular alike. A three-member group is a very tiny part of the universe, and two of the threesome were already dead. But I found their story affecting. It had reminded me of the weavers I had met in Bhagalpur, in Bihar, who observed *shaheedi diwas* 'martyrdom day' to commemorate the day on which two weavers—one Hindu and the other Muslim, Shashi Kumar and Jahangir—were killed 'by a single bullet' from the police who fired on the weaver's demonstration against the government. The weavers were very poor. Their looms had been destroyed in the Hindu-Muslim riots. They were agitating for electric supply to be restored to their neighbourhoods. The police had fired on workers who could not be divided by religion. The relationship between the Hindus and the Muslims in their community, one weaver said, was like that between the warp and the woof.

6

A Nation of Converts

On the evening of my arrival in Karachi, Nani asked me to sit beside her on the sofa. She was my wife's maternal grandmother. Nani said to me that she was going to have a party that night in my honour. She wanted me to meet everyone in the family. The people who were coming to dinner that evening, she said, had been informed of Mona's marriage to me the previous year. She said in Urdu, 'I told them that the groom is from Hindustan. And then I told them, "He has accepted Islam."'

Nani said that people had congratulated her. She said, '*Sabhi mujhe mubaarakbad dene lage. Log kehne lage ki Mona ko janaat milegi*' (Everyone began congratulating me. People said that Mona will get admitted into heaven now). I think Nani knew that I did not think of myself as a Muslim. Her account about the guests for the dinner that night was her way of orienting me to her world. It was all right. I remembered well that when my visa application for my Pakistan visit did not go through the first time, then on the second application, in the box marked 'Religion' I had written 'Hindu converted to Islam during marriage'. The words didn't fit in the box and I filled the margins so that anyone reading the form would notice what I had written. We all have our ways,

I guess, of dealing with the world. I didn't tell any of this to Nani.

That evening, when people came to dinner, they were polite and even affectionate. Many of them did not call me by my usual name. They called me Safdar. When dinner was over, one guest, my mother-in-law's cousin, turned in my direction and asked loudly: 'Safdar, how did your parents take the news of your conversion?' It was difficult for me to tell her that I had never thought that I had converted. At the same time, I was not opposed to being considered a convert either. As to my parents, I didn't know what they thought. I hadn't told them anything about it at all.

'Marriage among Hindus is no simple matter,' writes Mahatma Gandhi at the beginning of his autobiography. But, in the case of my marriage, distance made matters very simple. My parents and the whole of my family except for a younger sister were in India. I was living in New Haven in the US. It happened that I was the only one making decisions for myself. It was only when I was at the home of Mona's parents in Toronto—deep into the discussion of dates suitable for our marriage—that I decided to inform my parents of my decision to marry. I called them in India to give them the news. Two years before this happened I had told my parents in a letter of my having met Mona in New York City. I had written to them that she was a Muslim and, in fact, a Pakistani. Then, I had called my parents to talk to them. My father had rightly anticipated that I might be concerned about their opposition to my being in love with a Muslim. He came to the point immediately. He said, 'You have our blessings.' My mother too could not say no. But she had been a bit reluctant. She said, 'Yes ... but can't you find anyone from ... ?'

Later, when I called them from Toronto, I had only mentioned that we would get married in a simple ritual arranged by Mona's parents. I also said that when the two of us visited India, we could have another ceremony in my hometown, Patna.

Ten days later, I was married. Several of Mona's relatives came to the wedding. I was alone on the groom's side. It was a bright, warm day. Mona and I went to the office of the marriage registrar in North York in Toronto. The large modernist building, looming beyond several water fountains, was set at a distance from the main street. Inside, there were many offices. Mona, wearing a bright blue sari, walked to the window marked 'Tax and Water Inquiry', and then we were pointed in the right direction. An Irishman who was now settled in Canada officiated. He filled out our religions—'Hindu' and 'Muslim'—on the marriage form and asked, 'Isn't that a bit like a Catholic marrying a Protestant back where I'm from?'

After we drove back to the home of Mona's parents, we also had a brief Islamic ceremony. One of Mona's uncles officiated as the qazi. Both Mona and I were required to simply say 'yes' thrice to the question about our intent to marry. There were two lines from the *Qur'an* that the qazi asked me to repeat after him, and I did so, haltingly. The name that was used for me during this wedding ceremony was Safdar Ali. During the previous week, while I was in New Haven, I had got a call from Toronto. Mona sounded a little upset, but then her mother came on the line. I was asked to choose a Muslim name. It was explained to me that in Pakistan a marriage of a Muslim to a non-Muslim is not recognized. So, it was suggested, perhaps I could choose a name that could be used during an Islamic ceremony. Mona's mother said that they had thought the name 'Aftaab' would be suitable because it resembled my present name. I said no. I chose the name 'Safdar' after Safdar Hashmi, a dynamic, young theatre activist in India who had been killed on the streets outside Delhi by political goons.

A friend of mine in New Haven, a Hindu, when he heard of this said that this was Muslim design to convert me. I called a Muslim friend of mine, Raza Mir, and he started laughing on the phone. He said, 'Of course, this is a conversion, bastard ... . *Yaar*, these Muslims ... .' And then he laughed some more.

I was a little disturbed by all this, and it was one reason, I think, why I didn't pressure my sister in Virginia to try hard to come for the wedding. If this was indeed a conversion, I thought she might be uncomfortable with it. No one from Mona's family had actually used the word. It is possible that they didn't want to think in those terms, just as I didn't, though that is what they wanted it to be.

But I had by now become interested in the example of conversion in a nation where people increasingly identify themselves in religious terms. More accurately, the erosion of pluralism means that one participates in a kind of negative identification. As Eqbal Ahmad put it, this means saying that 'we are so-and-so because we are not the Other. We are what we are because we are different from the West, or from the Muslims, or from the Hindus, or from the Jews, or from the Christians'. In such a scenario, I wanted to see people in society who could boldly stake claims to many identities, many communities.

During my visit to Karachi, after I had finished speaking to students at my wife's former school, a boy had come up to me and asked a question. He first apologized for asking me what he thought was a personal question, and then he asked if I had converted. I had repeated to him the lines of poetry written by my friend Ajai Singh in Lucknow: '*Main aadha Hindu hoon, aadha Musalman hoon / Main poora Hindustan hoon*' (I am half a Hindu, I am half a Muslim / I am the whole of India). I told the boy about Nani calling me Safdar. I told him I could see myself being called Safdar. However, I was also the one who responded to the name I have had since I was a boy. I was not one or the other, I would be happy to be both. The boy had smiled, showing his braces, and then run away to join his friends.

The school boy, his curiosity and his politeness, were not what my mother-in-law, Ammi, had in mind when, just before my departure for the subcontinent, she called to tell me that I must pick up a few 'basics' of Islam before I went to Pakistan. She was thinking of those who would spot me as someone who was trying to pass off as a convert. Those who would demand faith. When Ammi spoke of her fears, I began wondering if she hadn't, in fact, had this fear in her heart all along, and whether it wasn't a part of the unspoken reason why she had wanted me to be, at least in part, Safdar Ali. On the phone she recited the *qalma* and I wrote the words down. *La Illaha Illallah Mohammed-ur-Rasulallah*. There is no God but Allah, and Mohammed is his Holy Prophet. As it was the month of Ramzan during which I was going to make my visit, she told be about the prayers (five in number, *fajar*, *johar*, *asar*, *magrib*, *isha*) and the parts of the faith (five in number, *namaaz*, *roza*, *hajj*, *zakaat*, *imaan*).

Although I have been employing the word 'conversion' and describing it as a desirable goal, it is perhaps not the right word for what I have in mind, which has more to do with a notion of plural identities. But conversion does help me attack the intransigent border between religions, or at least the sense of religion being a fundamental, unchanging reality. My choice of the word is also partly a protest against V.S. Naipaul's dismissal, in *Beyond Belief*, of all Muslims who are not Arabs as 'converts'. He writes that Muslims in a country like India or Pakistan—because they are converts to Islam—have an unreal sense of who they are. Their condition, Naipaul writes, has 'an element of neurosis and nihilism'. Such a way of thinking is troubling for me because it says that Muslims have no local histories, they are only tied to an elsewhere in Arabia. This is not only wrong because it erases the centuries of adaptation and growth of Islam in places like India; it also plays into the hands of the right-wingers like the VHP which don't tire of calling present-day Muslims 'outsiders' or 'invaders' in India. Against Naipaul's idea of purity and fixity in religion, it is necessary to see how communities have grown historically in dialogue with each other. Their influences are mixed and shared. They have long-standing histories in the places where they have flourished. If you go far back in time, surely all of us are converts.

*

A few months after my visit to Pakistan, a version of what I have written above appeared in an Indian newsmagazine, *Outlook*. I was nervous about the publication of this account of the weddings in Toronto. My parents had welcomed and supported my marriage with Mona, but they didn't know anything about my having entertained any thoughts of being called Safdar.

The news was going to shock them, I was quite certain of that, but I didn't know how I could broach it in a letter or on the phone. An essay making a moral case for a more fluid understanding of religious identity was, by default, now going to be my way of informing my parents about what had happened on my wedding day. I had doubts about this approach; it seemed academic as well as cowardly. But I hid behind my rationalizations and decided that this was the best that I could do. Yet, as the date of publication drew nearer, I grew anxious and called my parents in Patna. My mother was at home. I told her that I had written an article which was to appear the next day; it was provocative, I added, and that it would be disliked by many people. I did not say to my mother that I was most worried about *her* response and much less about the anonymous others. Later, when I got her letter, I realized that I had not only offended her. I had also hurt her.

The letter that came from her had been written in rage. A cousin of mine had called my mother and told her that she wanted to marry a Christian colleague. This was news to me. The girl's own brother had said that the family should disown her. My mother had spoken to my cousin on the phone and offered her support. My mother's letter recounted this story and then my mother reminded me that she had supported my decision to marry a Muslim— a Muslim who also was a Pakistani—*even though I was her only son*. When Mona had spoken to her on the phone, my mother had said, 'You are God's greatest gift to us.' Mona had not been asked by my parents to change her religion. My mother now wondered why I hadn't been given the same freedom. Switching to English, my mother had written, 'Please don't glorify your marriage as one between a Hindu and Muslim; it was a marriage between a Muslim and a Muslim.' The letter touched briefly on the case of the young Hindu woman on our street in Patna who had jumped from the roof when she had been unable to marry her Muslim lover. My mother informed me that the man's family had wanted the girl to convert, and she asked rhetorically why the question of conversion needed to come up where there was love between two people. And then, once again using English, my mother had written that I had broken her heart.

I felt sad, of course. But I also remember being uneasy about the irony in the situation. I didn't regard myself as a convert. I knew even before I had begun reciting the qalma that I would use it to make an argument about our mixed identities. I hadn't succeeded. Clearly, I was being seen as having exchanged one fixed identity for another. There was no real fluidity in my condition. At least, not in the eyes of the others. Somewhere in her letter, my mother had written, 'Henceforth, you have no right to criticize Hinduism ... .' *We Hindus never ask others to convert, but the Muslims are fanatical about demanding exactly that.* This issue, offered only in a veiled way in the letter, was amplified in the scores of hate-mail that I received from people I did not know. And at moments, remembering the two or three Hindu friends who had told me their stories about their failed affairs with Muslim women, I too nursed the same doubt. But what in my mind remained a doubt was present in the letters that came my way only as hate. Hate and certitude. The votaries of Hindutva seemed to ask me the same question about Muslims again and again: You call us fanatics, you traitor, but who is the fanatic now?

There was a phrase of V.S. Naipaul's, from his novel *The Mimic Men*, that came back to me, '... the convert, suspect to both the faithful and the infidel.' It was a precise, evocative description, and it touched on a fear inside me, a fear that arises from the feeling that one does not belong anywhere. But there was no danger of my claiming that space for myself; I did not think of myself as a convert and I couldn't even describe myself as religious. Mine was a more secular claim about how different religions are a part of our lives and that, especially in the context of the Indian subcontinent, the fact of mixed influences as well as historical co-existence is indubitable. I wanted to echo the sentiment that I had heard voiced by the writer Intizar Husain: 'I am a Muslim, but I always feel that there is a Hindu sitting inside me ... I still feel that I am an exile who wanders between Karbala and Ayodhya.' Husain was born in India and migrated to Pakistan after the Partition. He lives in Lahore and is one of Pakistan's leading writers. I was struck by the beauty of his words, and his sense of sublime rootlessness. In his worldview, the sense of belonging to different places, also distant places, was not a sign of neurosis but his humanity. Unlike those who are repulsed by divided loyalties, Husain celebrates his ties to the places that are a part of his past. Even his exile is a pleasant longing for the places to which he belongs.

In their own way, my parents had expressed a similar ideal when they had written warm, loving letters to Mona after our marriage in Toronto. But there was a crucial difference between Husain and my parents. For Husain, who drew his inspiration from the eclectic faith of the Sufi preachers, religious identity in the subcontinent was a shared tradition and, as a result, he described himself as both a Hindu and a Muslim; in contrast, for my parents, it was a modern political identity, as citizens of a democratic India, that allowed for a Hindu and a Muslim to marry each other and by sanctioning my marriage they were declaring a break from the past.

Mona's Pakistani parents too, I'd suspect, in wanting me to marry their daughter under a Muslim name, were also honouring their own adherence to a modern political identity, as citizens of an Islamic state where marriage between a Muslim and a non-Muslim was banned. Whatever religious ideas they might have had was overlaid with anxieties about life in a theocracy. Indeed, this became clear to me when Mona's mother, after reading my article in *Outlook*, wrote to say that the previous week in Canada she had told her class of forty-five students about her Muslim daughter's marriage to a Hindu man. She had added in her letter, 'I know I could not have done this in Pakistan without fear.'

I could recognize that fear. It was at its most abstract the fear of persecution felt by the religious minority, although I recognized it because it is the fear felt *on behalf of* the religious minorities that informs the secular tradition in places like India. This fear is what I have been taught to empathize with. It doesn't teach me much about belief, but it instructs me about rights. All my talk about all of us being converts is an attempt to have us grasp as a part of our cultural common sense the truth of our syncretic tradition, but what I would more readily die fighting for is the constitutional right for minorities to worship or demonstrate their faith or lack of it without fear and with equal protection under the law.

One day during my first visit to Pakistan, in a house in Karachi, I had begun reading the current issue of *Newsline*. It featured a special section on minorities in Pakistan. One brief, three-page story was on Hindus. The photograph on the story's opening page was a black-and-white image that showed a temple being demolished. The picture was a bit fuzzy, but nevertheless chilling. Amidst rubble and dust, the temple's tip had just begun to tilt. A man stood on the top, balanced like a monkey. I was immediately reminded of the demolition of the Babri Mosque in Ayodhya. This destruction must have been carried out in revenge. I flipped the page. There was another picture. This showed the back of a man, in black tank-tops and trousers, running with a tin bucket. Ahead of him was a woman in a pink sari. In her left hand, she carried a red tin. There was smoke and what might have been rubble around them. The caption said, 'Hindu residents of Ranchore Lines attempting to douse the fire in a temple set by a Muslim mob.'

The report itself said nothing about the destruction of temples. There are 2.7 million Hindus in Pakistan and the story was about the deaths of young Hindu women there. The story mentioned a young woman named Mohni who had married a Muslim man. She had declared in court that she had converted to Islam. But soon after that she was divorced. Mohni married another Muslim man from the same neighbourhood as her former husband. It was rumoured that she had been sold by her previous husband's family. This marriage ended too, and Mohni married a third time. Once again, there was talk of money being paid. Six months later, Mohni was dead. Her parents believed that she had been killed. Her husband claimed she had committed suicide.

The report mentioned many cases—'in the last couple of years, at least three dozen girls'—of young Hindu women who had been abducted. They had converted, voluntarily or otherwise, and had married Muslim men. Often, when parents were led to believe that their daughter had eloped with her lover, she had, in fact, 'been abducted and either forcibly married to Muslim men, sold to them, or even murdered'. The report presented as a boxed item one incident: 'In 1988, a Hindu woman, Daya Kumari was kidnapped along with her two young daughters, from her house in Shahi Bazaar. Her spouse lodged an FIR against the abductors, but not only was no action taken against them, Kumari's husband was told that his wife and daughters had converted to Islam and Kumari had married one of her abductors. He was not allowed to meet either his now "ex-wife" or his daughters, on the grounds that she was now "na-mehram" as far as they were concerned.' The un-named 'they' suddenly appeared to my mind as the people around me: and I became, in my own mind, identifiable only as a Hindu.

'They' were the entire nation that surrounded me and regarded me as the enemy who had no place in this land. I thought of the men I had seen at Karachi aiport. They were dressed in shalwar-kameez like ordinary Pakistani men but folded their hands in the Hindu greeting. They said 'namaste' to each other. They had been maybe five or six of them. That gesture had appeared so foreign in Pakistan in a way that a Muslim greeting never did in India.

Or did it?

That question stopped me. It is true that while reading the *Newsline* report about the treatment of Hindus in Pakistan, I had felt threatened, and more than a little diminished. I had felt this way even though I have never identified myself primarily or only as a Hindu. But, the next moment, my anger had given way to a more uncertain emotion when I thought of the Muslims in India. I was left asking myself, 'Was this how Muslims felt in India?' If not on a day-to-day basis, then maybe during a riot?

*

Mona's grandparents, Nana and Nani, were my hosts in Karachi.

Nana would sit on his sofa all day, drawing incessantly on his pipe. Above his head hung a large poster with the photograph of Einstein. On it were printed the famous scientist's words: 'I want to know God's thoughts ... the rest are details.' I seem to remember that Einstein, mimicking Nana sitting beneath him, also clenched a pipe between his jaws. Nani was not keeping well—she passed away when I was working on this book. But she would be up late into the night, working on a short story in Urdu about two destitute children she had adopted when living in a small frontier town many decades ago.

One evening in Karachi, when I came back to the house, I saw that Nana and Nani had a visitor. The visitor was Nani's elder brother. His name was Khalid Ishaq. I had read about him in Naipaul's *Among the Believers*. I recognized him not from his name but from what was said about his library at the moment we were introduced. Naipaul had written that he hadn't been prepared for the number of books he saw in Ishaq's house: 'Books filled room after room; case upon case, case in front of case; yards and yards of shelves, and cupboards in front of the shelves.' Ishaq had told Naipaul that Islamic institutions served some emotional needs, particularly of equality. The mosque served that role. He had said: 'The servant here brings us tea and sweets. That is his job. But he also knows that on another occasion we can be men together and he can sit with me.'

On the evening that I found them together, Ishaq and Nana were discussing aspects of Islam and the codes of finance and banking approved under the religious edicts. I knew nothing about the subject and stayed silent. Ishaq ignored me. When he had left, Nana said that Ishaq was among the most prominent lawyers in Pakistan. Then, he began telling me about Ishaq's wife who had died of cancer a few months earlier. He said that she was a very affable woman but—and here Nana looked at my face for a moment—she would not let anything from India enter her house. He said, 'If someone gave her a sari that had been made in India, she would return it.' She had suffered during the Partition. Her family had migrated from India. When they were making the journey into Pakistan, I was told, a mob had pulled out her two young brothers from the train and killed them in front of her eyes.

I asked Nana and Nani where they had been during the Partition. They were living in Lucknow in India. On 14 August, the official day of independence for Pakistan, they had put up a Pakistani flag on their house. There was no rioting in Lucknow. Nani had gone out into the market. She had stitched a new purse for herself which was made of green velvet. On that she had embroidered, with silver thread, a crescent and a star. People stopped her and congratulated her. Even Hindus, Nana said, offered her sweets. Only fifty miles away, in Kanpur, there was rioting. Punjab was burning.

Nana was in his early twenties at that time. He had a degree in psychology. He had just got a job as a psychologist in the government prison. Nana had decided that they were going to stay in India, but his resolve didn't last long. Lucknow was calm, but both Nana's and Nani's parents, far away in Pakistan, were very anxious about their safety. Nana said to me that many Muslims, who were nationalists and staying back in India, would joke about Pakistan. There was a professor in Aligarh Muslim University who would say: 'Miyan, you will indeed get a job in Pakistan but the currency that you will receive will say "I shall pay to the bearer rupees five, inshallah, if God wills."'

Nani was stabbed in a train by a Sikh who had wanted her bag. He stepped on her when she resisted and this later on led to chest problems. Nana's father was also attacked. In between these personal details, Nana would offer statements that would be more general in nature and I didn't always know how to interpret them. Nana said, 'Sikhs raped a lot of women. Fear releases the matured egg: the chances of a raped woman getting pregnant is a hundred times higher. I was told this by a man in London.'

A boy who was a former convict and one of Nana's students in his classes in prison took the responsibility of taking their boxes to Pakistan by train. Nana said, 'He was a confirmed criminal but he used to call me his father.' Nana and Nani went to Delhi to see if they could travel on a chartered plane. They left Lucknow secretly, only informing their Hindu neighbour, Mr Chandra. Then, they gave bribes to different Muslim politicians, hoping to get a place on a plane, but they simply pocketed the money and nothing ever came out of it.

There was going be a long wait in Delhi. The couple went to a hotel they knew about but found that it was now in Hindu hands. It was full of refugees who had fled Pakistan. Nani put a bindi on her forehead and they registered as a Hindu couple, Mr and Mrs Kapoor. People thought that Nana and Nani were Hindu refugees who were like so many others who had just arrived in Delhi. But there was always the threat of being found out. People wanted to know what part of Lahore they were from. Any answer that Nana and Nani gave could reveal to the others that they were lying. If they told the truth and mentioned the name of the locality in which they had lived in Lahore the others would immediately suspect that they were Muslims. One day a woman passing in a car saw Nana enter the hotel. Her name was Mrs Raza and she had known Nana in Lucknow. Mrs Raza followed him into the hotel and asked for him at the desk by his real name. Nana and Nani were thrown out of the hotel.

A psychology professor of Nana's, a Hindu whose name was Parshuram, took them to a Methodist minister. The priest was a black man from America who gave them shelter for three days. Nana and Nani were required to say grace at breakfast before eating cornflakes. For lunch and dinner, they ate canned tuna fish. After three days, they were on their own again. Luckily, they found two friends at Delhi's All India Radio. The man was a Muslim, his wife a Hindu. Nana and Nani stayed with them. Here too they continued to eat what the Methodist had given them:

cornflakes and canned tuna. Their hosts were having problems in their marriage. There was no conversation between them. They sat around—the man and his wife— and drank whisky. The tension was unbearable. Nana and Nani felt that they had reached an end. Nana sold a stopwatch and some of Nani's jewellery. He gave the money to a man who was the personal assistant to a Muslim minister in Nehru's cabinet and was able to finally get seats on a plane.

The two of them had waited in Delhi for sixteen difficult days. When they landed in Pakistan, Nana had only Rs 7 with him. His family's house in Lahore had been destroyed, but they were able to find the new quarters where his parents and sisters had moved. The young man from Lucknow had brought their boxes from India; those boxes were all the property they had. The former convict wanted Nani to feel comfortable in her new house. So, he went ahead and stole jewels that belonged to Nana's mother. He brought money to give to Nani, but he had to be fired instead. In the new Pakistan, Nana joined the civil service. Nani was pregnant with her first child when they crossed over into India. A boy was born to them a few months later. That son is now a chief justice and it was his letter that had helped me get a visa to visit Pakistan.

When Nana had finished talking, I began to narrate to him a story I had read about those who did not make their way across the border. This was the remarkable account that Urvashi Butalia, in her book *The Other Side of Silence*, had written of her uncle who had stayed behind in Pakistan when the rest of the family moved to India during the Partition. This uncle was the younger brother of the writer's mother. His name was Rana. He lived in

Lahore and had converted to Islam. Rana had forced his mother to stay behind with him in Pakistan; it was felt in the family that he had done this in order to inherit the house in Lahore that was under the old woman's name. Butalia's grandmother had been a pious Hindu. She too had converted to Islam, or more likely, she had been forced to convert. This was part of the pain of the Partition that had remained in Butalia's family. There had been no contact between the two families for forty years, although there had been rumours, at different times, about the death of Butalia's grandmother. Then, Butalia travelled to Pakistan and went to meet Rana, her uncle, whom she called Ranamama.

When Butalia was in Pakistan, she felt that she had come home. A daughter of refugee parents who had fled during the Partition, she was coming back, for the first time, to the home that her mother had left forever. Rana told his visiting niece that although Lahore was the only home he had known, it was India that he regarded as his home, his country, his land. He had visited India only once. Rana said that he listened to the Indian news everyday. He secretly cheered for the Indian cricket team. Butalia had once asked Rana, after he had been recounting his life to her, why he was telling her all this. Rana had replied, 'My child, this is the first time I am speaking to my own blood.'

Rana also told his niece that he had not 'slept one night in these forty years' without regretting his decision to stay behind in Pakistan. When asked why, he offered this explanation: 'You see, my child, somehow a convert is never forgiven. Your past follows you, it hounds you. For me, it's worse because I've continued to live in the same place. Even today, when I walk out to the market I often hear people whispering "Hindu, Hindu."'

I was telling Nana this story because I found in it a damning intimation of how religious identity frames individuals in fixed ways. These marks become the sum total of anyone's identity during riots. Your neighbour is no longer a person who is a father, or a friend, or a working man with interests that you share. He is suddenly without any history. Or the only history he has is the one that says that he is a Hindu or a Muslim. But this need not happen only during riots. In fact, right-wing political dominance in both India and Pakistan during recent years has meant that ordinary time, the span of days of empty normalcy, is filled with instances that show how social identities are being shrunk to the narrow dimensions mandated by the communal nation-state. With the rise to power in India of the BJP, what is increasingly and often violently evident is the power of a nakedly majoritarian polity. As the writer Mukul Kesavan puts it, 'The BJP *is* a Hindu party, or at least a party that affirms Hindutva, an inclusive ideology which grants Muslims and Christians the right to be Hindus in India.'

Across the border in Pakistan, the mullahs have been asserting a stridently Islamic identity, more Arabic in character than in any way shaped by Islam's long history in the subcontinent. In Lahore, the veteran Pakistani journalist Ahmed Rashid had told me, 'Shared culture is anathema in Pakistan. Nobody wants to hear about it as Pakistan is struggling still to find its own identity and is debating whether it is an Islamic or a modern secular state.' Rashid said that the debate was still being fought but nobody wanted to be reminded that the Pakistanis might share a culture with India. The two sides were united on that. He said, 'Pakistan has over the years tried to root itself in other cultures such as the Arab world after the loss of Bangladesh in the 1970s and in Central Asia in the early 1990s, but that is only avoiding the issue of what is Pakistani culture and what are its roots.' The result was that Pakistanis might watch Indian movies or sample other cultural offerings from India, but this didn't mean that there was going to be any acknowledgement that the two nations share a culture.

In her book, Butalia had written that her mother had gone back to Lahore for a brief visit decades after the Partition. Lahore was the city of her childhood and youth. She found it had changed completely. Butalia had noted down the words her mother had said to her: 'I visited many places I had known well, but nothing was the same: this wonderful cosmopolitan city had now become a Muslim one. Loudspeakers called the Muslims to prayer ... shops, streets, everything was different.' I repeated this to Nana. He listened as I said that the turn towards a more fervent religiosity in both places, India and Pakistan, was accompanied by an assertion of a more purist identity. The antidote to this would be a clear recognition of the ways in which our cultures were syncretic. But Nana would not agree with me. He was a proponent of universalism. He said that a surgeon doesn't think in terms of a Hindu kidney or a Muslim kidney—all human kidneys are the same to him. 'If you examine the question of religion in depth,' he said, 'instead of ideas of mixing, you arrive at a sense of their unity.' And then, perhaps because he thought that I was anxious about my own place in Pakistan, or more likely, as a Hindu in his large Muslim family, he remarked that I could not be considered an outsider because of my faith. He took down from his bookshelf a leather-bound volume which I saw was an English translation of a book called *Gulshan-e-Raz*, or The Mystic Rose Garden. It was composed in AD 1317 by Sa'd ud din Mahmud Shabistari. The verse that Nana wanted me to read was about idols and the charge of infidelity. I am not religious but it is true that the strict followers of Islam would consider me an infidel and a kafir. The lines that Nana was pointing out to me were giving a different kind of benediction. Shabistari had written that both infidelity and faith were manifestations of God and part of a shared universe:

Consider well, O wise man,
An idol as regards its real being is not vain.
Know that God Most High created it,
And whatever comes from the Good is good.

*

I had grown up hearing stories about the violence of the Partition. Stories of conversion were a part of that larger tale of violence. This is what I have believed as a Hindu. No one ever *chose* to convert. It was a choice that was forced upon you. If you were given any choice, it was only the one between choosing Islam and choosing death.

In 1997, in the fiftieth year of the Indian independence, *Outlook* magazine published accounts of what it called the 'sufferers and survivors' of the Partition. One detailed narrative was provided by a Sikh woman, Jeet Behn, who was only a little girl in 1947. She was a part of a large family of Sikhs in a village near Rawalpindi where they had owned farmland and brick kilns. When the riots started, a Muslim neighbour gave them shelter. The door of the room in which the Sikh family was hiding had been barricaded by their host with bags of grain. There were twenty-one people in the family: a grandmother, five girls, six boys, Jeet Behn's parents, her two uncles and their wives, also the son, a doctor, of an elder uncle who had come visiting with his three-year-old boy. A mob of around five hundred came for them the following day. Jeet Behn said, 'They jeered, yelled that if we came out, ate halal meat, converted to Islam, we'd be spared. Father refused, yelling back that we'd prefer to die.'

The roof of the room was made of straw and mud. A part of the roof caved in because someone was trying to get inside. Jeet Behn's father gave each person a kirpan, the small ritual sword worn by the Sikhs, and told them that if the mob broke down the door, they were to stab themselves on the left side of their bodies. Jeet Behn remembers, 'My mother, nursing my three-month-old brother, threw herself at father's feet, saying, "Save this child. Agree to convert." Father ignored her. When she repeated her entreaty my elder uncle got up, slashed her neck with a kirpan yelling, "*Yeh kehna haraam hai*" (This is blasphemy). She died instantly.' After this, her father put his wife's blood-soaked scarf or dupatta on the tip of his sword and ran out of the door into the mob. Knives and swords were plunged into his body. Then it was the turn of Jeet Behn's eldest uncle who rushed out and was similarly cut down. When the doctor cousin got up to fight next, his wife stopped him, saying that he should first kill them. 'He stabbed her, killed his three-year-old son, stabbed each one of us. I still carry that kirpan scar on my scalp ...' Jeet Behn said. He would not kill his mother. He said, 'No dharma tells me to do this.' He was lynched in seconds. The last to leave the room was the old grandmother. This is how Jeet Behn, who was only six years old at the time, recalled the scene: 'She tottered out, frail but resolute, saying, "*Kaisi ladai ladney aaye ho? Mujhe apne bacchon ko ek baar dekhna hai*" (What kind of war is this? Let me at least see my children once). They ripped out her earrings, bangles, gold chain. And as she stood there bleeding, stoned her to death.' Then, before the mob turned away, leaving Jeet Behn behind for dead, the mob slaughtered the Muslim man who had given the Sikhs shelter.

About a decade earlier, the broadcast of the television mini-series *Tamas*, based on the novel of the same name by Bhisham Sahni, had made Indian as well as Pakistani viewers familiar with the story of the ninety Sikh women of Thoa Khalsa. These were the women from a village near Rawalpindi, who had jumped into a well to die and thereby preserve their religion and their honour. Feminist scholars like Urvashi Butalia, Ritu Menon and Kamla Bhasin have collected oral testimonies of survivors, both men and women, and each of these testimonies lead to troubling questions. The women who were abducted have been lost to history, their stories drowned in silence; and those women who were killed by their own families have become symbols of sacrifice and their deaths turned into tales of martyrdom. But, what would have happened if the women had not been sacrificed? Butalia answers that question, 'In all likelihood, they would have been raped, perhaps abducted and further violated, and almost certainly converted. All of these were tantamount to death.' This was the logic of the men. But if that was not troubling enough, what made such reasoning even more compromised was that women were considered dispensable. According to Butalia, 'In many villages where negotiations had taken place, often women were traded in for freedom.' The point is not simply to say that the women were mere victims of the men in their own families in places like Thoa Khalsa, but to see that, as Butalia puts it, 'the lines between choice and coercion must have been more blurred than these accounts reflect'.

These lines remained blurred even in the cases of women who were abducted and forced to convert. As many as 75,000 women are said to have been raped and abducted on both sides of the border during the Partition. When families began reporting missing women to the police, the task of preparing a list of such women was assigned to the Edwina Mountbatten's United Council for Relief and Welfare. The sheer enormity of the number of missing women made it necessary for the prime ministers of both India and Pakistan to meet in Lahore in September 1947. A joint declaration was issued at that time: 'Both the Central Governments and the Governments of East and West Punjab wish to make it clear that forced conversions and marriages will not be recognized. Further, that women and girls who have been abducted must be restored to their families, and every effort must be made by the Governments and their officers concerned to trace and recover such women and girls.' A few months later, in December, the Inter-Dominion Treaty was signed which expressed agreement between the two countries regarding the steps to be taken for recovery of abducted women. Still later, in December 1949, the Abducted Persons (Recovery and Restoration) Bill was passed. But, as Butalia points out, the affected women themselves were not allowed to exercise any option. A Muslim woman who had been rescued in India would be sent to Pakistan. And a Hindu woman found in Pakistan would automatically be brought across the border to India. As the riots in Punjab had started in March, it had also been decided that any women seen in the company of a man from another religion after 1 March 1947 would be presumed to have been abducted. To quote Butalia again, 'No matter what the woman said, how much she protested, no matter that there was the odd "real" relationship, the women had no choice in the matter.'

The truth was that in many cases women protested and refused to go back. They had entered into relationships with their abductors or with the men who had bought them at a price. Mridula Sarabhai, an Indian social worker who played an important role in the recovery operation, was told by a young woman whom she had gone to bring back from Pakistan:

You say abduction is immoral and you are trying to save us. Well, now it is too late. One marries only once—willingly or by force. We are now married—what are you going to do with us? Ask us to get married again? Is that not immoral? What happened to our relatives when we were abducted? Where were they? ... You may do your worst if you insist, but remember, you can kill us, but we will not go.

Another social worker, Krishna Thapar, who had been assisting in recovering abducted women was asked by the twenty-one Muslim women she was taking back to

Pakistan, 'Why are you destroying our lives?' Thapar told Ritu Menon and Kamla Bhasin that those young women had been living with Sikh men and were happy. The women were taken to Pakistan against their will because the law required it. The social worker reported that the women kept shouting at her, 'Who are you to meddle in our lives? We don't know you, what business is it of yours?'

Over almost ten years after the Partition, about 30,000 women were recovered from both countries. The total number of Muslim women recovered from India was 20,728 and the number of Hindu and Sikh women brought from the other side was 9,032. If there was resistance on the part of the abducted women to return to their former homes, it wasn't only because some of them had settled into a new life. In many cases, there was fear of rejection, and it was not unfounded. In India, the emphasis on purity and the fear of pollution meant that many Hindus were unwilling to take back their daughters and wives who had been with Muslim men. Kamlaben Patel, who had worked in the relief camps for women, told Menon and Bhasin:

A Hindu woman felt that she had been made impure, had become sullied, was no longer a *pativrata*. A Muslim woman did not feel like this. It was not in her blood, it is in our blood. We feel we have been polluted, we are no longer worthy of showing our faces in public. How can we face our families now when we go back? We would reassure the woman saying, 'See how many times your father has come to fetch you.' Even then they would feel ashamed of themselves because this tradition is so deeply ingrained in us. And Muslim women were not stigmatized by society.

Prime Minister Nehru made a public appeal through newspapers in January 1948, saying that he found 'most objectionable' the behaviour of those who did not accept in their homes their abducted relatives. He said that 'these girls and women require our tender and loving care'. Mahatma Gandhi made a similar plea: 'I hear women have this objection that the Hindus are not willing to accept back the recovered women because they say that they have become impure. I feel this is a matter of great shame.'

*

The most celebrated story about abduction in the literature of the Partition is 'Lajwanti' by the Urdu writer Rajinder Singh Bedi. In the story, the people of the Mohalla Shakoor locality elect the social worker Babu Sunderlal as the secretary of the committee which would work for the rehabilitation of the women who had been abducted and raped. Sunderlal wins by a majority of eleven votes because his own wife Lajo—Lajwanti—has been taken away.

Lajo was a 'slender, naïve, village girl; she was supple, tender and fresh, like a young mulberry bush'. Nonetheless, she could lift heavy loads and do hard work. She even tolerated the beatings that Sunderlal gave her. Now she is gone and Sunderlal joins the processions in the morning through the city streets, the chorus chanting 'Honour them, give them a place in your hearts.' Some people are irritated by all this, but the campaigning has its effect, and some of the families of the locality agree to take back their women who are brought in trucks. Sunderlal and his comrades shout slogans 'Long Live ...' till their voices turn hoarse—

because there are always some women whose husbands or brothers or parents refuse to even recognize them.

Lajo is not among those brought back by the social workers. Sunderlal throws himself back in his work, speaking and pleading with everyone who will listen. He gets involved in arguments, trying to tell people that the women who were abducted are innocent and any society which questions them or refuses to accept them is morally corrupt. Sunderlal joins the morning procession and sings with zeal but also a great deal of pain in his heart.

Then, Lajo returns. She is part of a group of women who are exchanged at the border by both sides. Lajo is afraid because Sunderlal had always mistreated her, and now, since she has been with another man, she does not know how he will react to her arrival. Her appearance surprises Sunderlal. He had expected her to look thin and wilted, but she looks brighter than before and has even put on some weight. He wonders if she has been forced to return by the Indian government.

The story's writer is at pains to tell the reader about the ways in which Lajo has missed Sunderlal and how he fails to read the signs of pain and humiliation on her face. The brightness of her look is only the result of a fever. Sunderlal takes Lajo's hand and brings her home. He does this despite the fact that there are people who say things like 'We don't want these sluts ... they were defiled by Muslims.' Sunderlal is ecstatic that his wife has returned. However, he no longer calls her Lajo. He thinks of her as a goddess, and accordingly calls her 'Devi'. He does not beat her any more.

That is the gist of the story. Sunderlal doesn't allow Lajo to tell him much about how she has suffered. She feels weighed down by what remains unshared and it also fills her with apprehension. Lajo realizes that she will never be Lajo again. Her husband does not divide the burden of her pain. He only wakes up early to join the procession in which he sings for the sake of the women who have been abducted.

The story is very moving in its details and also sharp in its delineation of the inability on the part of men to deal with women's sexuality. Sunderlal, for all his humanity, is like the men who took Lajo away. He is not at ease with her sexuality and can deal with what he experiences as her violation only by turning her into a goddess. When we read that Sunderlal 'made her feel as if she was something precious and fragile like glass, that she would shatter at the slightest touch', we also know that there is no sex between the couple any more. The trauma of sexual violence has given way to the alienating distance of sexual sublimation.

While I like Bedi's reading of sexuality, I find his story intriguing for its absence of any anxiety about conversion. At only one point in the story is there the faintest hint that abductions were also most often accompanied by religious conversions, but even this might be my own attribution, in the scene in which the writer describes Lajo's return as witnessed through Sunderlal's eyes: 'Her head was covered with a red dupatta like a typical Muslim woman, and one end of it was thrown over her left shoulder ... . She was in no condition to think about the basic differences between Hindu and Muslim culture or worry whether her dupatta had to be thrown over her left or her right shoulder.' Perhaps Bedi is only making the point that the real difference between Hindu and Muslim culture might be as simple as whether an innocent girl tosses the end of her scarf over the left or the right shoulder. It is equally plausible, however, that by paying attention only to sexuality and not to religion, Bedi was making the stronger ideological point that in the context of the new nationalist politics, both were interchangeable. Hindu women could only be with Hindu men: this basic identity secured for an emergent nation a sense of legitimacy. Without boundaries at all levels to demarcate difference there would be no nation.

But was this need felt only with the coming to being of a fragmented nation which had a large population of displaced refugees? Commenting on the recovery of women, Menon and Bhasin write that even in the mid-nineteenth century, the birth and consolidation of the Arya Samaj and the formation of a Punjabi Hindu consciousness betrayed a nervous concern over 'Muslim and Christian inroads into Hinduness, and the erosion of Hindu dharma, values and lifestyle through steady conversion to those two faiths by Hindus'. The formation of Pakistan, accompanied by what was seen as territorial loss, could have only heightened this anxiety. The task of recovering abducted women was 'a symbolically significant activity'. The exercise afforded the consolation that conversion was not irreversible. As Menon and Bhasin put it, 'it would seem that the only answer to forcible conversion was—forcible recovery'. Like the contemporary efforts to recover sacred Hindu sites, it was an attempt to proclaim that it was possible to restore history to an imagined wholeness.

The reality can be different. As a result of the violence and dislocations that resulted from the Partition, there are now people on both sides of the border who are related by blood but who do not share a nation or a religion. The newsmagazine, *India Today*, went in search of such families during India's fiftieth anniversary in 1997. A brother and sister that they located were brought to meet each other for the first time since 1947. The seventy-five-year-old, Shamli Bai, a Hindu from Rajpura, held her brother, younger by four years, for a few minutes at the Wagah border. His name had changed from Punnu to Sheikh Imam Buksh, of Maouza Kot Khalifa in Pakistan. When they were separated after their ten-minute meeting by the border guards, Imam Buksh said to Shamli Bai, 'Sister, destiny separated us, but the Almighty has united us.' His sister told the reporter, 'He is the same Punnu I had left behind fifty years ago. So what if he is a Muslim now? It has not changed his blood.'

The reality of such divided—and shared—lives challenges the assertions of fundamentalists in both India and Pakistan. And it is remarkable that in such stories religion does not come up as an issue between the people. I find that fact even more moving than the obvious love and pain that is bared by these accounts of reunions.

In 'Pali', Bhisham Sahni's marvellous short story, one reads of a boy Pali who is accidentally abandoned by his Hindu parents and adopted by a childless Muslim couple. A search party from India finds him. Years have passed in between. Two sets of parents love the boy—that is not the boy's tragedy, however. His real tragedy is that those who are in a position of religious as well as bureaucratic authority in both India and Pakistan want him to choose between his two identities. The *maulvi* in Pakistan had seen to it that Pali was circumcised and that he recited the qalma; in India, under a pundit's gaze, his head is shaved and a *hawan* is lit to purify him. When the story ends, the boy is supposed to have come home; away, in a village in Pakistan, a woman wipes her tears again and again.

*

My own story took one more turn two years after my marriage in Canada. I got married again in India. This time Mona and I went to Patna and we were bride and groom in a Hindu ceremony that was organized on the small lawn outside my parents' home. A priest chanted the proper shlokas in Sanskrit. The sacred fire was burning, spreading the smell of sandalwood and ghee. The two of us walked around the fire seven times while the guests assembled there tossed flowers in our direction. Mona had never seen a Hindu wedding before, except in Bollywood films and Attenborough's *Gandhi*. She enjoyed the ceremony very much. I had wanted to please my parents. We had had a Muslim nikaah, it was considered right that we have a Hindu shaadi.

The traditional way of holding inter-religious marriages— and even the inter-caste ones when there is opposition from the families of those getting married—is to have them solemnized in court. Many decades ago, back in 1942, Jawaharlal Nehru's daughter Indira wanted to marry Feroze Gandhi. As Gandhi was a Parsi, or a man of Zoroastrian faith, there was a great controversy. According to a biographer of Nehru, M.J. Akbar, the future prime minister of India was 'certain that Hindu chauvinists would pounce upon this inter-religious marriage as a "betrayal" of Hinduism'. Nehru was averse to 'alienating himself from Hindu sentiment so sharply. Yet, his conscience would not allow him to forbid the marriage'. Although Akbar does not mention it, there were rumours in some quarters that Feroze Gandhi was a Muslim, a rumour that persists in right-wing Hindu circles today. On 26 February 1942, Nehru issued a statement to the press about his daughter's engagement. The details of the press release appeared the next day. (This announcement shared space with news of Japanese advances in the war and the anticipation that Churchill was to break his silence on India; in Delhi, *Gone with the Wind* was playing in Regal Theatre and *Jhoola*, starring Ashok Kumar and Leela Chitnis, was to be released the next day.) 'A marriage is a personal and domestic matter affecting chiefly the two parties concerned,' the statement began. Then, Nehru went on to say, 'Feroze Gandhi is a young Parsi who has been a friend and colleague of ours for many years, and I expect him to serve our country and our cause efficiently and well. But on whomsoever my daughter's choice would have fallen, I would have accepted it or been false to the principles I have held.' Nehru also mentioned that Mahatma Gandhi had blessed the proposal. Akbar writes, 'Yet it was not as principled as all that. The ceremony was not under the civil act but through Vedic rites—for which purpose Feroze had to go through the process of becoming a Hindu. A concession was made to the hate-mail ... .'

In Vikram Seth's well-known novel *A Suitable Boy*, which is set in the 1950s, the protagonist Lata falls in love with a young man whose name is Kabir. Unlike Lata, Kabir is a Muslim. When Lata's mother, Mrs Rupa Mehra learns through someone that Lata has been going for walks with a male friend, her mother demands to know his name. Lata tells her that his name is Kabir. Mrs Mehra doesn't realize—in the same way that Lata first hadn't—that Kabir is a Muslim. She asks, 'He has a name, doesn't he? What is he—Kabir Lal, Kabir Mehra—or what?' Lata closes her eyes and offers the Muslim last name, 'Kabir Durrani.' Seth writes, 'The three deadly syllables had their effect. Mrs Rupa Mehra clutched at her heart, opened her mouth in silent horror, looked unseeingly around the room, and sat down.' When she is able to collect herself, the mother says, 'A Muslim! What did I do in my past life that I have brought this upon my beloved daughter?' Lata had begun to feel 'alarmed and miserable' even before the conversation had started. Not too long after, she breaks off her relationship with Kabir.

Seth tells his readers that 'Mrs Rupa Mehra was not more prejudiced against Muslims than most upper-caste Hindu women of her age and background.' This only raises the question: how common were marriages between Hindus and Muslims at that time? When I was growing up, I knew of no such couples. That might have been indicative of a less open time as well as my own closed social setting. Today, I know of at least a dozen such cases where a Hindu is married to a Muslim. There must be many, many more. Charu Gupta, in her study of colonial Uttar Pradesh, the same region in which A Suitable Boy is set, finds 'elements of defiant love and sexual pleasure in the face of a culture that continually sought to restrict them. Elopements and conversions hint at love and romance'. Gupta writes that particularly 'in a communally charged atmosphere, when abductions and the maligning of the Muslim male acquired importance', inter-religious alliances could be seen as attempts to establish a different world.

Women in the earlier part of the twentieth century were increasingly stepping out into the public sphere. The national movement as well as the world of print culture offered a new sphere of activity for them. For men and women to enter into relationships that were transgressive was a part of this emergent picture. Yet, faced with the threat of these changes, it was also easy for patriarchal chauvinism to try to seek reactionary coalitions. According to Gupta, 'anxieties about alliances between lower-caste Hindu women and Muslims could be used to win lower-caste men to the cause of Hindu unity'. This meant that those who stepped outside the fold faced condemnation and exile. This situation altered in later decades, but still held considerable power, especially over young women who had few resources of their own. When Kabir asks Lata why she can't be with him, she replies, 'Because of my family. However much they irritate me and constrain me, I can't give them up. I know that now. So much has happened. I can't give up my mother—.' Another way to put this is that Lata cannot have her mother giving up on her. She ends up marrying a suitable boy, someone who is from her own Hindu Khatri community.

We begin to see that behind the accusations against Muslims wanting to forcibly convert Hindus is a different kind of coercion. This is the coercion of the Hindu community that fears the taint of pollution. As Seth writes in his novel, 'The more Mrs Rupa Mehra thought, the more agitated she became. Even marrying a non-Khatri Hindu was bad enough. But this was unspeakable. It was one thing to mix socially with Muslims, entirely another to dream of polluting one's blood and sacrificing one's daughter.'

The cultural studies scholar Gauri Viswanathan, commenting on the appendix to the 1901 Census that lists individual cases of conversion in Bengal, writes that though 'romance is presented as the main motive for conversion, the play of human desires and feelings has no place here'. In the enumerated instances of mixed marriages between Hindus and Muslims, Viswanathan only finds 'examples of exile, excommunication, and existential isolation, as marital union is achieved only by conversion of one partner to the religion of the other'. This is a strong but persuasive reading of inter-religious marriages. Let's imagine for a moment that Lata would have converted and married Kabir. According to Viswanathan, the potential for this marriage to serve as 'a model of cultural syncretism' would not last because it would be unable to challenge 'the irreversible loss of community caused by romantic attachments'. Based on her reading of the latent plot lines described in the Census, Viswanathan's claim is that it is not the impulse of desire that prompts Hindus to convert to the religion of their spouses but, instead, the more depressing fact that they lose their place in their home community because of their romantic choices. The criminal here is caste. To quote Viswanathan, 'the real cause of conversion still continues to be a condition that is built into Hinduism: namely, its ability to turn caste members into outcastes through mere contact with non-Hindus'.

Conversion can be seen differently, not as violence but as movement and fluidity. This is Viswanathan's larger argument. B.R. Ambedkar, the great political leader of the untouchables or Dalits in India and the architect of the Indian constitution, converted to Buddhism in 1956. In Ambedkar's case, conversion was a break away from the inhumane hierarchical structure of Hinduism and, equally important, a step towards what Viswanathan calls 'the construction of a moral community'. In the decades that followed, the impulse present in Ambedkar's move resurfaced in the Dalit community and sparked controversy, most strikingly when hundreds of villagers in Meenakshipuram in southern India converted to Islam in 1981. Extremist organizations like the VHP have, in recent years, whipped-up the rhetoric of Hindusim being under attack by saying that Muslims and Christian minorities have been trying to convert poor Hindus. Beginning in 1998, many churches were attacked and razed to the ground. In response, the Indian Prime Minister, Atal Behari Vajpayee called for a 'national debate on conversion'. The following year there were attacks on nuns in Haryana, Madhya Pradesh, Rajasthan and Gujarat. Early the same year, an Australian priest was burnt in his car along with his two young sons. It is impossible to say whether Prime Minister Vajpayee's call actually signalled the government's desire for such attacks, but it has certainly legitimated a wider, and often violent, questioning of the presence of Christians and other minorities in India.

Most recently, the state of Tamil Nadu passed a law banning religious conversions 'by force, allurement or fraudulent means'. This cannot by itself be considered bad—except that, in the past, any conversion has been seen as a forcible one. In the case of the Dalits of Meenakshipuram who converted to Islam, groups like the VHP and the RSS were quick to charge that the conversions had been forced, that money from the Gulf had played a big role in it, and that Islamic groups had duped the Dalits with cash. One of the journalists who critiqued the myths around conversion was P. Sainath. In Sainath's reports, one learned that it was not cash but caste that had forced the Dalits to convert. The Dalits of Meenakshipuram were fed-up of oppression. One man in that village, when asked by the journalist whether the offer of money had lured the Dalits away from Hinduism, said: 'Nonsense! Money played no role. I did not convert, so I can say so easily. Two sisters of mine converted. What money? I would know. Even my grandparents had once thought of conversion. Oppression alone was the reason.' Others who had converted spoke of the humiliation of the 'two-glass system' in the tea-shops and the harassment at the hands of the police and the landlords. Conversion was a step towards gaining self-respect.

Indeed, as Sainath reported, the villagers saw immediate results. One young villager, who later reconverted to Hinduism because of his father's wishes, spoke about his experience after the conversion to Islam: 'Nobody worried about us when we were miserable within Hinduism. No one protested when we suffered untouchability. But once the conversions took place, they were all worried about us. The RSS and others came running then.' The villagers also gained a new bargaining power with the administration. There had been no roads or tap water in the village. But, following the conversion and the attention it attracted, the government officials began to offer the Dalits what they had needed for so long. In this context, the charge that the villagers were duped by outsiders with foreign money infuriated the villagers because it presented them as ciphers and put them back in the same position in the social hierarchy where they had been exploited for centuries.

Would the converts like the ones that Sainath had met in Meenakshipuram not also have a sense of multiple identities? After all, there were now in that village where families had some members who were Muslim and others Hindu. There was even inter-marriage between them. I remembered Intizar Husain whose sentiment I had liked so much: 'I am a Muslim, but I always feel that there is a Hindu sitting inside me ... I still feel that I am an exile who wanders between Karbala and Ayodhya.' When I repeated these lines to Sainath, he was not as taken by them as I was. He did not believe that every Indian would say that there was a Hindu inside them. 'I do notice that a few elite Muslims do say things like this now and then,' he said, and added, 'If you asked the neo-Buddhists, for instance, if there is a Hindu within them, you'd receive a very, very different reply. Possibly a violent one.'

Sainath was also approaching my questions from the viewpoint of those who were rejecting a religion because of what they had found oppressive in it. I understood this point. He clearly saw that conversion for such individuals came as a dramatic release and a restorer of dignity. One could not expect such converts to be very happy to declare their love for both Ayodhya and Karbala. But, as a concession to the viewpoint from which I was coming, Sainath said, 'If, however, you're talking about gentle, complex symbiotic relationships between people of different faiths, unusual commonalities, sure, those are present. Look at the tragedy of the *gurbani* singers in the Sikh gurudwaras at the time of the Partition. How many know that these people were Muslims, several of them from families which played that role in a hereditary way. There's a beautiful side to the whole thing.'

The real ugliness, Sainath said, was that the cancer of caste afflicted people of all faiths in India—Hinduism, Christianity, Islam, Sikhism, and even Zoroastrianism. Conversion was a way out, but not for too long. 'Changing one's religion is a very, very difficult thing to do,' Sainath said. 'It's the very last thing they discard. So when they do so, it is entirely in anguish and disgust. When they can simply no longer bear the oppression of caste.' This remark made me think of what had happened less than ten days prior to my exchange with Sainath. A BJP leader in central India by the name of Dilip Singh Judeo had reconverted more than 2000 Christian adivasis or aboriginals to the Hindu faith. In a giant stadium, in the presence of the press, and in front of twenty-five hawans with sacred fire burning in them for purification, Judeo had passed out a nylon sari or a cotton dhoti to each reconvert as a mark of a symbolic shedding of the old garb of Christianity. The entire cynical exercise, it was very clear, paid no heed to the reality of caste inequality. There was a question for me there. What were the chances of my having married, instead of a well-educated, upper-middle-class Muslim, a poor Dalit?

7

In Bad Faith

In the days following the September 11 attacks, I would read the newspaper every day, looking for stories. On 3 October, there was a report that several children in a school in Brooklyn had falsely claimed that their fathers had died in the Twin Towers. The children had done this, the newspaper said, 'in a muddled attempt to identify with classmates who actually had lost parents'.

A few days later, I was sitting in a meeting at my university, a sheet of paper in my hand. The sheet that I held had a glossary of terms printed on it. Item number 23 read: 'Muslim [MOOS-lim]: A follower of Islam. One who submits to God's will.' There were other terms on that list, words like 'Hajj', 'Hijab', and 'Jihad'. Students sat on either side of me. A white American woman wearing a headscarf—I later learned that she was a professor at the university; she had converted when she married a Muslim man, an immigrant from Egypt—was addressing us. Professor Kuhn spoke with great zeal of the ways in which her religion represented love, and compassion, and peace. She said that she doubted if the hijackers on September 11 had really been Muslims; after all, they had consumed alcohol and paid lap-dancers in a Florida bar.

With her face wrapped in a stern, mid-western sanctimony, Professor Kuhn was trying to convey a sense of injury. Her voice sounded, by turn, indignant and hurt. The crude glossary had been discarded. What we now saw was that the concerns around September 11 were being reduced to the idea that our speaker had of her own victimhood. Muslims the world over, she said, were being seen as terrorists. In America too, ordinary Muslims going about their daily business had been assaulted. The professor had herself received an e-mail message that was filled with hate, and she feared for her own and her children's safety.

It was of course right to protest attacks by bigots. And it was also necessary to raise our voices against the bristling national-state machinery which had declared its intent to curb civil rights, and, in its more imperial guise, drop bombs on innocent people. I am sure that most people in the audience that day, including me, had gathered for that very purpose. But in what was being said there was no acknowledgment of the plain shock of what had happened and how disturbing and depressing it all was. Instead, we were getting a little dose of identity politics. Like all those who had wrongly reduced Islam to a religion of terror— and its followers to a horde of suicide bombers—Professor Kuhn was erasing all complexity of experience from the faith she was seeking to defend. In her story of Islam, there were no contradictions, no traditions of internal dissent, no real history, no ugliness, and therefore, also no beauty. There were no people in Islam, there was only Professor Kuhn. Even worse was her audience. Like the children in the Brooklyn school, identifying with their aggrieved classmates, it wanted to be one with the wronged

Muslim, that vast, faceless collective subject now presented as Number 23 on our glossary list.

Who is a Muslim?

The terrible events of September 11 had made it necessary for Americans to ask this question. The logic of that questioning meant, however, that answers were already in place—and rarely were these answers provided by Muslims themselves. On those rare occasions when we saw the Muslims on our television screens, especially Muslims from other countries of the world, their responses were predetermined by what had happened on that September morning. It was as if the Muslims of the world were being asked to explain the sum total of their lives and their daily realities in relation to that singular event. (Often, even this chance was not given to them. The mother of a young woman who had died at the World Trade Centre, when asked to speak about Muslims in an HBO documentary, said, 'I want them tortured ... men, women, children.' It was impossible not to feel immense sadness for everyone concerned.) When they appeared on our screens, Muslims were being put in the absurd position of having to either condemn or celebrate that overwhelming occurrence: the fact of two jets, carrying passengers and loaded with fuel, crashing into buildings filled with people. To be a Muslim was to simply serve as the explanation for why what happened had happened.

Several weeks after September 11, I was on a visit to Pakistan. One evening, I was in Lahore, on my way to a dinner. The car belonged to a friend of mine who is a well-known editor and journalist. I was being driven through a crowded street, and I began to look at the row of road-side flower-shops. The vendors had arranged roses, lilies and marigolds under the light of bright, naked bulbs. Currency notes of various denominations were woven into the fat garlands of tuberoses that hung from bamboo poles. There were dainty bracelets, made from small chameli blossoms, for guests to wear during weddings that were under way that night all over the city.

Earlier in the evening, I had made my first contact with a leader of the fundamentalist jihadi group that, a few weeks later, was responsible for the kidnapping and then the murder of the American journalist Daniel Pearl. I had given the man my name—which would have revealed to him that I was an Indian and a Hindu—but I wasn't worried about it much. I had told myself that the 'fundoos' would not harm a journalist. As the hours passed, there were more calls and cellphone numbers exchanged, and a little before midnight, anticlimactically, the meeting was cancelled.

If I remember that evening, it is for something more ordinary that happened as I was sitting in the car looking at the flowers outside. My host's driver Qasim—a slight man, in his late twenties, with a thin moustache—quietly asked me where it is that I was visiting from. I told him that I was a writer living in the US. He turned his face to me and said in Urdu, 'The Americans are the true Muslims.' I did not understand this. The attacks in New York and Washington DC were still fresh in everyone's minds. I had also seen the images from the streets of Lahore and the rest of Pakistan, of bearded men shouting slogans in support of the Taliban. Qasim said, 'The Americans have read and really understood the message of the *Qur'an*.' I was baffled. But Qasim explained his point to me. He said, '*Woh log apne mulaazimo ke saath*

sahi salook karte hain. Woh unko overtime dete hain'
(The Americans treat their workers in the right way. They
pay them overtime).

Ah, overtime! Fair wages, just working conditions, true
democracy. There was little place on American television
in all that talk about terrorism for this plain man's sublime
understanding of his religion. Or for his deeply human
and compassionate sense of the goodness of the American
people. In fact, here was the proper antidote to Professor
Kuhn. Islam in Pakistan had not freed Qasim, and he
wanted his minimum wage! As far as Qasim was concerned,
it was others in his own country, his fellow Muslims, who
were the oppressors. On the other hand, the fair-minded
employers of the poor in America, such as they were,
when they died, were going to be gathered in the arms of
the angels and wafted to heaven.

Qasim's view of the world and religion could be
considered simple-minded and wrong. But, I believe that
his judgement is no more misplaced than the generalizations
about opposed civilizations made by the pundits and
politicians in the aftermath of September 11. Indeed,
Qasim's tale had conveyed something else to me. Religion
was not much more than the stories you told yourself
about the world, and Qasim's account was interesting
because it had surprised me. His story was surprising—
although not in a way that the hate of the hijackers had
been to so many—and this gave it significance. It spoke to
me of the need to listen to the stories that people tell
about themselves and how they imagine their place in this
world.

*

Who is a Hindu?

This question would not have occurred to me in my childhood. Hinduism was simply the faith of my ancestors and my parents. Till I was well into my teens I prayed to Hindu gods and goddesses. Even when I felt faith dropping away from me, and I was left only with the encumbrance of minor superstitions and doubts, I still didn't have any reason to ask the question I have posed above. There were more important questions to be addressed. When I was in college, the world of secular struggles opened in front of me, and the personal drama of faith did not possess its hold any more. It had become important for me to name injustice in the society around me as evil, not my tiny little contracts with my personal gods about whether I could resist temptation or not. There was another gift that the end of adolescence brought me. I saw that those who prayed seemed mostly to be in need of things—a job, a groom for their daughter, a licence to sell cooking gas, a safe journey—and I had decided after a lot of vain striving that I needed nothing. For several years, while I remained in college, I became an austere drop-out resigned to inevitable failure. I saw that those relatives of mine who were the most venal were also the most diligent in offering their prayers and making religious sacrifices. A corrupt uncle often had a priest staying at his house on a semi-permanent basis. I found it enormously liberating to turn my back on this world of cravenness and hypocrisy. At yet, even for me, my identity as a Hindu was assumed as a given, like my name, and it remained so despite my rejection.

But, no longer. The rise of the vicious right-wing Hindutva ideology to a position of dominance has meant that a very particular definition of Hinduness is being foisted on me. I am told that if I do not agree with the agenda of the rulers I am outside the fold. It is almost as if I am not even offered the choice to protest and say no. To make it worse, I feel that I cannot speak loudly *as a Hindu* because I have not, after all, even visited a temple for a long time. I remember that I had taken to sitting by myself in the car outside, prepared to wait for my parents when they would stop at a neighbourhood temple in Patna. Thugs have entered the temple now and driven everyone else out. All I am allowed to do, it seems, is turn my face away and quietly leave.

This realization did not come slowly to me. It arrived as a shock on 6 December 1992 when I first heard that a mob of Hindu karsevaks had demolished the Babri mosque in Ayodhya. That day I learned that Hinduism had already been defined for me and without seeking my consent. I had been defeated and I had not even made my move yet.

The destroyed mosque had been built in 1528 by Mir Baqi under the orders of India's first Mughal emperor, Babar. The Hindutva leaders claimed that the mosque had been erected after destroying a temple that had stood there to consecrate the place where the mythical Hindu god Ram had been born. This conflict was not a new one. According to Richard H. Davis, back in 1855, a group of Sunni Muslims had attacked the Hanuman Temple close to the site where the mosque had formerly stood. The Hindu ascetics who occupied the temple repulsed their assailants. During the revolt of 1857, the priest of the Hanuman Temple took over a part of the mosque compound and erected there a raised platform which, he claimed, marked the birthplace of Lord Ram. In the 1880s, a Hindu priest demanded that a temple be built over the platform but the British authorities turned down this request. There were no rival disputes for the next fifty years. In 1934, there were Hindu-Muslim riots in the area, and the mosque's dome was damaged. However, the government quickly repaired it. Then, two years after India got its independence, the Babri mosque was broken into at night. This was in late December 1949. The intruders placed the idol of an infant Lord Ram inside the mosque. This development was regarded as a miracle by the Hindus, and as act of sacrilege by the Muslims.

The next day, thousands of Hindu devotees came to Ayodhya, drawn by the news of the appearance of Ram, chanting religious songs and raising religious slogans. The government official who was directed to remove the idols from the temple did not do so. The reason for this lay in the fact that the official's wife had organized an *akhand kirtan*, an uninterrupted recitation of prayers and religious songs, which made it impossible for any such move to be undertaken. The official himself had his strong ideological reasons for inaction. He was to later join the Jan Sangh, the precursor to the present-day BJP, and become a member of the state legislative body and later also win a seat in the national Parliament. Leaders like Nehru and Patel were able to check the spread of further troubles over this demand, but in 1950, a court order allowed the Ram idol to remain inside the mosque. Neither of the two communities could effectively use it as a place of worship.

The Babri mosque returned to the national stage several decades later in the 1980s. In 1984, the VHP adopted a resolution demanding what it called a liberation of the Ram birthplace in Ayodhya. In the summer of that year, the VHP established its militant wing, Bajrang Dal, a group which was to play a decisive role in the mosque's destruction in 1992. I was a graduate student in America when the Ramjanambhoomi movement for a temple to be built over the Babri mosque had gathered force. In 1989, I read in the newspapers that the Sangha Parivar had begun a campaign to collect a small amount, Rs 1.25, from each family in a door-to-door campaign. Bricks with the name of Ram inscribed on them—the bricks were called *Ram shilas*—were carried in processions and consecrated at public pujas. Bricks made of precious materials, including gold, were also donated by rich Hindus living abroad. The sacred bricks were going to be used to build the temple at the site of the mosque that had not yet been brought down. This was a massive mobilization campaign through which anyone who had contributed to the construction of the temple was also being inducted as a partisan in the army of Hindutva. The BJP-VHP combine was preparing its grassroots support-base as well as its electoral vote-bank. There were riots in many parts of India as the processions with the *Ram shilas* passed through the cities and the countryside. In Bhagalpur, only a few hours from my hometown, more than thousand people, mostly Muslims, died after one such procession came to town. I would get to witness the havoc, which the riots had caused in Bhagalpur, when I went there some months later, during my summer break, to write an article for a newspaper. The broken homes in the small villages which were miles away from Bhagalpur, away from the urban centres which had been the traditional space for Hindu-Muslim violence in India, stood as evidence of the murderous success of the Hindutva campaign.

That same summer, the then prime minister, V.P. Singh of the Janata Dal, who was in a multi-party coalition with the BJP and the Communist Party, announced that he would implement the recommendations of the Mandal Commission. The Commission had proposed that 27 per cent of all jobs in the Central government as well as public corporations be reserved for those belonging to what are called Other Backward Castes. Singh had sought to undercut the growing base of the BJP-VHP by alienating the upper caste Hindus from the lower castes which formed the vast majority of the Indian population. In response to this populist move, the Hindutva leaders took the initiative back by having one of their senior leaders, L.K. Advani, undertake a rath yatra. The rath or chariot, designed to resemble the chariots driven by warriors in the Hindu epics, was actually a DCM-Toyota van. It was decorated with the Hindu Om and a profusion of lotuses with eight petals, the electoral symbol of the BJP. Advani was accompanied by young men dressed to resemble the monkey guards who formed a part of the army of the monkey-god, Lord Hanuman, Ram's trusted lieutenant. The chariot-van was fitted with loudspeakers that relayed the speeches of the leaders as well as militant religious songs.

In his book *The Hindu Nationalist Movement in India*, Christopher Jaffrelot writes that 'demonstrations of religious fervor and militancy became mingled'. There were many on the streets of cities and towns who approached the DCM-Toyota chariot as a sacred vehicle with hands folded or holding flowers, incense and coconuts. There were also young men, like those in Jetpur, near Rajkot, who offered Advani a jar of their own blood. Similarly, at Ujjan, the

BJP leader was presented with arms and welcomed by youth who put a tilak of blood on his forehead. The youth, many of whom had been initiated into the Bajrang Dal, were armed with primitive weapons like bows and tridents which are associated with ancient Hindu epics like the Ramayana. In fact, the BJP procession as well as the responses of the public on the streets was overdetermined by the collective experience, in the years leading up to these events, of having watched the national broadcast of Hindu epics on government-owned television. These weekly broadcasts of serialized episodes were watched by billions of devoted fans and this had created what one writer called 'a shared symbolic lexicon around which political forces could mobilize communal praxis'.

It wasn't simply that Lord Ram or his monkey-warriors had become so familiar to the Indian masses; it was more that the BJP propaganda, working on what the televised serials had made available to them, projected an image of a militant and masculinist Ram. It was a new and charged image of an old and revered religious icon. Anuradha Kapur, writing in the *Times of India* (1 October 1991), commented: 'The transformation of the Ram image from that of a serene, omnipresent, eternally forgiving God to that of an angry, punishing one, armed with numerous weapons, wearing armour and even shoes, is truly remarkable.' As to the question about where this 'new Ram, laden with all manner of martial gear' came from, Kapur's answer was that the cultural emergence of a 'militaristic and virile Hinduism' had been made possible through the broadcast of Ramanand Sagar's *Ramayana* and B.R. Chopra's *Mahabharata*. Advani's procession exploited the imagery made available by television for

Hindutva's more overtly political ends. The rath yatra produced a narrative of national resurgence that had as its goal the liberation of Ram's birthplace from those who were invaders. Muslims living in present-day India were cast as the alien outsiders. Hindus began to see themselves as those who had woken up from a long slumber of weak-minded passivity.

Everywhere the rath yatra went, it brought social conflict in its wake. In Bihar, however, the procession was stopped and Advani was arrested. A few days later, on the day that the procession was to have reached Ayodhya, Hindutva activists broke into the Babri Masjid and wrapped saffron cloth around the spires of the mosque. The Sangh Parivar had succeeded in making its first assault. Two years later, this process reached its conclusion. On 6 December 1992, more than 300,000 people had assembled in Ayodhya. A mob of activists broke down police barricades and, using hammers and pickaxes, iron rods and shovels, they took five hours to bring down the old mosque. Before the day was over, the construction of a new Ram temple had begun amidst the rubble. There were riots in many parts of the subcontinent. Over the next few months, in the ensuing violence in India alone, 1700 people were killed and about 5500 injured. The new Hindu had arrived.

*

After the destruction of the Babri mosque, and the riots and the killings that followed, an Indian newsmagazine asked architects and artists to contribute ideas suggesting how the disputed site could be used. There were calls for shrines that could be built to serve as sacred places for both faiths. For example, an artist from Bihar visualized a temple and a mosque facing each other, surrounded by fields of marigolds and date palms.

There were many fatuous proposals too. A steel mobile structure rotating from a central axis which would represent permanence and change. There was another design proposed for a structure that was inspired by the interlocking double helix of the DNA molecule because that is the substance that life is made of. A postmodern artist wanted hundreds of cubicles to be made available for people to build personal shrines. This artist had said that people visiting Ayodhya could buy or rent these little spaces and make their own shrine. The suggestion was followed by the bold declaration that in a few years this space of small cubicles would become a celebration of common faith.

I couldn't but laugh when I had read all this. Was there no awareness on the part of educated, well-meaning, presumably creative people that Ayodhya was a place where powerful ambitions and deep resentments had found expression? In the political naivety of those responses lay an instance of the sanitization of violence from the liberal imagination—not only of the violence of the mosque's destruction, but also the complex and ongoing violence in an unequal and changing society. How was a fifty-foot high steel mobile structure going to engage, much less displace, the distortions that had fixed the Muslim as the enemy in the imagination of millions of Indians?

Perhaps the only sane suggestion came from a humble auto-rickshaw driver who had suggested a Ram-Rahim hospital to treat the good and bad alike. He, unlike all the others, had at least allowed for violent opposition to his scheme and even proposed a cure. He had said, 'Make a hospital on the site, I say ... and if anyone tries to break it, we should break their hands and legs ... . Of course, the hospital should treat them later!'

I had gone to Ayodhya one summer after the Babri mosque had been demolished. The other visitors waiting in the line that afternoon were Hindu pilgrims. They wanted to catch sight of what they believed was Ram's birthplace. The policemen first made us pass through metal detectors—I had to even leave my notebook and pen with the cops—and then pass into what was a grill-iron corridor. We were surrounded by metal rods on all sides. The narrow corridor stretched past a small structure to the right which was covered with a canvas canopy. This was the temple that had been hastily erected by those who had brought down the mosque in December 1992. Everyone who was in the line ahead of me folded their hands and bowed to the invisible idol of the infant Ram. There was pride among the people, and also devotion, in having visited the birthplace of Lord Ram. The rubble somehow remained invisible to the holy tourists. And then we were back in the open, back in the company of policemen and the monkeys that swung from branches or stared down from the tall walls of surrounding buildings. The whitewashed walls were covered with graffiti, large black letters in Hindi, promising that the Ram temple would be built where the mosque had stood.

There, in the lane, I peered at a bioscope show, paying Rs 2 to watch. While a man held a large basket lit from behind by the sun, I put my eyes against an opening and watched a crude slide-show of images of the demolition.

But I wanted a keepsake, and so, for Rs 10, I bought a small picture-book. It said on its cover *Sri Ayodhya Bathed in Blood*. Inside, there were images apparently of the Ram idol that had been installed inside, a black figurine of a boy standing with his elbows pressed to his sides and the arms stretched in front. The head was round, as if the boy had been shaven, and his eyes, the whites glowing against the black surface of the face, were spread wide in an expression of amazement. There was a picture of a monkey, which had been photographed on the dome of the mosque, clutching the saffron banner, and the monkey was identified in the picture as Lord Hanuman, the monkey-god follower of Ram.

There were several images in the book from the day of the mosque's demolition, images of the milling crowds of karsevaks with yellow and orange headbands. These images of young men from small towns, their hair cut in imitation of Bollywood's men of action, straining their necks to keep their faces in front of the camera, seemed to me to better reveal the violence that had befallen Ayodhya than the artsy proposals I had discovered in the newsmagazine. Instead of abstractions about spirituality and faith, here were men in denim trousers and shirts, seizing power by tying an orange band around their forehead and waving an iron rod in their hand. You could not but ask if they each had access to good education or high hopes of finding employment. I was reminded of Gérard Heuzé's study on the right-wing Shiv Sainiks of Chattisgarh. His research shows that they were mostly poorly educated youth, with little knowledge of English, who were either unemployed or frustrated in their meagre jobs. They longed 'to be the hero of a Bombay film in which violence leads to justice'.

In Muslims, these men had found their cardboard-cutout villains. As I looked at the photos of the young men, I asked myself what had been their bargain with God? In the thin, frenzied faces, there was such desperate assertion! When those men raised their hands in the photographs, were they declaring their passion or, more simply, just calling attention to themselves?

There were many photos of the activists who had been shot dead by the police.

The pictures of the dead karsevaks in Ayodhya were not, however, from the day on which the mosque fell down. The local police in Ayodhya had hardly acted when the barricades were overrun and the mosque destroyed. Around two o'clock in the afternoon that day, Advani had urged the mob to block the Faizabad-Ayodhya road so that the federal police, including the Rapid Action Force, could not advance to the site. But, it had been the local police itself, the Provincial Armed Constabulary, which had fired on the karsevaks two years earlier, on 30 October 1990, when the saffron warriors had clambered on to the dome of the Babri mosque with the intention of destroying it. On that occasion, many activists had died. The VHP had claimed that there were fifty-nine people killed while the official figure had been fifteen. It was the photographs of those dead youth that I was now seeing in the picture-book that I had bought. It was important to note this because the police had been asked to shoot during the earlier occasion—because the state administration at the time was not in the hands of the BJP. The riots in the wake of Advani's rath yatra had polarized Hindu society and allowed the BJP to emerge, in 1991, as the second-largest party in the national Parliament and also as the

victors in four other states, including the largest state of
Uttar Pradesh where Ayodhya was located. The events of
6 December 1992, were also in part the result of the active
failure of the machinery of the state. The arrival of the
new Hindu has been facilitated by the connivance in many
places of a communal state apparatus.

Let's consider the riots that broke out in Bombay after
the mosque came down in Ayodhya. On 7 and 8 December,
Muslim demonstrators were targeting policemen and Hindu
temples. The first casualty of the riots in Bombay, on the
evening of 6 December itself, was a police constable. As
Clarence Fernandez and Naresh Fernandes reported in the
Times of India, on the morning of 7 December, four Bombay
policemen, trapped by a Muslim mob in their station in
a locality called Kherwadi were told by the thousand-
strong crowd, 'Police in Ayodhya just stood by and let the
mosque be demolished. We're going to get you now.' But,
in the days that followed it was the policemen who reacted.
As Christophe Jaffrelot describes the situation, 'it became
less a case of Hindu-Muslim conflict than Muslims against
the police or vice-versa. Of 202 casualties—the official
toll—132 died in police firing and 51 in mob violence, of
which 98 and 32, respectively, were Muslim'. The riots
lasted till 16 December and, according to Jaffrelot, 'revealed
the depth of the communal bias of the police as well as
its lack of preparedness'.

And yet, nothing that had happened in the earlier
riots in India, including Bhagalpur where the men from
the Bihar Military Police had targeted Muslims in 1989,
could match the malevolence displayed by the police in
Gujarat in February and March 2002. The riots there
had begun after a train-car of Hindu activists returning

from Ayodhya had been set on fire by Muslims in the town of Godhra in Gujarat. Over the next few days, mobs of Hindutva cadres raped and murdered with impunity. More than a thousand—some estimates were as high as 2000—Muslims were killed in Gujarat. The killers taunted their victims with the chant 'Yeh andar ki baat hai, Police hamare saath hai' (It's known on the inside/the police is on our side). As if to show that there would be many more Ayodhyas, the rioters demolished hundred of mosques. Slogans in praise of Lord Ram were scrawled on the walls of a few mosques and, in others cases, temples were built to replace mosques. The rampaging mob used sophisticated explosives and gas cylinders to burn Muslim homes and businesses; in doing this, they were assisted by computer printouts listing information about the ownership of the properties which had been supplied by the municipal authorities. The Human Rights Watch published its report on the killings under the telling title 'We Have No Orders to Save You: State Participation and Complicity in Communal Violence in Gujarat.' The nature of the complicity of the communal state was described in the report's following statement:

In many cases, the police led the charge, using gunfire to kill Muslims who got in the mobs' way. A key BJP state minister is reported to have taken over police control rooms in Ahmedabad on the first day of the carnage, issuing orders to disregard pleas for assistance from Muslims. Portions of the Gujarati-language press meanwhile printed fabricated stories and statements openly calling on Hindus to avenge the Godhra attacks.

Twenty-seven senior police officers who had tried to control the riots and book influential persons responsible for the mayhem were transferred from their posts. Teesta Setalvad, a human rights activist, wrote that one of the most disturbing aspects of the violence was 'the manner in which the police force wilfully abandoned the state and its citizens to the depredations of homicidal mobs'. In places like Danteshwar in Vadodara, Muslim policemen were assaulted by their Hindu colleagues. There are no Muslims in positions of authority in the police force in Gujarat. Almost a decade ago, during the Bombay riots, Setalvad had taped several police wireless messages which revealed 'a deep and abiding anti-Muslim hatred' among those entrusted with the task of protecting all citizens. In Gujarat, this bias took a more blatant form. For Setalvad, this gross failure on the part of the state was 'an extreme example of the complete politicization of a police force that functions as per the dictates of the ideology of the government in power and not on constitutional principles of equality and discrimination'. It is the dereliction of duty by the state, and, in fact, its active hostility, that made the riots in Gujarat a state pogram against Muslims.

As a result, it is not surprising that the people's expectations from their own government are dismally low. Thus it is that when Harsh Mander, a senior officer of the Indian Administrative Service, resigned to protest the bureaucracy's abdication of responsibility in Gujarat, he was immediately hailed as a hero. Mander represents the apotheosis of the secular consciousness. In his honourable civic response, the liberal Indian imagination found its finest expression. It is also true, however, that while

Mander's is a voice of morality and conscience we also find it easier to venerate him as a saint than to put pressure on the government for its sins. There is no doubt in my mind that every Indian should expect and get fair and accountable treatment under the law. That is the meaning of Mander's resignation, and we should all seek police reform as well as punishment for those responsible for the killings in Gujarat. But, I want more. It is true that as a citizen of a secular democracy, I demand transparency from the government—but, as a Hindu, I also want to understand what it is that I can expect from myself and others of my faith.

*

As a Hindu.

I feel ambivalent about that phrase. A Hindu. I am one, and I am not.

The ambivalence is appealing from the position of a writer. Writing allows you to inhabit different points of view and, in this context, the task of mediating the contradictions of belief and secular existence calls for the accommodation of opposed worldviews. Not having to choose one identity over another can actually be a salutary response to a situation where there is a murderous zeal prompting you to choose an identity to the exclusion of all else. Particularly as a writer, it appears to me that in a world where belief is being taken hostage by fundamentalists and where secular or worldly reason is the weapon of the powerful, the exploration of doubt or what I would call the benefits of half-faith holds a promise that one cannot possibly ignore.

In the days following the worst violence in Gujarat, Ramachandra Guha wrote that the VHP and its cohorts needed 'also to be condemned by the Hindu middle ground, the millions of thus far silent Indians who have seen their ancestral religion taken over and grossly distorted by a bunch of power-hungry individuals'. Guha was putting moral pressure on those who thought of themselves primarily as religious Hindus—and not as, in his own words, secular democrats, or non-denominational patriots, or as pragmatic businessmen. Guha used the example of the well-known writer U.R. Anantha Murthy who, as someone well-versed with Hindu scriptures, had recently appealed against the bid to build a Ram temple where the Babri mosque had stood. Anantha Murthy had said that 'unlike Islam and Christianity, Hinduism is not a historical religion. It does not need to know where or when Rama was born. The Rama for whom thousands of men, women and children have been killed is not the Rama our saints and poets have praised or the Rama whom Gandhiji called out to when he died. I request you not to support this murderous campaign'. In his own essay, Guha had gone on to criticize the Ayodhya campaign in strong terms. 'The temple, were it ever to be built,' he wrote, 'will not be a celebration of divinity but, rather, a chilling testimony to manufactured violence and consciously willed murder.'

The middle ground, then, was not to be confused with compromise. And this move was a correct one. The brutal and inhuman practices of the Hindutva followers in Gujarat did not call for any expressions of sympathy or support. Any condemnation could only be offered in clear and unequivocal terms. And yet, by calling on Hindus and by citing Anantha Murthy's letter which had been written to a religious leader, Guha was widening the middle ground. He was speaking from a place where belief was being mobilized to protest against its own distortion. This was an invaluable supplement to the powerful voices that had been raised from the dry land of secularism.

The most challenging space of scrutiny that one can occupy is the place where one is both oneself and the enemy. One good example of empathetic fiction is the story 'Does Anyone Have the Strength?' written by the Kashmiri writer, Akhtar Mohiuddin. The story begins with the following line: 'He stepped into the bus and it seemed that a rose had suddenly bloomed in it, as if a shining star had torn a hole through the clouds and emerged to dazzle the firmament.' It is a small boy who has come and sat next to the man who is the narrator. The man yields the window-seat to the boy; the man now sits between the boy and his mother. As the story progresses we learn that the boy is fascinated with every sight that passes his window. The narrator is spellbound by the boy. The bus passes a funeral procession. The mother of the boy asks him not to look that way, but the narrator doesn't want the boy to be frightened. He offers him a verse from the *Qur'an*. The mother's acute consternation at this makes the narrator aware that he is seated next to Hindus. He has made a mistake. But he is at ease. He tells himself that it does not matter. The boy is clearly dear to him. He reasons to himself, 'A rose is a rose, no matter what you call it by. Will a change of name lessen the brightness of the Morning Star?'

The narrator tries to make conversation with the boy, in order to win his trust, but it only makes things worse. There is further confusion when the boy stonily repeats

the Hindi name for a temple that they are passing by
while the narrator tries to tell the child that the Kashmiri
name means the same. Then, the narrator catches sight of
the boy trying to hide from him as he folds his hands and
bows to the temple. A huge weight suffocates the narrator.
He knows that the boy sees the devil in him—the devil
that makes grown-up men do violence to children. He
very much wants someone to speak up for him. 'Will
someone who still has strength of utterance left, tell this
child that he is the Morning Star of my firmament, and
his mother the mark of obeisance on my brow?'

This story is remarkable, and I'd even say rare, for several
reasons. It does not speak in a secular language. It is
delivered in the voice of a religious man who is at ease
with his own belief. But his belief also translates into an
idiom that includes those people who, particularly in the
context of the Kashmir Valley, are seen as being caught in
violent conflict with him. But, the bridging will not happen.
And the story recognizes that. A deep abyss has opened
between the narrator and the boy. It will not be closed
easily. At this time, all that the narrator can do is offer
testimony or make an appeal. I am very much taken by
the fact that even at the moment of his futility—that
wonderful last line!—the narrator does not abandon the
language of his truth. 'Will someone who still has strength
of utterance left, tell this child that he is the Morning Star
of my firmament, and his mother the mark of obeisance
on my brow?' In other words, the narrator does not become
secular. He makes religion human and urgent without
making it political.

I envy the man in the story his language. I cannot speak
in it. It is an alien tongue for me because I was taught to

think and talk in a language of law, rights and rationality, even though all around me are also the signs of faith and the passionate striving towards transcendence. My appeal to the boy, if I was sitting in the narrator's place, would have been voiced as a citizen of a secular democratic state. It would have been a strange language to adopt in those circumstances, particularly if what divided us was religious difference. I would not be able to speak like the narrator because I do not have his beliefs. I could only articulate, as I have said above, my ambivalence. This would mean leaving behind also my secular speech. If I'm going to be as truthful to my own condition as the narrator is to his, then I must speak not in the language of rational certainties but in the faltering vernacular of doubt and half-faith. *I am a Hindu, and I am not.*

In an essay published soon after the demolition of the Babri mosque, Rustom Bharucha had written that 'in the name of vigilance' what had emerged among intellectuals opposed to fundamentalism was 'an unusually emphatic rhetoric'. Everyone had become busy asserting a tough secularism. Bharucha commented, 'An emphatic rhetoric, it is assumed, can only be dealt with emphatically. An eye for an eye, a tooth for a tooth, man against man.' In contrast to that, Bharucha was calling for an engagement with the ambivalence of faith. In India, he argued, gods refused to die and so it was necessary to deal creatively with the ways in which belief found place in the secular world. As one of his examples, Bharucha had chosen, like Guha, the writer Anantha Murthy who wrote about Hinduism as a 'critical insider'. The Kannada writer had dramatized in his novels the pitfalls of imposing a superior rational consciousness on others. This was attractive for

Bharucha because it exposed to question the ethics of one's intervention and the validity of one's action. Anantha Murthy is a writer who writes out of doubt and half-faith. Doubt not only about secular rationality but also about ritual and religion. This made for a particular kind of vacillation—which some are bound to call inaction. But I see in the mobility of doubt the true conditions for not only flexibility of critical response but also openness to the complexity of human experience.

*

In July 2001, the Indian and Pakistani leaders met for talks in the city of Agra. The Indian Prime Minister Atal Behari Vajpayee was playing host to Pakistan's President General Pervez Musharraf. Public expectations ran high. As the Pakistani human rights activist Asma Jehangir put it just before the summit opened, 'If the talks fail, the two leaders must take the blame for playing with the emotions of one billion people.' The summit *was* regarded as a failure. The two sides could not come to an agreement even on a joint communiqué at the end of meeting. As one Indian newspaper put it, 'They broke the ice, then froze.' There were complaints that too much space was being invested in highlighting trivia: 'What Musharraf ate, what he wore, and all that nonsense. If the talks resulted in a joint statement, master chef Jiggs Kalra could have very well claimed that it was the crushed pearls or whatever in his cuisine that did it.' This was probably a reference to the reports in the press that the special delicacies served at lunch when the summit started included tandoori prawns laced with a pinch of fired coral, and a dish of apricots and lamb sprinkled with powdered pearls. The exotic food for the summit was designed to be therapeutic, 'the ingredients drawing on the ancient Ayurvedic system of healing'. The attention being paid to even such matters as the facial expressions of the two leaders was perhaps silly, but it also revealed the depth of interest that the ordinary people, on both sides of the border, had in securing peace. A fifty-six-year-old businessman in Karachi told a reporter, 'Despite my poor health, I have been watching various television channels the whole night, just to hear some good news.'

The public interest in the talks was not merely sentimental. Concrete proposals that had been advanced by peace groups in the subcontinent included the demand that India and Pakistan not deploy the nuclear weapons that they had tested in 1998. The demand was also made that both countries agree to keep their bombs at reasonable distance from missiles or aircraft so as to allow time for mutual consultation that could act as a check on jittery responses. The threat of war between the nuclear neighbours inevitably raised the spectre of nuclear catastrophe. Two anti-nuke activists, Praful Bidwai and Achin Vanaik, have pointed out that a nuclear weapons explosion in any city in the Indian subcontinent is likely to be 'particularly harrowing' because of the density of population in the urban centres, their poor medical and civic infrastructures, the existence of flimsy shanty towns, and many other features. Thus, peaceniks from both sides joined hands to ask their leaders meeting in Agra to work on a treaty to keep each other informed of any ballistic missile flight tests and work towards nuclear risk reduction. Appeals were also made for the signing of a no-war pact which would forbid, among other things, military incursions across the border, state-support for cross-border militancy, sabotage, blockades and disruption of river waters. More than twenty NGOs, including the Pakistan-India People's Forum for Peace and Democracy as well as Women's Initiative for Peace in South Asia, urged greater people-to-people contact between the two nations. Indeed, in the days immediately prior to the Agra Summit, more than 200 organizations came together to sponsor a Pakistan-India People's Solidarity Conference in New Delhi.

But this did not prevent the expression of more medieval gestures of enmity. Ten members of the Shiv Sena used Ganga jal to purify Mahatma Gandhi's memorial site at Delhi's Raj Ghat after General Musharraf had sprinkled rose petals there. This had actually been a retaliatory move. During Prime Minister Vajpayee's Lahore trip in 1999, after his visit to the Minar-e-Pakistan, the site commemorating the Muslim League's signing of the declaration demanding a new country, the members of the right-wing Jamaat-e-Islami performed a ritual cleaning of the monument. The behaviour of the fundamentalists on both sides of the border would prompt the belief I first heard articulated by an editor in India—that wars between India and Pakistan are Hindu-Muslim riots fought with tanks and fighter planes. In fact, every occasion for even an ordinary exchange becomes a way of waging war by other means. In that mindset, the division is not only along territorial but also religious lines, ignoring the fact that India has the third largest population of Muslims in the world. One of my memories of the 1997 celebration of fifty years of independence for India and Pakistan has been the words of the RSS leader from Delhi, B.L. Sharma

'Prem', who is a self-identified 'fundamentalist by birth, instinct, training': 'We believe politics must be Hinduised, Hindus must be militarized ... I only live for the day when the *tiranga* (the Indian tricolour) will be unfurled on Pakistani territory. We should be like the Israelis. They greet each other with a "Next year in Jerusalem"; we should say "Next year in Lahore".'

Such declarations are in bad faith for their blatant misunderstanding of the nature of religion in India or even the role of democracy and sovereign nationhood. But there is also a more banal misreading of contemporary realities hidden in such remarks. Cotton, wool, leather, tea, and cardamom easily make their way across the borders of India and Pakistan—in addition, of course, to the armed militants aided by the Pakistani Army who regularly infiltrate into the Kashmir Valley. According to a study released before the summit in Agra, India's imports from Pakistan had gone up by 350 per cent in the previous five years; Pakistan's imports from India during that same period had increased by about 150 per cent. During 1998–99, according to the Federation of Pakistan Chamber of Commerce and Industry, Indian exports to Pakistan were to the tune of 154 million dollars. The flow of goods from Pakistan to India was worth around 186 million dollars. In 1999, the Kargil war broke out between the two countries. But, difficult as this might be to believe, the volume of trade between India and Pakistan increased rather than stopping or declining. The sad part is that even this exchange languishes at less than 5 per cent of the potential trading capacity of two countries which is estimated to be about 5 billion dollars a year. In the absence of a policy that allows for greater movement of both people and goods, the people remain trapped in the situation described by a customs official in the Bollywood film *Gadar*: '*Hindustani cheeni hamari khaayenge aur hum paan ke patte unke, magar ugglenge dono nafrat*' (The Indians will eat our sugar, and we their betel leaves, but both will spew hatred for the other).

The quotidian world of trade and commerce returns us to a welcome consideration of the necessities required by the wider populace despite the waging of destructive wars by our leaders. The war in Kargil had started after General Musharraf, the then army chief, had sent his troops to capture the mountainous border territory inside Indian Kashmir. Reviewing that history in the pages of the *New York Review of Books*, the Pakistani writer and journalist Ahmed Rashid has written: 'By now, after three and a half wars with India (counting the fighting in Kargil), most Pakistanis are fed up with the Kashmir issue and would much prefer that the money spent on the 500,000-strong Pakistani Army be spent on roads, schools, and hospitals.' Rashid admitted, of course, that the voicing of such opinions in his country is considered 'treasonable' by the army which views Kashmir as 'a sacred Islamic cause'. It is also worth remembering that while President Clinton offered to write off Pakistan's 3 billion dollar debt to the United States if Prime Minister Nawaz Sharif desisted from nuclear testing, Sharif went ahead anyway because of the pressure being exerted by Islamic groups. And yet, the truth is that there have been many notable men and women of religion from both faiths who have powerfully addressed the cause of peace. There have been those who have highlighted the common people's economic needs over any distant, sacred causes.

In April 2003, I heard Barbara Metcalf, a well-known historian of subcontinental Islam, speak at a university in California. The subject of her talk was Maulana Husain Ahmad Madani (1879–1958), a distinguished scholar and political spokesman who played an important role in the Jami'at Ulama-i-Hind (the Association of Indian 'Ulama) for four decades after its establishment in 1919. Metcalf's admiration for Madani was based in the fact that he 'had responded to the changing circumstances of the day with hardheaded pragmatism'. Madani was a religious leader who was modern in that he posited a view of national life in which citizens of disparate faiths would together fight for justice and against exploitation. Although Madani would speak as a cleric who believed in democracy, Metcalf's account made it clear that Madani was important for another reason too. He had provided a narrative for Muslims to find home in India.

Around the same time in history as Madani, hardline Hindu nationalists like Vinay Damodar Savarakar were giving expression to the theory that India was a Hindu land, sacred only to Hindus. Savarkar is a revered figure among the Hindutva rank and file and, even though he was a suspect in Mahatma Gandhi's assassination, his portrait now hangs opposite Gandhi's in the central hall of the Parliament in Delhi. He and his followers deeply resented what they thought of as Gandhi's 'appeasement' of Muslims in the subcontinent. In his 1923 book, *Hindutva: Who Is a Hindu?* Savarkar made it clear that he believed India's minority Muslim and Christian communities possessed 'all the essential qualifications of Hindutva but one ... they do not look upon India as their holy land'. He wrote, 'Their holy land is far off in Arabia and Palestine. Consequently their names and their outlook smack of foreign origin. Their love is divided.' (This is in strict contrast to someone like Jawaharlal Nehru who, as the first prime minister of India, was to later tell a correspondent on 13 November 1955: 'Muslims can certainly look to Arabia as the country which was the fountainhead of their religion. That is natural. But politically the citizens of each country look to that country and not to another. Christians, no doubt, look to Jerusalem as a city connected with the founder of their religion, but politically and culturally they look to their own countries. There is no conflict between these two approaches.') Metcalf explained that the narrative of colonial history, first given shape during the eighteenth century, had vilified the Muslims as foreigners, thereby making the British appear less intrusive and even benign. It is this key element that had been appropriated by the Hindu nationalists and is today repeated in equally virulent terms by the spokesmen of groups like the BJP.

Madani's response to the writings of the likes of Savarkar was especially novel. He had described Muslims as the original inhabitants of India. This was because Adam, the founder of the Islamic prophetic tradition, after his expulsion from paradise, had descended on Adam's Peak in Ceylon. His descendants—which would mean all humans—were in a sense also Indians, with Muslims certainly claiming pride of place in that land. What was even more startling, and even affecting for me, was Madani's point that Muslims stayed in India after their deaths. Unlike the Hindus and Zoroastrians, the Muslims buried their dead so that 'even after death, a Muslim remains attached to the soil'. While a Hindu might be reincarnated in other lands, the grave of a Muslim remained in its fixed location. A fixed, and apparently, also an active location. For the dead person, Madani explained, the 'grave is like a Radio Station ... where messages are received and transmitted', particularly as others pray and do good works on behalf of the deceased.

I have not done justice to the range and richness of Metcalf's historical analysis or her pointed assessments of the current climate in which Muslim protest is rendered mute by interpreting it as fanaticism. But I seized upon the details of Madani's fabulism because of its extraordinary pathos. Madani's account of the Muslim's grave in India was more than anything else a defence against being rendered homeless in the land of one's birth. The story sought to bring into being, solely on the strength of the writer's will, an imagined community of the living and the dead.

There is fabulism also in the stories of the Hindu right. Consider the Taj Mahal which served as a backdrop for the Vajpayee-Musharraf summit in Agra. As Tim Edensor relates in his book, *Tourists at the Taj*, visitors to the monument subscribe to myths long propagated by Hindu nationalists. One tourist told Edensor: 'Well, it's an excellent building ... but people should remember that it's a Hindu temple dedicated to Shiva. If you read about it you will find this is the truth. It's something that was taken over by Shahjahan. The Moghuls were cruel tyrants who oppressed the Hindu masses. The Mohammedans converted all these temples into mosques. You will find that one of the rooms in the Taj is locked. Inside you will find a Shiva.' What makes Madani's story different is that when I heard the historian presenting it, I didn't think of it as a weapon in the arms of an aggressive majority. It wasn't an example of the myth-making of the mighty. There was such invention and delight in the idea of the radio-station—a touch of modernity too!—and I saw it as a defence against the rage and the humiliation of not being believed all your life when you say: 'I belong here'.

*

On the first anniversary of the attacks on September 11, I sat at my desk while the radio brought the report from Ground Zero. At the site in New York City, the name of each person who died was read out in a solemn procession of grief. Among the nearly 3000 dead there had also been numerous Indians and Pakistanis, and I heard and connected with those names at the memorial service.

And then I suddenly thought of my driver Qasim in Lahore with his praise for workers being paid overtime in America. I wanted to tell him of my reading in a newspaper about a Bangladeshi waiter, Sultan A. Salim. Sultan used to work at the Windows on the World restaurant in the World Trade Centre. He stayed back from work on September 11. As a result, Sultan did not die, but now he is without a good job. He is finding himself unable to make ends meet. He had told the reporter, 'If I had died, my family would be okay. They would have a million dollars and they would be fine. They would not have me, but what good am I now?' This is an unusual thought. It reminds you forcefully of the carnage of poverty, and it compels you to think of Sultan first as a human with a need for work. Does it really matter that he is a Muslim?

It is that question, however, which has become central after September 11. In giving importance to that question, the meaning of terms like 'Islam' or 'Muslim' is also assumed to be transparent. These words are being equated with terror. Qasim and Sultan aren't asked to explain what they believe in, what their needs are, and how their dreams are like billions of other human beings the world over. In a Pakistani newsmagazine, a few months prior to the first anniversary of the attacks, I had read about seven men who had been killed in Macedonia. The men were all young; six of them were Pakistanis, and the seventh, Indian. They were described by the Macedonian authorities as Islamic extremists. Pamphlets had been recovered from the dead men. The Arabic-language pamphlets, the authorities claimed, provided the names of other terrorists and the dates of previous meetings. The pamphlets were seen as having established the link of these young men with the Al-Qaeda network. The Pakistani newsmagazine had gone ahead and obtained copies of the alleged pamphlets. There was only an invitation to a *majlis-e-aza* (a Shia religious gathering) in Gujranwala, Pakistan, and the names on the invitation were the names of the meeting's organizers and speakers. The other 'pamphlets' were nothing more than a verse from the *Qur'an* and a copy of *Nad-e-Ali*, which as the report put it, is 'a document found in every Shia home'.

The men had no identity papers on them. It was the pamphlet about the meeting that had led the reporter to Gujranwala and he was able to identify all the dead within a week. The men had crossed into Greece illegally to find work. Some of the men had earlier been deported from Iran and Turkey for trying to work as illegal immigrants.

The brother of one of the men who had been killed said that the dead man had paid 1,100 dollars to a smuggler to get into Turkey. The smuggler had demanded additional money to find entry into Greece. The reason why the men were in Macedonia was that they had hoped to make their way into Greece by walking undetected for some days through the mountainous terrain. If they had succeeded they would have saved nearly six hundred dollars. The report had quoted a *Wall Street Journal* reporter who had said that the shooting of the men might have been an attempt to convince the West that the ethnic Albanian minority residing in Macedonia had attracted Islamic extremists from outside and security in the region was now threatened. The West could now be expected to provide aid for that country's homeland security.

Albert Camus, in his Nobel lecture, had said, 'By definition the writer cannot serve those who make history: he serves those who have to live it.' In all the reports that were published after the events of September 11, I must confess that I would read newspapers and look for stories that would tell me about people, ordinary people, whose lives had been overtaken by forces that they were powerless to anticipate or oppose. Everything that has happened since then, in Afghanistan and then in Iraq, has deepened that sense of inadequacy and pain which had suddenly become a part of the lives of people in cities like New York. The greater tragedy is that for people in the rest of the world this script has been a more familiar one and it goes on being repeated, ad nauseam.

To follow the dictum that Camus had outlined means, in this context, to describe how individual lives have been pinned under the weight of ideological judgements. The likes of Samuel Huntington ignorantly dismiss economic conflicts and also produce gross generalizations about millenarian conflict between Islam and the West. How is a person looking for bread in Iraq while bombs are falling around him fare against his depiction as a warrior in the 'clash of civilizations'? Huntington had borrowed that phrase from Bernard Lewis's study of what he called 'The Roots of Muslim Rage'. These thinkers are anachronisms. As Edward Said has pointed out, Orientalist learning had been premised 'on the silence of the native, who was to be represented by an Occidental expert speaking ex cathedra on the native's behalf, presenting that unfortunate creature as an undeveloped, deficient, and uncivilized being who couldn't represent himself'. Of course, it has now become inappropriate, Said writes, for white scholars to speak on behalf of 'Negroes'. Or for others to pontificate about the Oriental's mentality. But not for the likes of Lewis. According to Said, Lewis has even performed such 'philological' tricks as 'deriving an aspect of the predilection in contemporary Arab Islam for revolutionary violence from Bedouin descriptions of a camel rising'.

Once you have depicted the whole of Islamic culture as irrational, it becomes easy to bomb Baghdad and to allow the gutting of the National Library and Archives. And when history has been turned into ashes, what remains in its place is Disney. People get reinscribed into the fantasies of the conquerors. During the recent Iraq War, the Amnesty International had expressed concern at the report in the Norwegian newspaper *Dagbladet* which showed American soldiers escorting naked Iraqi prisoners through a park in Baghdad. In one of the photographs accompanying the report, a young Iraqi man's naked chest had the following words written on it in Arabic: 'Ali Baba—Thief'. This was an example of demeaning treatment of prisoners, of course. But it was also evidence of how the old Arabian tale of Ali Baba, turned into a popular cartoon by Disney, served as the only mirror in which the US soldier could recognize an Arab man. Would the marines have known about a book called *Arabian Nights*, and, if they did, would that have moved them to protect any of the libraries in Iraq?

When reading about the episode reported in the *Dagbladet*, which had gone largely unremarked in the mainstream US media, I was reminded of Jon Lee Anderson's story in the *New Yorker* about the sacking of Baghdad. Anderson described a visit to one of Saddam Hussein's palaces where a marine told the photographers not to take pictures of the troops because they were 'Intel'. Anderson wrote: 'A Marine officer was reading a copy of *Playboy* as he defecated into a milk crate. He waved when we passed. Some young marines hanging out around a Humvee festooned with photos from what looked like a perfume ad asked me if I have any news from the war.' Were there no readers in the army of the victors?

My search actually unearthed the name of an Indian soldier in the US army who was carrying books to the war. But the details of this revelation left me feeling decidedly ambivalent if not also depressed. A news report in *India Abroad* had it that a soldier in the US army, Nishkam Gupta, believed that his fight in Iraq was also a struggle for India. His parents, Arun and Renu, told the reporter that Gupta's participation in the war in Iraq was 'a part of his desire to fight the larger war against terrorism, a war that would directly benefit Hinduism and its cause'. The proud parents also said that their son had founded a chapter of the Hindu Students Council and that the books he had taken to the war with him were the Gita, the Ramayana, the works of Swami Vivekananda and a tract called *The Hindu Mind*.

I do not know Nishkam Gupta, but in him I recognized a dangerous condition. I saw the narcissism of a narrow cause, bred among immigrants bound up in their own insularity, projected into the arc of a super power's triumphalist career. Bush searched for power and oil, and claimed it was for the Iraqi people; our own long-distance nationalist packed his bags for Iraq, and declared that it was for India and the Hindus. Hindutva appeared as a little sticker stuck on an American cruise missile.

To my mind Gupta's beliefs revealed little more than bigotry, and the surest sign of that was present in the young man's reading choices. Judging from Gupta's booklist, one couldn't but feel that he was utterly incurious about the place he was visiting or the people at whom he was to be pointing his gun. How had this happened?

In 1893, Swami Vivekananda, whose writings Gupta had taken with him to Iraq, travelled to Chicago to speak at the Parliament of World Religions. During one of his interventions, he presented the assembled delegates a fable. A small frog lived in a well. One day, another frog which lived in the sea fell into the well. The small frog said, 'The sea! How big is that? Is it as big as my well?' The frog from the sea laughed at the question and explained that the well was tiny when compared to where he had come from. 'But,' said the frog of the well, 'nothing can be bigger than my well; there can be nothing bigger than this. This fellow is a liar, so turn him out.' Vivekananda told his audience that the Hindu, the Christian, the Muslim, each person was sitting in his 'own little well and thinking the whole world is my little well'. This story is appealing as a narrative about close-mindedness, but it is inadequate to explain the bigotry I find in some Hindu minds outside India. We are no longer in our little wells. But it is as if the encounter with the outside world has pushed us back into more and more hardened forms of thinking.

In an essay on diasporic Indians, Vinay Lal informs us that after the destruction of the Babri mosque, the Hindus in Southern California, describing themselves as 'Concerned NRIs [Non-resident Indians]', could do no better than take out an advertisement in the *Indian Express* deploring the government's short-lived ban of 'nationalistic [Hindutva] organizations', and urging their 'brothers and sisters in India' to aim at the 'restoration of common sets of values and laws based on the 6000 year heritage', There was no concern shown for the nearly 2000 Indians killed in the riots. Lal writes, 'As if in anticipation of questions about their entitlement to intervene in the politics of the homeland, the Californian Hindus argued that "of the one million NRI's living in the United States, over 900,000 call Bharat [India] as [sic] their Mother. Hindus have only one place (other than Nepal) to call home. Their roots are in Bharat." What about the remaining 100,000? Our remote-control nationalists are claiming the right to call Muslims from India 'anti-national'!

More recently, a group of activists working on a campaign called 'The Foreign Exchange of Hate' revealed that Hindutva groups in the US and UK were raising money to fund religious extremism in India. A group called Ekal Vidyalaya Foundation of USA had raised about 500,000 dollars for starting tribal schools in India. Smita Narula, a senior researcher at Human Rights Watch, told a reporter from *Philadelphia Inquirer* that 'The schools ... help to create a cadre of foot soldiers to fight against the constructed enemies of Hindutva, in this case Muslims and Christians.' Narula also pointed out that the extent of tribal participation in the Gujarat riots in 2002 had been unprecedented—a sign that the Hindutva propagandists were now gaining success where, in earlier times, it was arguably the Christian missionaries who had exercised greater influence.

According to the activists who have exposed the diasporic funding of extremist campaigns in India, the greater part of 5 million dollars raised by one US based charity for relief and development projects in India went to a network of nationalist groups. The reporter from the *Philadelphia Inquirer*, Gaiutra Bahadur, said that she was present at a meeting in New Jersey where the chief guest was Ashok Singhal, the VHP leader who is among those accused of having master-minded the destruction of the Babri mosque. At the meeting, his host, a gynaecologist named Veena Gandhi, made a pitch for donations: '365 dollars a year for one school. A dollar a day, for which we can't even buy a Coke in New York. Talk to your friends. This is our debt to our country where we were born.' I have long wondered about the processes through which the soft emotion of nostalgia is turned into the hard emotion of fundamentalism. In the story that Bahadur recounts from the meeting in New Jersey, the change is visible when the demand for a dollar a day gets transformed into the claim made by the gynaecologist that 'Hindus have always taken a beating because we are supposed to forgive ... . You cannot be tolerant to the point of being a coward.' This is familiar. The incitement to violence through the cry that we have been weak. What is also being increasingly familiar is the transition of the old fundamentalism into a more fashionable one. Hindus needed to unite throughout the world, Ashok Singhal said to the reporter, because there was a cultural onslaught against them. He said, 'People can understand more because of September 11. America has suffered the first onslaught by the jihadis. We have been suffering this onslaught for the last 1000 years.'

8

The Blind Men

At the end, I must return to the beginning. The riots in Bhagalpur had started on 24 October 1989 and went on for almost six weeks. There was a fresh outbreak of violence in March the following year and a few more people died. More than 11,500 houses had been damaged in a large area covering 200 villages. The total death toll was around 1000—with only less than half those bodies being recovered. The missing bodies had either been hidden in fields or thrown into the Ganges. The riots were said to be the worst in the country since the killings and the devastation that took place in 1947.

The first piece of journalism I published in India was a report on my visit to Bhagalpur. The article had appeared in the Sunday magazine of the *Indian Express* in September 1990. In a sense, then, my life as a writer began in Bhagalpur. I had actually been away when the killings were going on there. As a graduate student at an American university, I would sit in a library where the newspapers arrived from India more than a week late, reading reports that were filled with the corruption of death. I learned from news reports of a rumour that Hindu students had been killed in Muslim-owned dormitories or 'lodges' and thrown into wells. Both All

India Radio and the BBC had broadcast this fiction, and a new wave of violence had been unleashed. One reporter writing for the *Hindustan Times* wrongly said that a Muslim cleric had exhorted Muslims to kill Hindu men and rape Hindu women. The reports, even when accurate, often appeared confusing to me: in that quiet basement library, I read one story about the arrest of the peace committee that had been formed by both Hindus and Muslim members of the local community. I also read that the right-wing Hindu party, the Jan Sangh, forerunner of the contemporary BJP, had also spread the rumour that one of the senior police officers in Bhagalpur, Naseem Ahmed, a Muslim, was in police custody because he had been caught talking to Pakistan on a wireless set. The riots appeared like a violent hallucination in the flickering light of rumours—and I couldn't help feeling that it is perhaps experienced as such, as cruel but also unreal, even by those who live through it.

This feeling returned to me when, a few months after the riots, I went to Logain. This was a village where about 170 Muslims had been attacked by a mob of about several thousand Hindus belonging to the surrounding villages. The killings had gone on for nine hours. The attacks were directed by the police officer who was posted at the *thana* there. Some of the corpses of the Muslims who had been killed were first dumped in two wells and a pond. Later, when the stench became unbearable, they were pulled out and buried in adjoining fields. The killers had planted cauliflowers in the soil above the decaying cadavers. In another report, the cauliflowers were changed to radishes. In the Parliament, one newspaper said, a legislator had spoken about the carrots that had been planted over the corpses. This lack of certainty about what it was that had really happened, made the events at once unreal and frightening.

When I visited Logain after the riots, I saw that the fields were filled with the water from the monsoon rains. A police unit had been posted there and the constable on duty told me that the job of the police was to make sure that what had been done to the Muslims did not now happen to the Hindus. There was only one surviving Muslim family in the village, however, and its members had fled the village. Who would have attacked the Hindus?

Twelve years later I went back to Logain. As my jeep slowly made its way on the muddy road to the village, I suddenly imagined the open mouths of dead children sprouting vegetables in the fertile fields. The hut that I had found vacant during my earlier visit now had a rickshaw parked in its front yard. Sheikh Nazim, the hut's owner, was digging a ditch when I appeared at his doorstep. Nazim is a thirty-five-year-old farmer. He lives in the hut with his wife and children and his old mother. I found out from him that he had married twice. His first wife and two children were among those who were killed in the riots. The Muslims of Logain had run and hid in their own fields when the mob appeared. Many, like Nazim's wife and kids, were killed in the fields and then buried there.

When he saw the mob approaching, Nazim had crossed a small river and fled to another village where there were more Muslims. He didn't return to his hut till twenty-two days had passed. There was a plot of land close to Nazim's house where weeds had grown knee-high. That was where twelve corpses had been found. The land belonged to Nazim and he had refused to use it again for farming. It didn't have the appearance of a cemetery but that is what it now was. A little distance away was the pond, round and filled with muddy green water, where other bodies had first been thrown and then pulled out and planted in the fields. And several furlongs away was another plot of land—a field about forty feet by thirty feet—where the men from the government had begun to dig a month after the riots and found that the stench of rotting bodies kept growing stronger. Fifty-two corpses had been found in that field. It was there that Nazim had discovered his dead family members. When I asked him what condition the bodies had been in, Nazim used an English word, saying, 'laash complete tha,' as in 'the bodies were whole'. He had also recognized on the corpse the yellow sari that his wife always used to wear. That plot of land too was now overrun with weeds. On the small embankment around the field grew large, trumpet-shaped flowers of a bright, violet colour.

As a compensation for the killing of his wife and two children, the government gave Nazim Rs 350,000 (in today's prices, a bit more than 5000 dollars), money that he used to buy more land in Logain. There was a reticence in Nazim's manner as he told me all this, but I couldn't also help feeling that he was without bitterness. Although he was a survivor of a massacre, he said that he did not feel threatened in the village. I still do not know how to understand this. Perhaps, it has to do with the small world of the village and the ease with which what is ordinary and enduring is able to reassert itself. It is also possible that Nazim, because he was a man, was able to more easily recreate the world that he had lost. He had remarried and produced children. With the money that came to him, he had bought more land and in a sense prospered from his misfortunes.

A sense of inhabiting an altogether different world, a world that had been irrevocably destroyed, would have to be found elsewhere. And I found it when I met Rasheeda in Bhagalpur one night. She was a well-spoken, beautiful widow with three college-going children. Her husband had been the *momin* at the mosque close by and when the riots started he was stabbed in the neck. Rasheeda had dragged her husband's bleeding body through the streets, hoping to get help but he had died in her arms. From the government she got just one-third the amount that Nazim had received as compensation because she had lost only one family member. But in her case the family had lost its breadwinner. Rasheeda was left with three children, all of whom were very young at the time of their father's death. She had decided quite early, Rasheeda said, that she would not speak to others about her woes. She said, 'By not telling my story, I would have my honour. If I were to reveal my difficulties, others would express pity, but they would do nothing else.' She bought sewing machines with the money that the government gave her and she began training young women in her neighbourhood to cut and to sew. Rasheeda also gave her daughters the same instruction, but her emphasis was on providing them an education. All her children became graduates in science. Rasheeda's daughters were not in purdah, and they talked about matters that concerned them with a great deal of independence and humour. But it was also clear from our conversation that their degrees were the only wealth that the family had. There were very few prospects of jobs for her daughters and Rasheeda said that she had no money for dowries for their marriage.

There was a touch of desperation when Rasheeda spoke of her children who had now grown up and were educated but had little by way of a future. We were meeting during a power-cut and a kerosene lantern sat smoking on the bed beside me. The smell of burning oil filled the hot, stuffy room. Rasheeda insisted on waving a straw hand-fan near me so that I would find the heat more bearable. Her young daughters stood in the half-shadows while their mother sat on the bed beside me. I would stare at the flame in the lantern and when I looked up at the people who were talking to me their faces would appear blotched with darkness. I heard Rasheeda ask me whether I knew of 'young, idealistic Muslim men' who would not demand dowry. You are a professor, she said in Urdu, you must have students. You have studied in Delhi. You must have friends there who are professors and have students. I nodded but knew that there was little I could do for Rasheeda. Perhaps she knew this too. As if wanting to explain things, she said in the dark, 'I have seen all the blood in the massacres ... . For a long time, all I would see in my dreams were the necks of my children. In all my dreams I would try to bend down and pick up my kids in my arms.'

*

It was the blind judge in Patna, a man from an old Muslim family, who told me that I must meet Mallika when I went to Bhagalpur, and when he began talking about her I remembered her name from the riots I had written about, the case of the fourteen-year-old girl whose right leg had been cut off by a Hindu mob with a machete. The judge, Mr Niazuddin, was sitting in his house in Pataliputra Colony. He wore a kurta which, although it was crumpled, was delicately embroidered and its buttons studded with shiny stones. Long grey hair curled above his head and gave him the look of a poet. On the wall was a full-length portrait of the judge's grandfather who had been a member of the Viceroy's Executive Council. There also hung on another wall a painting of the Kaaba in Mecca. It was late in the morning. The servant who brought the tea had the same name as I did, and this fact for some reason was less of a surprise for me than the fact that he was a Hindu working in a Muslim home.

The girl had survived. She had thrown herself into a pond that was covered with hyacinth—this detail came back to me whole as the judge began his story—and it was from there that she had been later fished out by a passing army patrol. Sixty-one people were killed in a village called Chanderi and Mallika was the only witness to the crime. This fact gave her importance in the judge's mind and that is why he was telling me about the girl who by now, I realized, must have become a young woman.

The judge had retired many years ago. He wore a pair of dark Raybans but I noticed that his left eye remained shut. The government had appointed him to the commission of inquiry on the Bhagalpur riots. When he submitted his report, a politician had tried to blunt the criticisms by pointing to the judge's blindness. ('He cannot read. How could he have written the report?') Mr Niazuddin scoffed at such objections. With a hint of pleasure, he told me of someone else who had said: 'This is not a report; this is a piece of literature.' Literature or not, the judge wanted me to know that he had indicted the administration for the massacres in Bhagalpur. By way of giving me an example, he mentioned that the district authorities had done nothing to curb the rumours that had sparked attacks in the early stages. The news, later found to be false, had spread that hundreds of Hindu students had been massacred in the Muslim localities. There were other rumours. The army had been fired upon by Muslims in a mosque. Pakistani as well as black flags had been hoisted over Muslim homes. Muslims had planned to molest Hindu women and the principal of a women's college had ordered the students to leave and thereby saved them from 'a fate worse than death'. Despite being false, these rumours had been widely reported, and the government had remained paralyzed. By contrast, the judge said, one need only think of Lord Mountbatten who, even though he himself wasn't sure of this fact, had announced on getting news of Gandhi's assassination that the Mahatma's killer was a Hindu. When the judge told me this story—and I didn't know whether it was apocryphal or not—I got a sense of the reason why he had relished the remark that his report on the riots had read like literature.

Mr Niazuddin wanted me to understand that not much had come out of the report he had submitted on behalf of the commission of inquiry. In the case of the village of Logain, for example, he had named the man who had been a sub-inspector of police there. When the riots had started, the police officer had used his revolver to kill Muslim villagers who were under his protection. Political manoeuvrings and bureaucratic corruption had allowed criminals to go free. Speaking of the police officer in Logain, Mr Niazuddin said, 'Till today he is at large.'

The judge's remark wasn't only about Bhagalpur. When I had gone to meet him, early in the summer of 2002, the violence against Muslims was still continuing in Gujarat. Those responsible for the riots and the killings had, for the large part, not been persecuted. The role of the ruling-party politicians as well as the policemen had led to widespread charges that the pogrom in Gujarat had been conducted 'under the benign gaze of the State and, at worst, with active State collusion'. The ideal of the secular state had proven to be a myth yet again. The judge, it would appear from what he was saying, had greater faith in the people themselves. Mallika had been offered money—and later threatened—by those she had named in her witness report of the massacre. They had wanted her to withdraw their names. But Mallika had decided that she would seek justice instead. In February 2001, more than a decade after the tragedy, the court had delivered its judgement. The killers of Mallika's parents, Bijli Singh and Rameshwar Prasad, had been sentenced to life imprisonment along with a third man, Shambhu Pandit, the one who had wielded the machete and maimed Mallika.

When I had first gone to Bhagalpur to write about the aftermath of the riots, people had told me to go to Chanderi. In the Muslim section of the village, I had seen a striking sight. All the houses were empty, but they had shiny new tin roofs. The roofs were a gift from the government. In the absence of the inhabitants, the only evidence of the violence was offered by the charred clothes, blackened utensils, and burnt paper soaked by the rain. And, of course, the new tin roofs. In an adjoining village, I had come across a man from Chanderi whose name was Mohammed Suleiman, and he said that when he had returned to his gutted home, he had been threatened. His former neighbours said to him, '*Hai baar marliye to tino ke chappar mil le, abki marbe ta chaandi ke dilaibe*' (This time when we hit you, tin roofs were given to you, next time we will hit you so much that you will get silver roofs).

A steel company had built forty-five houses for the Muslim inhabitants whose houses had been destroyed. During my last visit, I saw that those houses in Chanderi had now become old once again. Only a few of them were occupied. It was late evening by the time I could return to Bhagalpur and go to the part of town where Mallika lived. Once again, there was no electricity. It struck me that one was often blind in Bhagalpur, learning to recognize voices in the dark, walking gingerly forward with one's eyes shut in concentration. The man who had taken me to Mallika called out her name when we were in front of a half-built structure that was her house. A woman's voice rose in greeting from the space in front of us and then we heard her immediately shout to someone to bring a chair. But no one said anything about bringing a lantern or a candle. So we remained in the dark as we talked. In my pocket was a small torch and I held it over my notebook. Till the light in my torch went out, I sat in the chair that had been brought, listening to Mallika's voice and writing on the bright sheet of paper in front of me.

When the killings had started, Mallika saw her father being 'beheaded like a goat'. People were murdered and pushed into the pond. Mallika's leg was chopped at the very moment when she fell in the water. When she got up once, Mallika felt that she was standing in blood. She did not drown when she fell down again because she was held up by the corpses beneath her. A snake had wrapped itself around her wrist. Seven or eight hours passed, and when the army patrol rescued her, the major was very kind and caring in a paternal sort of a way. Later, he had asked the soldiers in his patrol if any one of them would volunteer to marry her. One did. He was Mohammed Taj of 3JK Rifles. Mallika got married after she was released from the hospital in Danapur. But, after three years, Mallika's husband disappeared with a good part of the money that she had received as compensation for her parents' deaths. Mallika believes that Taj became a separatist militant in the Kashmir Valley. She was left alone with two small children.

The kids, a boy and a girl, had been standing beside me, their faces pressed close to the small circle of light in which I was writing. Mallika said to them that I was their Mama, their maternal uncle, and because they had been learning these things in school she made them say 'Good evening' to me in English. Then, it was time for me to go and when I got up in the dark and the two children came close to me to say goodbye, I felt for my wallet and put the notes that I had with me in their tiny hands. I did not at any point see Mallika's face and for that reason she remained a bit of a mystery to me. Only once during the evening had I moved the light in her direction when Mallika wanted me to see her new prosthetic shoes—they had been expensive, she said, costing Rs 6000, and she had to get them from faraway Indore—and my eyes had travelled as far up as her damaged leg, brown skin sewn together under the amputated bone.

*

During my childhood, I had gone to Bhagalpur on different family occasions like weddings and engagements. I was not yet out of my teens when suddenly Bhagalpur became known all over India. A reporter had found twenty-five under-trial prisoners who had been blinded by the police. The year was 1980. For several days, the details of the story appeared on the front pages of the national newspapers. The eyes of the men had been pierced in most cases by long needles used to sew jute bags. The police had also used awls ordinarily employed by cobblers for making holes in leather. On the wounded eyes of the prisoners, the policemen then poured acid.

A month or so after the story about the blindings first appeared I accompanied my parents on a trip to Bhagalpur. My maternal uncle was the superintendent of the jail in which the blinded prisoners had been kept. We were on our winter vacation; in a few months, I was going to enter college. The day we arrived in Bhagalpur was the last day of the year. To celebrate the arrival of the New Year, we were going on a picnic the next day. In my uncle's house, police constables in brown overcoats peered into pots over dung fires that had been lit in the driveway. Rose and marigold bushes were in bloom in the garden. In front of the house was the town's airport—in reality, an open, unused field—and the winter mist spread across it just as the evening came. On the left I could see the red walls of the jail. There was a stairwell at the corner, and it led up to a tower where a guard stood with a rifle. When darkness fell, a searchlight in the tower swept the surroundings with light. My uncle, Keshav Mamaji, had only recently got the job and, when I went inside the house, I overheard him talking to my parents about the blindings.

Everyone was sitting in the living-room. My father had spread around him the new quilt that Keshav Mamaji's wife had presented him. The wool, in red and white, was woven to form the pattern of a tiger standing in the wild. I sat and examined my uncle's collection of vinyl records. The former superintendent had been transferred after the blindings became public. It was that same man, Keshav Mamaji's predecessor, who had informed the press as well as a human rights organization about the police crimes. The men had actually been blinded in the thanas, the police stations, and then brought to the jail to be admitted as under-trials. The former superintendent had got into a fight with the police and then given the story to the press. His government bosses had taken a dim view of this official vigilantism on the part of the superintendent and promptly sent him elsewhere to cool his heels. Keshav Mamaji made it clear that he was not going to be such a fool himself. He said to my father that the level of crime had gone down in the district since the blindings started. I entered the conversation and asked my uncle if he would take me inside the jail the next day. I was curious to see the blinded men. Before Keshav Mamaji could say anything, my father dismissed my request. He said, 'They are all notorious criminals.' Keshav Mamaji agreed with him. He said that the blindings had full support of the local public. There had been a couple of recent incidents—after the actions of the police had been reported in the press—in which mobs in small towns had blinded the criminals in their area. The implement used by the public, my uncle said, were thin aluminium spokes from a bicycle wheel.

I didn't get to see the blind men. Not too long after my trip to Bhagalpur, they were released from jail and sent for treatment, on government expense, to the All India Institute of Medical Sciences. Then, I joined college in Delhi and began to dream of becoming a writer. I went abroad and found work there. Years later, when I arrived in Bhagalpur a few months after the riots, I remembered the blindings from a decade ago, but I had no interest in them. I had told myself that my subject was the blindness that is the cause of religious violence. But the two had always been related. I discovered this the longer I spent in Bhagalpur. It started with my meeting with the blind men.

On the morning after my meeting with Rasheeda, I went with my parents to visit a relative who lived in a village beside the Ganges. The village was about an hour's drive away, but it had taken us longer. Then, we had to stop because, close to our destination, a bridge had collapsed. I could not see the truck in the water. But people were pointing at the spot where it had sunk in the muddy current of the Ganges. The truck was carrying petrol and the damaged bridge had given way under its weight. The house where we were going was just across the river, and we could see it from where we stood, but we would need a boat to ferry us to the other side. Beneath us, down an incline, was the river bank. Two men were loading computers on a boat: they stacked the hard-drives one on top of another like bricks, and then, showing greater care, picked up the computer monitors and put them in the section that was dry. The boat was small but a plank was laid on its side so that my parents and I could climb on board more easily. When we had taken our place in the boat on the opposite end from the computers, a young man wheeled on board his Hero Honda motorcycle and parked it in the small space in the middle. We were ready to leave, and the boatman, using a long bamboo pole, pushed the boat into the current.

The house loomed closer in a few minutes. It was owned by Raman, my uncle's brother-in-law. I recognized Raman above us, in his mauve shirt, waiting for us to come up the steep slope of sand. The village where Raman lives is located at the place where two small rivers feed into the Ganges. I had visited this house several times in my childhood, once spending over a month there in the summer when I was eleven years old. The village had changed over the last twenty years. The fields that I had been familiar with were now small construction sites where workers were loading concrete chips on trucks. Several brick-kilns had come up close to the house. As a boy I had walked barefoot over the hot ground and then jumped into the river. My acts at that time were witnessed only by the trees. Now, there was activity all around. The sand from the river-bed—and the clay fired in the kilns—was being used to build houses all over Bihar. The road leading to the house still had a few remaining mango trees but the tyres of the trucks had made small ditches beside the road and they were now filled with dirty water. Raman was proud of these changes; he was a building contractor. He looked at the computers being unloaded from the boat and told me that they had been donated for a school. He announced that he had a computer too, and his son used it whenever he came home from boarding school.

The blind men were seated in the shaded veranda of Raman's house. When we stepped into the veranda, they shook their heads in the air like cattle, trying to catch what we were saying, but I mistook their movement and assumed that they were uncomfortable in the heat. It made me conscious of how stifling the air was. There was a boy sitting among them. He was sighted and his big, alert eyes were fixed on my face. I looked back at Raman, and then at the men. One of them—I could see his pink eyeballs and the way the acid had burnt the flesh beneath one eye—wiped his face with a dirty, striped towel draped around his shoulder. I didn't immediately know what to say, and I turned to Raman and suggested that we take my parents inside the house. Raman nodded, and said to the men, 'Just a minute.' A dog was barking in the room behind the door. Raman took the dog, a white Pomeranian, in his arms. There was a generator in the house and Raman switched it on, so that he could then use the air-conditioner in his bedroom. I was sweating heavily and the cool air made me suddenly unwilling to step outside to talk to the blind men. When I joked about this, Raman said loudly, 'Why don't you just relax? I will have them fed lunch.' He stepped out of the door and began to give orders.

In a few minutes, Raman's daughter came up bearing a tray of soft drinks in her hands. I had last seen her as a child, and she touched my feet in greeting. Raman began removing the plastic cover from the computer on his desk. I asked him about the men waiting for me downstairs. How had he been able to contact them? Raman said, 'They were the most famous criminals in this area. They have become beggars now.' He told me that he had also been able to find Anil Yadav. 'He was the worst of them all,' he said, and indeed, when Raman took that name, it stirred a memory. I asked him to tell me more about Yadav. Raman first said that I should ask Yadav myself, but then he could not pass up the opportunity to tell us a story. The criminal gangs around Bhagalpur had used the *diara*—the stretch of fertile land that the river would reveal in the middle when the course of the water shifted or when it receded after a flood—to hide from the police and also to hide their loot. It was to the diara, Raman said, that Anil Yadav took the men he had kidnapped. He would have them tied to a stake and then use a razor to skin their soles. This was a persuasive method if you wanted to change someone's mind. But, Yadav didn't inflict death painlessly either. The brother of a local politician from the opposition had died at Yadav's hands. People said that his shins had been carved out with a knife and his flesh fed to the fish in the river.

I ate lunch. Raman had made friends at a nearby electric company. Its manager was a city man. It was his wife who had cooked the food for us. Rice and fresh fish curry was served with heaps of salad that had been cut in florid patterns. The food was delicious and Raman said that I would have to try the dessert after I had talked to the men waiting for me. I went down the stairs. The men had eaten. I sat down on a chair facing them with a notebook in my hand. The men, there were four of them, sat together on a large wooden bed. A window to my left let in light and some air. I began taking down the names of the men, and asked them to tell me their age.

The boy was sitting closest to me. The name of the blind man sitting next to him was Lakhan Lal. He was old, the man said, close to sixty. Lakhan Lal's hair was white and he wore a white shirt and a short white dhoti wrapped around his waist. The boy beside him was his grandson. The old man had been caught stealing and had been blinded. Sitting to their right was a man who wore dark glasses. His clothes were cleaner, and he had a well-trimmed moustache. His name was Ram Swarup. He said he was fifty-five years old. He added that one of his eyes still 'had some light in it' and he was able to make out the shapes of things about two yards away. From the kind of Hindi he spoke, I judged that he was educated and that he could not have been a petty thief in the village. I mentioned this to a police officer later in Bhagalpur, and he said that Ram Swarup had been a 'rape master'. He would stop buses on the highway and force women to step down. The policeman made a point of saying that Ram Swarup would choose the most beautiful girl on the bus. He would rape his victims on the road, the girl lying on the tarmac beneath him. In Raman's house, however, Ram Swarup told me that he had been a gem trader. He was returning home after a pilgrimage when the police took him into custody and then blinded him.

I asked the man who sat behind Lakhan Lal with his eyes downcast to tell me his name and then realized that he was actually sighted: he was there as an escort, he simply pointed at the tall man next to him, the one I had earlier seen wiping his face with the towel. The tall man, to whom I now paid greater attention, was Anil Yadav. His curly hair was turning grey and he had a week-long stubble on his face. When I asked him his age, he said, 'Forty-five'. The police had blinded him on 6 July 1980. At that time, Yadav was twenty-three years old. Ten years later, he had got married. How had the marriage been arranged? The bride was an orphan, he said. Using an English word, Yadav said that she didn't have a 'guardian'. There was a marriage ceremony and the couple now has two boys.

Looking at Yadav, I said that the police had acted criminally and, of course, what had happened should not ever have taken place. But I was also curious, I told him, whether the stories were true, the stories that I had heard about the killings he had carried out. Yadav turned away from my voice and faced the wall close to him. 'I used to take my buffalo to graze in the diara,' he said. Silence sat like an invisible person among us. The faces of the other men remained expressionless. I saw that Raman was smiling. He pointed at Yadav with his finger, in order to encourage me to be persistent. But I couldn't repeat the question. After a minute, Yadav said, 'The government gives us Rs 750 every month. They should make it Rs 2000.' I was being given this information as a writer, and I understood that this was why the men were talking to me. I took down notes and made noises in my throat. Yadav began to speak again. He said, 'I am useless now, fit only for cutting grass.' He made a gesture, bunching the fingers of his left hand as if he were holding a clump of weeds, slicing with his right hand the empty air in front of him.

I asked Yadav to tell me what his eyes had last seen. He said he was in handcuffs in the courtyard of the Sabour police station. Then the constables—there were ten or twelve of them—tied his legs with rope. The time, he guessed, must have been around four in the morning. He remembered the mango tree in the courtyard of the station. The police inspector asked Yadav to tell him exactly how many men he had killed so far. When Yadav did not answer him, the officer pierced his right eye. Then, he used the acid. Yadav said that this hurt more. The first few drops made him feel as if he was on fire. He was able to get up on his legs—Yadav now stood up before me, his hands clenched beside each shoulder—and then he lost control and fell down. Once he was on the ground again, the constables held him down more strongly and the inspector blinded his left eye. I noticed that it was the right eye which had the extra fold of drooping flesh beneath it. It meant that when Yadav had thrown off the constables and got up, the acid would have bubbled down to the cheek and burnt the skin there into a small ball.

*

A storm was threatening to break over us when we were leaving Raman's house. The sky above the river was a mixture of brown and grey, and suddenly out of nowhere, two egrets flew past us with their legs seeming to touch the water. Then, I noticed that there was a stain spreading on Raman's shirt. In a moment or two, the first raindrops fell on me, and I turned to look at the Ganges. Rain broke the surface of the water around us and soon the brown expanse of the river was covered with tiny ripples.

We crossed the river in the rain. For a brief moment, the storm had made everything bright, but soon after the rain had stopped, darkness descended quickly. We were back on the road to Bhagalpur. At one place, some figures appeared in our path. A heavy man in a shirt and trousers, leaving his motorbike lying in the middle of the road where it had fallen, was slapping the driver of a tonga. The tonga-driver sat on his seat. He was holding the reins of his pony, allowing the blows to fall on him, and I wondered, for a moment, what it would take for him to let his whip fly over the face of the man who was assaulting him. We kept on driving. The headlights picked out insects dancing in the dark. The endless insects in the humid night and, lining the highway near the hamlets we were crossing, the women in saris who wait for the cars and trucks to cross before they can squat down again. Men can use the fields freely in the day, but women learn to wait till night falls to go out to sit beside the highway. When the lights of the cars approach in the pitch dark, the women stand up and turn their faces away. The passenger in the passing vehicle sees only the saris and, among the folds, the women's hands in which are clutched small flashlights.

It could have been the women by the wayside that made me aware that it was only men who had been blinded by the police in Bhagalpur. I was also remembering, I think, the blind girl in J.M. Coetzee's *Waiting for the Barbarians*, who is seduced by the magistrate responsible for rescuing her after she had been tortured. In his apartment, the old magistrate rubs almond oil on the barbarian girl, bathes her broken body, and soon he begins to make love to her, but what he wants to know is what the torturers have done to her eyes. Her blindness is a mystery to him. As long as she doesn't tell him anything about it, he feels restless and empty. He is haunted by bad dreams. Then she offers him a few incomplete but frank details. She tells him that they had used a fork with two blunt teeth. They put the fork in the coals and then held it close to her eyes. There is a worm-like mark in the corner of one eye where the fork had touched the girl, but she says that they did not want to burn her. They held her eyelids open and forced her to look at the red hot fork. The girl tells the magistrate that there is now a blur in the middle of everything she sees.

The novel had begun with an image of the girl's torturer, the notorious Colonel Joll from the Third Bureau. In fact, there is a question in the magistrate's mind—when he first sees Joll—about the latter's eyesight. This is how the novel begins: 'I have never seen anything like it: two little discs of glass suspended in front of his eyes in loops of wire. Is he blind? I could understand it if he wanted to hide blind eyes. But he is not blind. The discs are dark, they look opaque from the outside, but he can see through them. He tells me they are a new invention.' As the novel proceeds, and Colonel Joll unleashes his terrible violence, it is impossible not to be reminded of the magistrate's innocent question in a new way. 'Is he blind?' This question might justifiably be asked about his prejudice or his brutal arrogance, but Colonel Joll does not offer any opportunity for scrutiny the way the girl does—after all, the magistrate is able to look into her eyes, and even discover the mark which reminds him of a decapitated caterpillar. This much is at least possible, despite the girl's silence and her mystery. Joll, on the other hand, allows no reciprocal gaze. There is no return of looks. The torturer remains undecipherable behind his opaque glasses.

In Bhagalpur one day, I tried to find my Colonel Joll. In meetings with journalists and administrators, I kept asking if there was in the city a police officer who had been held guilty of blinding criminals. Later, a man came to see me where I was staying; he was plainer than Joll, altogether without mystery and almost harmless, but he presented a more complicated case for me. He had been the officer in charge of the Sanhaula police station and his name was Parmeshwar Prasad. When the blindings came to light, he was suspended from duty and subjected to an inquiry from the intelligence wing of the government. For ten years, he was without a job. Prasad was not a very well-educated man, and he was already in his sixties, but he remembered the ranks of all the policemen who were indicted in that case and the details of the judgments that were read against them. His felt that his life had been made a part of a farcical political tamasha. He recalled the politician from Bihar who had appeared in parliament in Delhi with a bandage tied on his eyes. When he spoke of the politician's antics, Prasad laughed. And I laughed too, and, in the pause that followed, asked him to tell me about his tools for blinding. He smiled and said with what I am tempted to call humility, 'Sir, I had used the needle used to sew jute bags. I kept the acid in a small bottle which had its own rubber dropper.' The bottle had originally contained medicine for the eyes, and all that had needed to be done was replace it with acid. Prasad squeezed together the fingers of his right hand to indicate how the drops of acid would be put into the eyes.

This prompted another question in my mind. When I was a child, the only occasions on which I had heard the word 'acid' was when the sweeper came to clean the toilet-bowls. I had found out that it was sulphuric acid that was easily available for such purposes. When I asked Prasad if that indeed was the chemical that he had used, his eyes widened and he laughed once again. 'No, no,' he said. The type of acid chosen by the police was the weaker liquid that jewellers use to clean gold. The other kind of acid, he corrected me respectfully, 'would have melted the prisoner's brains'.

Prasad lost his levity when I asked him if any of his superiors knew what he was doing. He said he was bitter that all senior police officials who had been aware of the blindings had permitted men like him to be turned into scapegoats. The superintendent of police in Bhagalpur had suffered at the hands of the criminals: 'His brother had been cut open at a factory and his body thrown into the Ganges.' Crime was flourishing, and the public wanted the police to put a stop to it. That is why a hundred thousand people had turned out on the streets of Bhagalpur to show support for the policemen when their jobs were taken away from them. In the years during which he had been suspended, Prasad said that he had lost all his savings. His son, his first-born, had died soon after his graduation. There were other regrets. If he had not lost his job, he would have retired at a higher rank, as a police inspector. He would have had a bit of standing in society. When I asked him why he thought he was justified in taking a man's eyesight, Prasad hesitated and then appealed to my sense of justice. 'Not one of them'—and here I am translating from a common Hindi expression he had used—'was washed in milk.' He meant to say that all of his victims were villains. Anil Yadav, he claimed, would chop off a person's leg in public, secure in the knowledge that there wasn't anyone in Bhagalpur who could do anything about it.

For a few minutes, we talked about the circumstances in which Prasad had been able to return to work after ten years. He began to talk of the riots in Bhagalpur, and I felt that I had met Prasad before, and then, a bit abruptly, I lost any interest in proceeding with our conversation. Prasad saw me looking at my watch. I said that we should end our meeting, I needed to drive my parents to lunch. Prasad stalled. It seemed he wanted to say something else. I noticed that although he wore a baseball cap on his head, which gave him a jaunty look, he was an old man with a ragged grey moustache and shaky speech.

Prasad's eyes were rheumy, and he wiped them with the back of his hands, but now I saw that he was crying. He bent down and hugged my feet. He said, 'Sir, you can be of help to me.' Although his own life had been destroyed, he said, he did not want anything for himself. He had one remaining son. It was possible for the government to grant Prasad a licence to be a vendor of revenue stamps. If he got this licence, his son would have employment, a vending stall in front of the courts, selling the stamps that are used on all official forms and affidavits. He knew that I had recently interviewed the superintendent of police. Would I not put in a word when I spoke next to the police chief?

I put my hand on Prasad's arm, and promised that I would do what he wanted. I was like Coetzee's magistrate, solicitous, seductive, and a little guilty.

*

After having been under an order of suspension for nearly ten years, Prasad had been admitted back into the police force. Riots had broken out in Bhagalpur. The bloodbath during these riots was so widespread that it was said to be the most serious outbreak of conflict between Hindus and Muslim since the conflagrations that had accompanied the Partition of India in 1947. Prasad told me that when the senior police officers found out that he had been one of the men convicted in the blinding case, they knew that he was tough and could be sent to work in the troubled areas. He returned to work in a city caught in a communal frenzy.

Then Prasad started on another story about his toughness. There was a young Muslim man in town who had eloped with a Hindu girl. Prasad had caught them and given the young man a good thrashing. The name of the Muslim youth was Rupu Khan. There remained the matter of the Hindu girl. Prasad said that the girl was in love with the Muslim, and when they ran away, they had got married. Her father was a local, upper-caste politician. Prasad had had the girl brought to the police station and, in front of her father, he began beating the girl with a cane. I asked if the father didn't protest. Prasad laughed again in his self-bemused way. He said, 'I had asked the girl's father to sit quietly and allow me to take care of business.' The girl recanted. Her love story was beaten out of her. The rumour of her marriage to the Muslim was given a swift burial. Her father was very grateful to Prasad. Not much later, he got his daughter married to a Hindu of their own caste.

It was Prasad's narration of this story that had made me glance at my watch. I had claimed that I needed to take my parents to lunch. The truth was that only a few days prior to my meeting with Prasad, I had heard the same story, but the person who was telling it to me had been the mother of the murdered Muslim youth. The old woman's name was Bunni Begum. She was a widow. I had gone to meet her because she was a survivor of the Bhagalpur riots in the winter of 1989. Bunni's fingers were crooked—with one or two of them missing—because she had tried to push away the sword that the attacker had pressed against her throat. She was trying to save herself and her sister from a large Hindu mob. The women had been hiding with other Muslims in the house of their neighbour, a Hindu politician, when they came under attack. I was trying to get Bunni to talk to me about what had happened during the riots, and she told me about the blunt instrument that would not kill her, and that as long as she could hear her own cry she knew that she was still alive. The struggle with her assailant had taken place on a staircase. On Bunni's shoulder and neck were the pitted marks of her wounds, the loose skin bunched around gashes in the flesh.

But Bunni also wanted me to hear another part of the story. The local leader in whose house she had been hiding was 'a eunuch', she said emphatically, someone 'who was not man enough to be able to protect those whom he had given shelter'. Bunni wanted me to see the building in which she had almost died. I looked out past the faded curtain close to me—a goat was tied near the doorway and I had watched with growing alarm as it chewed on the blue plywood that it regularly bit from the door—and saw the large white house at the end of the street. The owner of that house, the politician, was an upper-caste Hindu whose daughter later fell in love with Bunni's son. The girl's name was Pinky. When Rupu Khan and Pinky ran away from home, the politician came to Bunni's house with a police officer. Bunni put her hand on the Qur'an and appealed to the men: she said to them that she had no knowledge of her son's whereabouts. The policeman began to beat her. Her son, he threatened, would be taught a lesson too, and, when Rupu Khan came back home two days later, the policeman stuck to his promise. Bunni covered her mouth with a corner of her brown sari, and let her eyes fill with tears. I looked up at the wall of the room. There was a photograph of a well-built young man standing next to the former film star Sunil Dutt. Bunni began to speak while half-crying. She said that there had been fears of a riot erupting between Hindus and Muslims, but it abated because the girl was back in her father's house. The public tragedy had been averted, but Bunni's family was not spared. Pinky's brother, the politician's son, came down the street with a gun. He called Rupu Khan out of the house and shot him from close range. The murderer was not punished; it was clear that the police had colluded with the politician. When Bunni ended her story, I understood why she had had her son's name painted on the wall outside. It was a way of making those who had killed her son look at his name every day when they made their way past her house.

It was only when Prasad was telling me his version of the story that I recognized him as the policeman in the tale that Bunni had told me earlier. I quickly saw that he demonstrated a link to the two species of blindness I associated with Bhagalpur: he was a policeman who had blinded the men in his custody and also someone who had, by his own admission, persecuted Muslims when the killings began in his town. Prasad would not have known, or even imagined, that I was married to a Muslim myself. The police officer who had helped me get in touch with Prasad was a distant relative of mine. This meant Prasad knew my caste. It is one of the first things people find out about you in Bihar. Prasad would have known that I was a Hindu who belonged to the same caste as the local politician whose daughter, he believed, he had saved from the clutches of a Muslim man. In his mind, I was certainly the right person to appreciate his deeds. Oddly enough, even Bunni had taken me to be someone other than what

I was. I had realized at some point in our conversation that she had assumed that I was a Muslim. This might have been because I was speaking to her in Urdu, and she had decided, quite understandably for someone in her milieu, that I was of her faith. So, every time she touched my knee and made a remark about the way the kafirs, the unbelievers, had mistreated her son, I felt the need to declare that I was a fake. I was only a counterfeit Muslim.

Later, when I thought about what had happened both with Prasad and with Bunni, I saw that my discomfort could not have been mine alone. It was a more general feeling which would be shared by all those post-Independence Indians who had grown up to regard themselves as secular. We had inherited the modern idea that in the governance of our country there would be a separation of the state and religion, but what it had really come to mean in our hearts was that we were to be suspicious of religion itself. Our names marked us as belonging to a particular religion, and we signalled this affiliation to those around us, but in our own minds we regarded ourselves as free from the biases of our religion and, indeed, even the entrapment of faith. Although we would not put it this way, what this meant was that we were above ordinary people. We were not to be included in the lay public's circle of assumptions. Ordinary people applied tilak and poured water over their stone-gods, and then murdered their fellow humans who practised another faith. In the name of religion, the people killed each other during riots. As left-minded secularists, we resisted ritual. We wanted to stand between the people and the riots. It is possible that my unease in Prasad's company, and also in Bunni's, was the unease of the liberal who regards religion as a dubious source of modern identity. However, it is also possible that my discomfort grew out of my desire to convey, and indeed to believe in, an idea of religion as humane and tolerant but I just didn't know how. It was much easier, then, to follow the path of the other secularists and simply focus on the violence and speak against the inhumanity of murder.

*

The afternoon when Prasad had visited me, I waited for him to leave and then stepped out of the room to find my parents.

We were staying at the government guest house, a run-down place with its own elaborately hierarchical bureaucracy. All through the day, government jeeps and Ambassadors would come to a stop outside the red cement steps of the guest house and guards would leap out to open the doors. In the room next to us was a former veterinarian who had turned into a state legislator after being thrown in jail for his involvement in a multi-million dollar 'fodder-scam'. This man held court each morning and evening in the shabby living-room on whose walls hung the portraits of the national leaders with pale yellow lizards sticking to the glass covering their faces.

That day, when Prasad left my room, I found my parents seated on the veranda outside. They were engaged in conversation with a man who had come to pay his respects to the veterinarian-turned-legislator. This man was a headmaster of a local school. I had seen him once before, scurrying across a dimly lit passage, and had assumed that he was a beggar. I realized my mistake when the introductions were made. I had assumed that because he had no legs and small stumps for hands, he was a beggar, but now when I saw the pens in his pocket, I knew that he was educated. The awareness that I had been presumptuous, and even prejudiced, made me a little resentful instead of generous towards him. I noticed that my parents had a pious look on their faces; they assumed this expression when speaking to religious swamis, academics, and those whose bodies were marked by disabilities. My mother said to the man with great solemnity, 'My son is a teacher like you.' I did not say anything. My father added, 'He is also a journalist. He is writing about violence.'

The headmaster's eyes lit up. He said that he had been given an award by the government; an article had been written about him in the magazine printed by the public relations department. He had tried to bring 'peace and harmony' between Hindus and Muslims in Bhagalpur. The headmaster urged me to write about him. He had been given a local award for having provided shelter to Muslim students in his own house during the riots. He would very much like, he said, to receive recognition from the national government. 'My life has been spent in hospitals,' he complained. He said that it was not till a couple of years ago that most of his sores had healed, the sores that were formed on his torso when he dragged himself on the floor.

It was difficult for me to be patient with him. I had decided that our headmaster was the mascot of the secular state. I could get from him talk about brotherhood and co-existence but absolutely nothing about the reasons that made one man kill another. I saw that my father held a piece of paper on which, I guessed, he had written down the man's address. I said to the headmaster that I was sorry but I didn't think that what I wrote would be useful to him in that way. It would not fetch him awards. The man looked at my father for a moment as if he wanted my bad behaviour to be explained by someone. I felt sorry for him. I looked at his slight body, bent like an old monkey's under the bald head, and prepared to change the subject. But the man didn't want me to say anything to soften the impact of rejection. He hopped down from his chair and with a mixture of awkwardness and agility disappeared down the corridor. My parents, embarrassed in my place, said nothing.

Prasad had wanted his stamp-vendor's licence. The headmaster wanted an award for his kindness during the riots. Bunni told me that she was in need of a telephone connection in her house. Rasheeda was looking for eligible bachelors for her unwed daughters. Anil Yadav wanted a more generous stipend from the government. I wanted stories from each one of them—and while they granted me my wish, I wasn't prepared to give anything in return. In my mind this made my mission purer. There was also the understanding that my writing was indeed all that I could offer anyone. I was writing about man's injustice to man. I did not say this to any one of them because I realized how little promise this had of saving them. So I did nothing. I felt that I was faithfully recording the pain of the people I met. That fiction was acceptable for a while, but there were also more concrete demands. At times, I felt that a subtle appeal was being made, and when I sensed this I would begin to withdraw. Often, however, there was a great temptation to show compassion or to win some love. In Bunni's case, for example, I thought of the

Rs 5000 (about one hundred dollars) that I was carrying in my bag. While she spoke to me of her need for a telephone, I played with the idea of making her happy by leaving that money as a gift. This old woman, whose thoughts wandered as she spoke to me, and who was speaking against the cruelties of Hindus, would probably be intrigued if she learned that I was not the Muslim that she had taken me to be. There would be delight about the money, and perhaps surprise that I was a Hindu. As it happened, I didn't leave her anything. Towards the end of our meeting, her son-in-law had arrived and begun to question me aggressively. The atmosphere had changed— no one was sharing anything any more, we were only suspiciously exchanging information—and I felt that my gesture would be misunderstood.

*

We left Bhagalpur in the morning, trailing for a long time, on the highway to Patna, a truck which had sawdust loaded in its back, like sand, and thick blocks of ice sitting in gleaming rows. The humid air around the translucent slabs of ice turned white and swirled in the wind. In small towns people waited patiently outside telephone booths which had names like 'Naaz Hello Centre' and 'Lokpriya Hallo Home'. My parents were in the back seat, lulled into sleep by the heat outside and the motion of the car. We drove past primary schools in the villages. No one was sitting inside the classrooms. The teacher and the pupils were crowded into the shallow verandas where there was some air and also light. The car in which I was travelling was air-conditioned and this single feature made my life a joy. In most circumstances, such a statement might appear to be an exaggeration or a mis-statement, but not on that occasion, when a steady rush of cool air seemed to offer me a natural protection not only from heat but also the surrounding poverty, wretched education, hunger, social conflict, and even bad spelling. I was leaving Bhagalpur behind me; I was leaving it behind in a bubble of comfort.

In the closing pages of *Vedi*, the childhood memoir by Ved Mehta, we read of the blind writer's visit to Dadar, in Bombay, where he had lived as a boy. Mehta was hardly four when he had lost his eyes to meningitis, and within a year, his father, who was an affluent public-health officer, decided to send the young Vedi to a boarding school. In the villages where he had toured, the elder Mehta had seen blind villagers being taken care of by their relatives. But these blind people, he thought, 'lived little better than wounded animals'. He decided to place advertisements in the 'agony columns' of newspapers in Bombay. That is how his son ended up at the Dadar School for the Blind, where the boy spent more than four years of his young life. The school was actually an orphanage for poor, blind boys. It stood between two huge textile mills and its aim was to teach its wards the skill of caning chairs. When Mehta, already an established writer in his forties, returned to the school from his home in New York, he found out that many of his childhood friends had died from consumption. A few of them had ended up as masseurs and physiotherapists. One was a teacher at a blind school in another city. There had been a girl named Rajas, someone whom Mehta couldn't remember very well, who now lived in a tenement. Mehta's memoir ends with a visit to the small, suffocating quarters in which Rajas lived.

It takes Rajas some time to place Mehta, and though she is thrilled, that feeling doesn't last very long. She begins complaining about hard times. 'I have three children to support,' she says. 'Come here, child. Say hello to your uncle.' Later, Mehta asks her whether she remembers anything about him at school. She tells him that he was 'a jolly child' but she can remember no more. Neither can he. When Mehta gets up to leave, Rajas 'starts whining like a street beggar'. What Rajas wants from her visitor is a Braille watch. Mehta leaves the room soon. As he rushes out, stumbling over people and animals, he knows that the begging tone has 'stirred up a still earlier memory and an old fear'.

The fear of becoming a beggar.

Since my early childhood I have looked as an outsider at others who have been intimate with that fear. These others have also seemed to carry a secret, a secret about life that has been denied me. I might have envied them that knowledge but what I could not have envied, not for long and certainly not in my later life, was their deprivation. I'm thinking of the blind men who came to our door, singing bhajans so that they could be given some money or food. In fact, what I have also learned as I began to travel and meet people was that violence adds insult to injury by turning its victims into beggars. I often saw this on the faces of the men and women who had suffered such violence, how they had quickly come to despise their experience because it had rendered them helpless, or had imposed on them the frustrating burden of having to weakly say no, over and over again, to offers of charity. The penalty of privilege, however, is to realize that violence is essentially democratic and it excludes no one: even to serve as its witness is to experience the erosion of one's humanity. A vacuum grows in the middle-class soul. The emptiness gets filled up with the sewage of guilt—guilt over one's lack of charity, or patience, or love, or even, let's not deny it, the absence of a more essential shame or culpability. That is where the writer's journey into the world ends. The discovery of suffering among others evokes in the soul an answering echo of sympathy. There are limits to the process, however, and it is easy to slip into either sentimentalism or recoil. All the truth and the pity of the world, instead of finding its way to a larger politics, gets reduced to a personal soap-opera of the self.

It is afternoon and I am lying shirtless under the fan in the guest house in Bhagalpur reading a magazine article about the soccer World Cup that has recently been played in South Korea. There is a knock on the door. It is the caretaker, a beedi tucked above his ear, with the news that a blind man is waiting outside for me. I go outside to look. There is a slight man with dark glasses dressed in a white shirt and a dhoti and beside him stand two girls. One of the girls is in her early teens, the other is younger, maybe six or seven. In a few minutes, we arrange ourselves under the portraits of the national leaders. I end up sitting close to the man. The girls, his daughters, sit on chairs facing me. The man tells me that he was blinded by the police on 6 October 1980. When the police took him into custody, they had found a few Italian moonstones in his pocket. He was accused of having stolen them. He was twenty-eight years old at that time and was working as a jeweller. He has been in jail once again since his blinding, on suspicion of robbery and murder. He was released after fourteen months.

I get these details from the man because I am asking him questions. He answers me in a very loud voice. I notice that the acid has left burn marks on the man's face, the lines appear a bit like brown frames of spectacles, stretching from the eyes down to the earlobes. It is clear that the acid has damaged the man's hearing. While the man and I talk, I do not look at his daughters. I do not want them to be a participant in whatever this exchange represents and I pretend that they are not there. As the man has been a jeweller I ask him the question I had asked Prasad. He tells me that it is not the acid used in cleaning gold that the policemen used; it was another sort, it is called *khatta tezaab*, sour acid, and anything stronger than that can be lethal. But the man shows impatience with these questions about the past. He has been told that I have been talking to those who were blinded by the police. He needs my help. His voice gets louder. He takes out a letter which has been folded five or six times. It is a letter written by the state food minister urging the district administration to assist the man and grant him a licence to sell oil. I learn from him that he already owns an oil store, selling kerosene and mustard oil. 'Our situation is not very good. We have been reduced to beggars,' he says. He wants something else now—and he uses the same words that I had heard Prasad use—a stamp-vendor's licence. I keep back the impulse to ask him if he had been blinded by Prasad. It is bizarre to imagine that both of these men, the victim and the victimizer, now have the same desire.

'I am not a government official,' I tell the man.

'I need your help, Sirji,' he says. I say nothing. He repeats the two words, 'Sirji, Sirji.'

I tell him that I will speak to the district collector. The man asks me for my business card. I have a packet of unused cards lying inside my room, but I do not move from my chair, and offer the excuse that I can't be of much help.

'I live thousands of miles away in America,' I say.

'Please take me to America,' the man says, 'please help me get my eyes back.'

His voice is more matter-of-fact than whining. It is also loud. It is very loud. I look at the girls. Both of them are looking at me, but I cannot read their expression. It is as if the man knows that I am looking at the girls, and he points at the one sitting closer to him. He says, 'Her mother will give one of her eyes, Sirji. Please take me with you America. Please, Sirji.'

I do not know what to say. I stand up, but I do not move away. I find the man's suggestion preposterous. I am aware that the girls are not looking at me any more. They understand I have to leave, I tell myself. The man reaches out with his left hand and finds my arm. He holds it in a loose, dry grip, as if he were measuring my wrist.

'Sirji, I will serve you for life. Please help me.'

I say softly that I will speak to the district collector. I say, 'That is all that I can do. You must understand this.' The man lets go of my arm.

He says, 'Sirji, one second ... .'

He says that he needs some money for the rickshaw fare ... or, he adds quickly, perhaps money for the girls' dresses.

There is anger, but also embarrassment, on the elder girl's face. Suddenly, I cannot believe that I have been having my little drama with the man at the expense of his young daughters. But I have no idea what else I could have done. I go around the man's chair and hesitate near the two girls. I resent being bullied by their father, but also feel pity for the two. I take out some money from my wallet, more than what would be needed for the rickshaw, I think, but certainly not enough for their dresses, and place it in the younger girl's hand. As I shut the door, I hear the loud, demanding voice behind me. 'How much is it—how much did he give?'

Select Bibliography

Ahmad, Eqbal. *Confronting Empire: Interviews with David Barsamian*. Cambridge, Massachusetts: South End Press, 2000.

Akbar, M.J. *Nehru: The Making of India*. New York: Viking, 1988.

Akbar, M.J. *The Shade of Swords: Jihad and the Conflict between Islam and Christianity*. New York: Routledge, 2002.

Alter, Stephen. *Amritsar to Lahore: A Journey across the India-Pakistan Border*. Philadelphia: University of Pennsylvania Press, 2001.

Ansari, Nasim. *Choosing to Stay: Memoirs of an Indian Muslim*. Translated from the Urdu by Ralph Russell. Karachi: City Press, 1999.

Bahadur, Gaiutra. 'Hindu nationalists tap immigrant guilt in U.S.', *The Philadelphia Inquirer*, January 17, 2003.

Basu, T., P. Datta, S. Sarkar, T. Sarkar and S. Sen. *Khaki Shorts, Saffron Flags*. New Delhi: Orient Longman, 1993.

Bhalla, Alok, ed. *Stories about the Partition of India*. New Delhi: HarperCollins, 1994.

Bhatt, Shakti. 'Duty calls. Indians head for battle', *India Abroad*, April 11, 2003.

Bharucha, Rustom. *The Question of Faith*. New Delhi: Orient Longman, 1993.

Bidwai, Praful and Achin Vanaik. *New Nukes: India, Pakistan and Global Nuclear Disarmament*. New York: Interlink Books, 2000.

Butalia, Urvashi, ed. *Speaking Peace: Women's Voices from Kashmir*. New Delhi: Kali for Women, 2002.

Butalia, Urvashi. *The Other Side of Silence: Voices from the Partition of India*. Durham: Duke University Press, 2000, c. 1998.

Chaudhuri, Amit. 'The suborning of saffron: How Hinduism became a rich man's religion', *Times Literary Supplement*, May 31, 2002.

Chowdhury, Srinjoy. *Despatches from Kargil*. New Delhi: Penguin Books India, 2000.

Gandhi, M.K. *An Autobiography Or The Story of My Experiments With Truth*. Translated from the Gujarati by Mahadev Desai, Ahmedabad: Navajivan Prakashan, 1981, c. 1927.

Gandhi, M.K. *Satyagraha in South Africa*. Translated from the Gujarati by Valji Govindji Desai, Ahmedabad: Navajivan Prakashan, 1960, c. 1950.

Ghose, Sagarika. 'Fighting Barista Brahminism?: The VHP and the Rise of "Shudra Hindutva",' *The Indian Express*, March 5, 2003.

Ghosh, Amitav. *In an Antique Land*. New York: Alfred A. Knopf, 1993.

Golwalker, M.S. *Bunch of Thoughts*. Bangalore: Jagarana Prakashan, 1966.

Gupta, Charu. *Sexuality, Obscenity, Community: Women, Muslims, and the Hindu Public in Colonial India*. New York: Palgrave Macmillan, 2002, c. 2001.

Hasan, Mushirul and M. Asaduddin, eds. *Image and Representation: Stories of Muslim Lives in India*. New Delhi: Oxford University Press, 2000.

Heuzé, Gérard. 'Shiv Sena and "National" Hinduism', *Economic and Political Weekly*, 3 October, 1992.

Horowitz, Donald L. *The Deadly Ethnic Riot*. Berkeley: University of California Press, 2001.

Huntington, Samuel. 'The Clash of Civilizations?' *Foreign Affairs*, Summer 1993.

Jaffrelot, Christopher. *The Hindu Nationalist Movement in India*. New York: Columbia University Press, 1996, c. 1993.

Kesavan, Mukul. *Secular Common Sense*. New Delhi, Penguin Books India, 2001.

Kureishi, Hanif. *My Son the Fanatic*. London: Faber and Faber, 1997.

Kumar, Krishna. *Prejudice and Pride*. New Delhi: Viking, 2001.

Lal, Vinay. 'North American Hindus, the Sense of History, and the Politics of Internet Diasporism', *Diaspora*, 2000.

Levy, Bernard-Henri. *Who Killed Daniel Pearl?* Translated from the French by James X. Mitchell. Hoboken, NJ: Melville House Publishing, 2003.

Lewis, Bernard. 'The Roots of Muslim Rage', *The Atlantic Monthly*, September 1990.

Ludden, David, ed. *Making India Hindu: Religion, Community, and the Politics of Democracy in India*. New Delhi: Oxford University Press, 1996.

Manto, Saadat Hasan. *Kingdom's End and Other Stories*. Translated from the Urdu by Khalid Hasan. New York: Verso, 1987.

Menon, Ritua and Kamla Bhasin. *Borders and Boundaries: Women in India's Partition*. New Brunswick: Rutgers University Press, 1998.

Mishra, Pankaj. 'Death in Kashmir', *New York Review of Books*, September 21, 2000. Also see Mishra, 'The Birth of a Nation', *New York Review of Books*, October 5, 2000, and Mishra, 'Kashmir: The Unending War', *New York Review of Books*, October 19, 2000.

Mishra, Pankaj. 'The Other Side of Fanaticism', *The New York Times Magazine*, February 2, 2003.

Naipaul, V.S. *Among the Believers: An Islamic Journey*. New York: Vintage Books, 1982, c. 1981.

Naipaul, V.S. *Beyond Belief: Islamic Excursions Among the Converted Peoples*. New York: Random House, 1998.

Nandy, Ashis. *At the Edge of Psychology: Essays in Politics and Culture*. Delhi: Oxford University Press, 1980.

Nandy, Ashis. *Time Warps: The Insistent Politics of Silent and Evasive Pasts*. New Delhi: Permanent Black, 2001.

Nehru, Jawaharlal. *Selected Works of Jawaharlal Nehru, Second Series, Vol. 30* (September 1–November 17, 1955). Edited by H.Y. Sharada Prasad and A.K. Damodaran. New Delhi: Oxford University Press, 2002.

Noorani, A.G. *Islam and Jihad*. New Delhi: LeftWord Books, 2002.

Noorani, A.G. *The RSS and the BJP*. New Delhi: LeftWord Books, 2000.

Pandey, Gyanendra. *Remembering Partition: Violence, Nationalism and History in India*. Cambridge: Cambridge University Press, 2001.

Rashid, Ahmed. 'Pakistan on the Edge', *The New York Review of Books*, October 10, 2002.

Rashid, Ahmed. *Taliban: Militant Islam, Oil and Fundamentalism in Central Asia*. New Haven: Yale University Press, 2001.

Reza, Rahi Masoom. *The Feuding Families of Village Gangauli, Aadha Gaon*. Translated from the Hindi by Gillian Wright. New Delhi: Penguin Books India, 1994, c. 1966.

Roy, Arundhati. 'Democracy: Who's She When She's at Home?' *Outlook*, May 6, 2002.

Ruthven, Malise. *Islam*. Oxford: Oxford University Press, 1997.

Sahni, Bhisham. *Tamas*. Translated from the Hindi by Jai Ratan. New Delhi: Penguin Books, 1988, c. 1974.

Said, Edward. 'Impossible Histories: Why the many Islams cannot be simplified', *Harper's Magazine*, July 2002.

Sainath, P. 'One people, many identities', *The Hindu*, January 31, 1999. Also see Sainath, 'Caste, not cash, led to conversions', *The Hindu*, February 7, 1999.

Sardar, Ziauddin. 'Mecca', *Granta*, 77, Spring, 2002.

Savarkar, V.D. *Hindutva: Who is a Hindu?* Bombay: S.S. Savarkar, 1969.

Schofield, Victoria. *Kashmir in Conflict: India, Pakistan, and the Unfinished War*. New York: I.B. Tauris, 2000.

Shabistari, Sa'd ud din Mahmud. *Gulshan-e-Raz, The Mystic Rose Garden*. The Persian Text with an English translation by E.H. Winfield. Date of Composition 1317. First published, 1880. Lahore: Islamic Book Foundation, 1978.

Sheikh, Omar. 'My Big Adventure', *Harper's Magazine*, January 2002.

Varadarajan, Siddharth, ed. *Gujarat: The Making of a Tragedy*. New Delhi: Penguin Books India, 2002.

Van der Veer, Peter. *Religious Nationalism: Hindus and Muslims in India*. Berkeley: University of California Press, 1994.

Varshney, Ashutosh. *Ethnic Conflict and Civic Life: Hindus and Muslims in India*. New Haven: Yale University Press, 2002.

Viswanathan, Gauri. *Outside the Fold: Conversion, Modernity, and Belief*, Princeton: Princeton University Press, 1998.

Vivekananda, Swami. *Vivekananda: The Yogas and Other Works*. New York: Ramakrishna-Vivekananda Centre, 1953.

Acknowledgements

This book began as an essay on the idea of the enemy. But it is also a report on violence in the Indian subcontinent. There are others, better qualified, such as social scientists, who have written on these matters with sharpness of insight. I, however have been interested not so much in outlining causes and cures, but in coming to an understanding of my own complicities and contradictions. Therefore, my greatest indebtedness is to those other writers who have produced literary narratives about encounters with people carrying the burden of their past and their prejudice.

Husband of a Fanatic was written with the aid of a Rockefeller Fellowship at the Center for Ideas and Society, University of California at Riverside, and a Resident Scholar Fellowship at the Institute for Arts and Humanistic Studies, Penn State University. The names of several persons whom I interviewed have been altered in the book. I need not change the names of those because of whom this book has found its present form: Gillon Aitken, Andrew Hsiao, Pankaj Mishra, Rob Nixon and Hanif Kureishi. Carlo Rotella is the kind of friend every writer must have. I am also indebted to Michael Vazquez, Michael Gorra, Mary Mount, Jean Tamarin and Ian Jack, all of whom read sections of the manuscript and provided lessons in style.

David Davidar and V.K. Karthika at the Penguin office in New Delhi provided enthusiastic support.

I also owe thanks to those who were of invaluable help in the cities and towns where I travelled and wrote: Raj Kamal Jha, Naresh Fernandes, Nira and Shyam Benegal, Shoma Chaudhury, Manisha Sethi, Ranjit Hoskote, Yashwant Raj, Shujaat Bukhari, Masood Hussain, H. Aram Veeser, Ashis Nandy, Rahul Roy and Saba Dewan, Mushirul Hasan, Raza Mir, Urvashi Butalia, John Hutnyk, Joseph Childers, Emory Elliott, Stephen Cullenberg, Cynthia Young, Toby Miller, Mahenaz Mahmud and Sanaa Ahmed. At Penn State University, I want to especially thank Jeff Nealon, Leisha Jones, Janet Lyon, Paul Youngquist and Michael Berube. Ashok Chowgule and Dinesh Agrawal of the VHP were gracious and helpful with information and contacts. My trip to South Africa could not have taken place without the help provided by Sanjeev Chatterjee. Harsh Kapoor deserves a collective vote of thanks for his selfless labours as a provider of information on the Internet. My parents, Ishwar Chandra Kumar and Lakshmi Nidhi, accompanied me to Bhagalpur when I was doing my research on the blind men.

For more private but also more abiding reasons, I want to thank my wife, Mona Ahmad Ali, from whom I have tried to learn about love and tolerance, not in religion but in everyday life.